WITHDRAWN

WITHDRAWN

THE ALLITERATIVE
MORTE ARTHURE
The Owl and the Nightingale

AND FIVE OTHER

MIDDLE ENGLISH POEMS

in a Modernized Version with

Comments on the Poems

and Notes

By John Gardner

SOUTHERN ILLINOIS UNIVERSITY PRESS
Carbondale and Edwardsville

FEFFER & SIMONS, INC.
London and Amsterdam

Library of Congress Cataloging in Publication Data

Morte Arthure.
  The alliterative Morte Arthure.
  (Arcturus books, AB116)
  CONTENTS: The alliterative Morte Arthure.–Winner
and waster.–The parliament of the three ages.–[Etc.]
  1. English poetry–Middle English (Modernized)
I. Gardner, John Champlin, 1933–   ed. II. Title.
[PR1203.G3 1973]   821'.1'08   73–7728
ISBN 0–8093–0486–4
ISBN 0–8093–0648–4 (pbk.)

ARCT
URUS
BOOKS ®

Arcturus Books Edition September 1973
Second printing May 1979
This edition printed by offset lithography
  in the United States of America

To Ken Morrow

ERRATUM

Page 86, line 3266: *For* On the wheel was a chair of chalk-white hues; *read* On the wheel was a chair of chalk-white silver

ADDENDUM

Page 86, insert between lines 3266 and 3267: And checkered with carbuncles of changing hues;

CONTENTS

Contents

PREFACE

THIS selection of Middle English poems is not meant to be representative of Middle English poetry in general. I have chosen poems (in most cases) which have real literary value and are so hard to read in the original that they are not as well known as they deserve to be. Another control on my selection is my object of presenting the poems as poetry. I do include one patently inferior poem, *The Thrush and the Nightingale*, because it throws light on *The Owl and the Nightingale*.

The poems brought together here do reflect a variety of medieval English ways of thinking and feeling. The neglected masterpiece *Morte Arthure* is the only "heroic romance" in Middle English—in other words, it is a poem in (roughly) the same genre as the French *Song of Roland*. *Winner and Waster* and *The Parliament of the Three Ages* are fine examples of that favorite medieval mode, the elegant, stylized debate. The lyric *Summer Sunday*, with its intricate repetitions of words and phrases, its close rhyming, its handsome use of traditional images, is a gem among medieval lyrics. The darker strain of medieval thought, hellfire terror, is represented here by *The Debate of Body and Soul*. And the lighter side of life in the Middle Ages comes alive in *The Owl and the Nightingale*.

Since I have modernized these poems in verse, it should go without saying that I have occasionally sacrificed literalness to preserve aesthetic qualities. For instance, in *Summer Sunday*, a tightly alliterated poem, I translate the phrase *I warp on my wedes* as "I caught up my clothes," not "I put on my clothes," which would be accurate but prosaic. I translate *to wode wold I wende* as "I would go to the groves in haste" not "I planned to go to the woods," a more accurate rendering but one which loses both alliteration and the excitement of the poet's opening. I frequently modernize *kene*, here and in other alliterative poems, as "keen," not "bold," which would be more correct. Certain nuances of modern *keen* are not too far from modern *bold,* especially when the adjective modifies some word like *warrior,* and retaining the original's *k* often means preserving the line's alliteration. Alliteration is not the only consideration, of course. *Keen,* like ME *kene,* has a thin, piercing quality *bold* does not have. Meaning in poetry often depends as much upon tone and cadence as on the exact denotation of words. A prose translation of *The Owl and the Nightingale* would miss the whole spirit of the poem.

Since the poems here are of various kinds, I have not followed the same principles in translating all the poems. In translating alliterative poetry I have not kept strictly to the laws of fourteenth-century alliterative verse but have kept the old laws wherever possible and elsewhere have simply tried for profluence and something of the characteristic stylistic effect—the flexibility of rhythmical pattern, the intensity of sound clusters, the frequent use of formulaic elements essential to the dignified cadence of the verse. In translating rhymed verse I have sometimes used half rhyme, as do the poets themselves, occasionally, and have in general kept the rhyme scheme intact. I have generally tried to avoid inversion and archaic language except where they serve not my own convenience but tone and meaning in the poem at hand. But the complexity of rhyme scheme in some of the poems—especially *The Debate of Body and Soul* and *Summer Sunday*—has sometimes forced me to awkwardness, even desperate mistranslation for a rhyme—so that the translations do not come as close to either the original spirit or sense as I would like. Elsewhere—for instance, in *Morte Arthure*—I have now and then revived an old word, or an older sense of a word still in use, because the special medieval sense of the word is central to the structure of the poem. No one nowdays would say "He rioted himself" ("he ran riot" does not mean quite the same), and the reader encountering the expression in a poem is likely to squint a moment; but the *Morte Arthure*-poet has developed a pattern of verbal relationships dependent upon the metaphor buried in this expression, a comparison between the cosmos, the state, and the elements in a particular man—and the only way I have found to keep the total pattern is to keep the archaic expression.

The least literal of the translations here is *The Owl and the Nightingale.* The best features of the poem are its humor, its drive, the precision of its comic imagery, and the inevitability and wild rush of its bombast. These are the features I've tried hardest to preserve. I have now and then allowed a concern with literalness to push me into odd rhyming, but not much further.

The reader perhaps deserves a warning against taking on faith all I say in my Comments. My object there is to offer a critical point of departure, that is, to offer a translator's judgments, not so much to survey the scholarship. I point out some of the various kinds of interest the poems have, and kinds of interest that, in my opinion, they do not. Needless to say, some of the interpretations here are not available elsewhere, but on the whole my concern has not been critical originality. I stand heavily in debt to all who have discussed or translated any of these poems before. More directly, I am indebted to Professors John C. McGalliard, J. L. N. O'Loughlin, and Donald R. Howard, who went over the manuscript of this book and made helpful comments. I must also mention my profound though indirect debt to Professor William Matthews, whose book on the *Morte Arthure* first called my attention to this little-read masterpiece and started me on this project.

For permission to reprint *Summer Sunday*, slightly revised from the introduction to my *Complete Works of the Gawain-Poet*, I am indebted to the University of Chicago Press, and for permission to reprint parts of my discussion of *The Owl and the Nightingale*, I owe thanks to the editor of *Papers on Language and Literature*.

John Gardner

Carbondale, Illinois
October 1970

The Alliterative Morte Arthure

THE
ALLITERATIVE
Morte Arthure

In nomine Patris et Filij et Spiritue Sancti.

Amen pur charite. AMEN.

Now great glorious God, through his own grace
And the precious prayer of his priceless mother,
Shield us from shameful deeds and sinful works,
And give us the grace to guide and govern ourselves
In this wretched world, that through virtuous living
We may come to his court, the kingdom of heaven,
When our souls shall part and be sundered from the body,
To dwell and abide forever with Him in bliss;
And grant me wisdom to bring forth words at this time
That are neither void nor vain, but glorify Him   *10*
And are pleasing and profitable to the people who hear them.

❡ Proem

ALL YOU who like to listen and long to learn
Of our elders in olden times and their noble deeds
How they were loyal to their law and loved God Almighty,
Hear me in courtesy, and keep your peace,
And I shall tell you a tale both true and lofty
Concerning the royal warriors of the Round Table,

The flower of chivalry and the first of chieftains,
Wary in their works and wise men of arms,
Doughty men in their deeds and fearful of shame,   20
Kind, courteous men who knew courtly custom;
How they earned many an honor by their fighting,
Slew King Lucius the Bad, the Lord of Rome,
And conquered the King's whole realm by craft of arms.
Harken to what I say, and hear my story.

❨ Arthur and the Messengers of Lucius

AFTER the great King Arthur had taken by conquest
Castles, kingdoms, countries more than a few,
And recovered the crown of his own rich realm
And all on earth that Uther had owned in his time—
Argyle and Orkney and all the outer isles,   30
And all the space of Ireland as the ocean runs—
And angry Scotland he ordered as he liked,
Conquered Wales by war and ruled at his will,
Made both France and Flanders fief to himself,
And both Hainault and Holland were held of him,
Burgundy, Brabant, and also Brittany,
And Guienne, and Gothland, and glorious Greece;
He governed in splendor Bayonne and Bordeaux
And the lands of lofty towers, Touraine and Toulouse;
In Poictiers and Provence he was recognized prince,   40
And Valence and Vienne, both lands of value,
And the wealthy earldoms of Auvergne and Anjou;
And by his cruel conquests men knew him king
Of Navarre and Norway, and Normandy as well,
Of Germany, Austria, and many another;
He won all Denmark, too, through dread of his power,
And also from Cadsand to Sweden, by his keen sword.
And when he had done all these deeds, he dubbed his knights,
Made duchies and dealt them out in diverse realms,
And made of his kinsmen anointed kings,   50
The bearers of crowns in whatever country they called for.
     When he'd ridden through these realms and ruled the people,

Then the royal lord rested and held the Round Table.
He sojourned all that season, to suit his pleasure,
In Britain, amusing himself as he best liked;
And later he went into Wales with all his men,
And with swift hounds he swung up into Swaldye
To hunt the harts up there in those high lands;
Rode in Glamorgan with joy, where there's always good sport.
And there by assent of his lords he established a city,   60
A place called Caerleon, with curious walls
On the beautiful river that runs so fair,
Where he might assemble his men to meet when he liked.
Afterward in Carlisle King Arthur kept Christmas,
This same famous conqueror, who was there called lord,
With his dukes and his douzeperes of diverse realms,
His earls and his archbishops and many another,
Bishops and vassals' knights and standard-bearers,
All who bowed to his banner and followed as he bid.
On Christmas day when these were all assembled   70
The splendid conqueror himself commanded
That every lord should linger and take no leave
Till the whole of the tenth day should be taken to its end.
And thus in royal array he held his Round Table
With splendid show and sports and sundry meals;
Never in any man's time was more festivity
Made in the western marches in midwinter.
     But on the day of New Year, at the dinner hour,
As the bold knights at the board were served their bread,
There suddenly came in a senator of Rome,   80
Sixteen knights at his side, who served only him.
He saluted first the sovereign, then all the hall,
King after king in order, and made his bows;
And Guinevere in her degree, he greeted as he liked,
And then returning to Arthur, he stated his mission.
"Sir Lucius Iberius, Emperor of Rome,
Salutes you as his subject, under his seal;
This is his claim, Sir King, with its stern words;
Think it no trifle; his shield is for all to see.
Therefore by lawful tokens, this New Year's Day,   90
I summon you, in this castle, to sue for your lands,
And command that on Lammass Day you give no excuses

But be ready with all your Round Table at Rome
To appear in Lucius' presence with your prized knights
At the prime of day—on pain of your lives—
In that famous capital come to the king himself
When he and his senators are seated at their pleasure,
To explain why you have occupied the lands
Which owe homage of old to him and to his elders;
Why you have ridden there, ruled and ransomed his people,   *100*
And murdered his mighty kinsmen, anointed kings.
There shall you give reckoning for all your Round Table,
Why you are rebel to Rome and rob her of rents.
If you dare to ignore this summons, he sends you this warning:
He will seek you over the sea with sixteen kings
To burn all the breadth of Britain, and break your knights,
And with rage he will drag you about like a beast where he pleases;
And you shall find neither sleep nor rest under heaven
Though you flee to a hole in the earth for fear of Rome.
For though you flee into France or even to Friesland,   *110*
He will drag you back by force and destroy you forever.
Your father paid fealty to us, we find in our rolls,
In the Register of Rome, as all may read.
Without more talk therefore we ask our tribute
Which Julius Caesar won with his courtly knights."
      The king looked down at the man, and his eyes were wide
And burned with rage as brightly as burning coals;
He cast colors as if bent upon cruel destruction,
And he looked like an angry lion, and gnawed his lip.
The Romans, terrified, fell flat to the flagstones,   *120*
As full of fear as men who are fated for death;
They cowered like dogs at the feet of King Arthur,
And by only his countenance they were confounded.
Then one of the knights rose up and wailed loudly,
"O King, crowned by Nature, courteous, noble,
For the sake of your honor, spare us, mere messengers,
Since we are here in your house and seek your mercy;
We live in the land of Lucius, the lord of Rome,
The mightiest man that moves on all this earth;
It is only right that we act as he requires: *130*
We come by his commandment; let us be excused."
Then the conqueror gave back scornful words:

6

"Ha! craven knight, you prove a coward!
There's one here in this hall who, if he were vexed,
You would not for all Lombardy dare look at."
"Sire," says the senator, "as Christ defend me,
The wrath of only your look has wounded us all;
You're the lordliest man I have ever looked upon.
And with no more than your rage you seem a lion!"
"You've summoned me," said the king, "and said what you please; *140*
For the sake of your sovereign lord, I suffer you the more.
Since first I was crowned in this country, and anointed with chrism,
No creature has ever raved on with such freedom before me.
But I shall take counsel now from anointed kings,
From dukes and from douzeperes and learned doctors,
Peers of the Parliament, prelates, and others,
And all the noblest knights of the Round Table;
Thus shall I be advised by valiant barons
And work according to the wish of my wise knights;
For honor's sake I'll waste no words on you   *150*
Nor willfully avenge my private wrath;
Therefore you shall linger here and lodge with these lords
For seven nights in peace, and rest your horses
And see what life we lead in these low lands."
And for Rome's royalty, richest in all the world,
He commanded Sir Kay, "Take care of these lords
And establish these valiant men as their station requires;
Make room for them at once in the high chambers
And let them be fittingly served in the hall after that,
And let them find no lack of food for their horses   *160*
Nor lack of wine or bread or the wealth of this land;
And do not stint on spices but spend what you please
And let magnificence rule, and may nothing be missing;
Keep my honor well and, sir, on my oath
I'll pay for your trouble with treasures to last you forever."
    The Romans are shown their rooms, made guests with the
                                                          others,
Served quickly, within these high walls, by gentlemen;
In chambers with wide chimneys they change their dress,
And the chancellor comes for them later with noble lords.
Soon the senator was seated as well as he could wish,   *170*
At the king's own table, with two knights serving him,

Two to him singly, as Arthur himself was served,
Richly on the right hand at the great Round Table;
For the Romans were held a noble race indeed
And men of the royalest blood to be found on earth.
And there the first course came, before the king's chair,
Boar-heads bright with grease and burnished with silver
Borne in by well-trained men in the fairest of robes,
A livery red as blood, and sixty at once;
Venison fat from the close season, spiced frumenty,   *180*
A glorious choice of wild game, beautiful game-foul—
Peacocks and plovers on platters of gold,
Wild pigs of porcupines that never saw pasture;
Then came herons in sauces, handsomely covered;
Great swans came swiftly, carried on silver trays,
Meat pies of turkey—taste them whoever likes!—
Well fashioned gumbalds, gracious gifts to the tongue,
Then shoulders of mighty boars, with the meat in slices,
Barnacle-geese and bitterns in pastried dishes,
And beside them broad young hawks—there were never better— *190*
And breasts of swine, all brilliant to men's eyes.
Next in flowed many fine pottages, more than enough,
With azure waves all over, and still in flame:
On each ornamental tower the flames leapt high,
And all who looked might well enough be delighted!
Then came cranes and curlews cunningly roasted,
And rabbits in excellent sauces, beautifully dyed,
Pheasants with fair decorations, aflame in the silver,
With yellow glazed custards and other good sweets enough,
With honey wine and Crete wine, skillfully run,   *200*
With spouts of clean silver, curious to see;
Alsatian wine and Spanish, and others as well,
Rhenish wine and Rochelle, no wines ever richer,
Rare vintages of Crete and of noble Venice,
In vessels of finest gold; quaff all who please!
The king's sideboard was all enclosed in silver,
In gilded goblets glorious of hue;
And the chief butler was a noble chevalier,
The courteous Sir Kay, who served the cups,
Sixty cups of a kind, designed for the king,   *210*
Curious and crafty and handsomely cut,

And every zone of them ranked with precious stones
So that poison might never be privily slipped inside:
For the bright gold, in its wrath, would burst into pieces,
Or the venom be made void by the virtue of the stones.
And the conqueror stood, himself, in gleaming array,
All clad in clean gold colors, together with his knights,
And wearing his diadem there on that splendid dais,
And was judged the mightiest monarch alive on earth.
    Then the conqueror spoke kind words to those lords   *220*
And encouraged the Romans with royal speech:
"Sirs, be of knightly cheer, and comfort yourselves!
We know nothing here in this country of curious foods;
In these barren lands we find no better stuff;
And therefore force yourselves, and eat without flinching,
And be satisfied with the feeble stuff before you."
"Sire," said the senator, "as Christ defend me,
There was never within Rome's walls such royalty!
There is neither prelate nor pope nor prince on this earth
Who could help but feel well pleased by these precious meats!" *230*
    After their meal they washed and went to the chamber,
This same great conqueror with a good many knights;
The worthy Sir Gawain leads Queen Guinevere,
Sir Ughtred on the other side, the lord of Turry.
They turned to spiced liqueurs unsparingly:
Malvesye and Muscadel, those marvelous drinks,
Rushed out merrily into russet cups
For each noble in turn, both Romans and others.
And now the sovereign, truly, to suit his pleasure,
Assigned to the senator certain lords   *240*
To lead to his proper place, when he asks,
With mirth and the melody of noble minstrels.
Then the conqueror afterward goes into council
With lords in his liege belonging to himself;
He goes with them gladly to the Tower of Giants,
With justices and judges, and gentle knights.
    Sir Cador of Cornwall addressed the king,
Laughing before him lightly, with a merry look:
"I thank God for that ogre that threatens us!
You'll be drawn to Rome, I swear, if you can't parley better! *250*
That letter from Sir Lucius has lightened my heart!

9

We've lolled like loafers here for many long days
With all the delights of the land and lordships aplenty,
Letting our hard-won glory go sliding away.
By our Lord, I felt ashamed for the best of our men,
And grieved to see them give up their great deeds of arms;
Now war is upon us again; all praise to Christ!
And once again we'll win it, by endurance and strength."
"Sir Cador," said the king, "your counsel is noble,
And you are a marvelous man for merry words;   260
You consider no cases and cast no further
But hurl in headlong, just as your heart desires.
I need to consider negotiating these matters
And first try talk of these tidings that trouble my heart.
You can see that the emperor is angered a little;
Indeed, from his servant he sounds like a man grieved sore.
His senator has summoned me, said all he pleased,
Scornfully here in my hall, with heinous words—
Spit on me with speech and spared me little;
I could scarcely speak from rage, my heart so shook.   270
He asked me like a tyrant for the tribute of Rome
That was taken brutally in my father's time;
In those days aliens, in the absence of all men of arms,
Took it from the commons, as the Chronicle tells.
But I have title to take the tribute of Rome.
My ancestors were emperors and owned it themselves,
Belin and Brennan, and Baldwin was the third.
They occupied the empire eightscore winters,
Each one after the other, as old men tell;
They captured the Capitol and cast down the walls   280
And hanged the head men there by the hundreds at once;
Then Constantine, our kinsman, conquered it later,
The heir of England and emperor of Rome,
He that conquered, by craft of arms, the cross
That crucified Christ, who is the king of heaven.
Thus we have evidence, and may ask the emperor
Ruling Rome what right he claims for himself."
      Then up King Aungers spoke and answered Arthur:
"You ought to be overlord above all other kings
As wisest and worthiest, mightiest of hand,   290
And the knightliest in counsel that ever bore crown.

I dare say for Scotland that we shall pay with interest
Those Romans who reigned and ransomed our elders
And rode in their wild riot and ravished our wives,
And without either right or reason robbed us of our goods.
And I shall make my vow devoutly to Christ
And to the holy vernicle, virtuous and noble,
For this great villainy I'll be fully avenged
On those venomous men with my valiant band of knights.
I'll back your defense in the fight they force once more   *300*
With fifty thousand men of fighting age,
Who'll set out in my service wherever you please,
To fight with your foes who unfairly deal with us."
    Then next the boarlike baron of Brittany
Counsels King Arthur, keenly entreating him
To answer the foreigners in the fiercest language,
To entice the emperor over the wall of mountains.
Said he: "I make my vow, verily to Christ
And the holy vernicle, never will I flee
For fear of any Roman that reigns on earth,   *310*
But he'll find me ready in array and found among the first,
No more daunted by the din of their dreadful weapons
Than I am of the damp dew when it drops to earth;
And no more shaken by the sweep of their sharp swords
Than I am by the fairest flower that grows in the field.
I'll bring to the battle bright-mailed knights,
Thirty thousand by count, all keen in arms,
Within a month and a day, to whatever march
You choose to assign them, whenever you shall please."
    "Ah! Ah!" cries the Welsh king, "Christ be worshipped!   *320*
Now we'll avenge in full the anger of our elders!
In Western Wales, by God, they carved such wounds
That all men weep for woe who remember that war.
I shall therefore furnish the vanguard myself
Until I have vanquished the Viscount of Rome:
He did me a villainy once at Viterbo
As I passed on a pilgrimage by Pontremoli.
He was in Tuscany at the time, and took our knights,
Arrested them without reason and ransomed them later;
I'll settle with him most surely, unreconciled   *330*
Until we ourselves have encountered in earnest once

And dealt out strokes of death with our dire weapons.
And I shall wage on your war, of my worthy knights,
From the Isle of Wight and Wales and the Western Marches,
Two thousand by tally, equipped with horses,
The worthiest warlords in all these western lands."
    Sir Ewain Fitz Urien then eagerly asks,
Cousin to the conqueror, courageous himself:
"Sire, if we knew your will we would do as you wish,
Whether this day's work be done or withheld until later,   *340*
We'll ride against those Romans and riot their lands;
We would all prepare ourselves to ship when you please."
    "Cousin," the conqueror said, "your words are kind.
If all my council agrees on attacking those lands,
When the first of June sets in we'll have struck them once
With our cruellest knights, as Christ is my defense!
To that I make my vow devoutly to Christ
And the holy vernicle, virtuous and noble,
I shall on Lammass take leave, to live at large
In Lorain or Lombardy, whatever seems best;   *350*
We'll march into Milan and mine down the walls
Of Petra Santa, Pisa, and Pontremoli;
In the Vale of Viterbo I'll victual my knights
And sojourn there six weeks, as it suits my pleasure,
And send in horsemen to the city and set my siege
If they fail to offer me peace in a fitting time."
    "Surely," says Sir Ewain, "I too avow
If ever I see that man with my eyes
Who occupies your heritage, emperor of Rome,
I'll try with my own hand to touch the eagle   *360*
He bears upon his banner, bright with gold,
And take it from all his nobles and tear it to bits
Unless he's rescued at once by a rout of good knights.
I'll support you in the field with fresh men of arms—
Fifty thousand men upon fair steeds—
To fight against your foeman as you see fit,
In France or in Friesland, fight whenever you please."
    "By our Lord," said Sir Lancelot, "my heart grows light!
I praise God for this love these lords have avowed!
If a lesser man may have leave to say all he likes   *370*
And not be ordered silent, listen to my words:

I'll be at that day's fight, with well-born knights,
On a swift running steed that's handsomely caparisoned;
Before other work begins I'll joust with that man
Among all his giants of Genoa, and others,
And strike him stiffly from his steed by the strength of my hands
Despite all the fighters of the field who follow in his army.
With my retinue in its gear, I'll count it a trifle
To take my route to Rome with my warloving men.
Within a week to the day, with sixscore helmets,   380
You'll see me on the sea, to sail when you please."
     Loudly Sir Lottes laughed, and loudly spoke:
"I'm glad to hear Sir Lucius longs for sorrow,
For now that he's asked for war, his woe begins;
But it is our fate to avenge the wrath of our fathers:
I make my vow to God and the holy vernicle,
If I may see the Romans, held so valiant,
Arrayed in all their ranks in a round field,
I shall, for the reverence of the Round Table,
Ride through all that rout, from front to rear,   390
Preparing roadways for others—and wide roads at that—
Running red with blood as my horse rushes.
He that follows my path and first comes after
Will find in my fareway many a fated man."
     Then the conqueror kindly thanked his knights
And gladly acknowledged their lordly vows:
"Almighty God give glory to you all
And grant I may never lose you while I reign in the world.
For you maintain on earth my honor and might;
All my honor in the lands of other kings   400
My weal and worth, and all this wealthy realm
That knows my crown, you've conquered like true knights.
No man who leads such lords need fear any foe
But is always fresh for the fight in the field when he pleases.
I need not fear any king alive under Christ:
So long as I see you sound, I'll need nothing more."
     When the council came to agreement they called for trumpets
And descended down to a dance of dukes and earls;
Again they assembled in the hall and eagerly dined,
All this worthy band with noble pomp.   410
Then the royal chief brought cheer to his knights

With the honor and pleasure of all his princely Round Table
Till seven days were done. The senator asks,
With grave words, for an answer to the emperor.
After Epiphany, when the opinion was brought
From the peers of the Parliament, the prelates and others,
The king in his counsel, courteous and noble,
Brings in all the aliens, answering himself.
"Hail to Lucius your lord: let him hear all I say:
If you are his loyal liegemen, let him know quickly,   420
I shall take my leave at Lammass and live at large
Delighting in his lands, with lords aplenty,
And reign by my royalty, and rest when I please;
Beside the river Rhone I'll hold my Round Table,
Receive the rents in full from all the realms
For all the menace of his might and maugre his eyes,
And thence march over the mountains to his main holdings,
To beautiful Milan, and mine down the battlements;
In Lorain and Lombardy I'll see that I leave
No man still living who follows Lucius' laws;   430
I'll turn in to Tuscany, when it seems to me time,
And ride those roomy lands with riotous knights;
Bid him, for his honor, come save whom he can
And meet me, if he's a man, in those main holdings.
He'll find me waiting in France, in those fair marches,
On the first of February, fare out whenever he pleases.
Before I am fetched out by force or forfeit my lands,
The flower of his fair knighthood will fall to its fate.
I promise him certainly, under my royal seal,
To besiege the city of Rome within seven winters   440
And so bitterly besiege him on every side
That many a senator will sigh for the sake of me.
My summons is certified, and you have been served
Safe conduct and credentials; go when you please.
I myself shall assign you lodgings on your way
From this place to the port where you're to cross;
I give you seven days to get to Sandwich—
Sixty miles a day—an easy matter—
But you'll need to speed on spurs, not spare your pony;
You go by Watling Street, and no other way.   450
Where night overtakes you, there you needs must stop,

Whether it's forest or field, and go no farther.
Tie up your horse at a bush with the bridle rein
And lodge yourself under a limb, as you see fit;
It is not allowed that aliens travel at night
To riot about in freedom in obscene bands.
Your license is limited in the presence of lords.
Now be loathed or prevented, whichever you please,
For both your life and your limb are hanging on it—
And would be if Lucius had laid on you the lordship of Rome   *460*
For if you're still found a foot this side of the sea
By the eighth day, at the time the undern is rung,
I'll have you beheaded on high and drawn with horses
And afterward hang up your corpses for hounds to gnaw;
Neither the rent or the red gold belonging to Rome
Will then prove sufficient, Sir, to ransom you."
    "Sire," says the senator, "as Christ defend me,
If I might in honor escape from here once
I would never for any emperor dwelling on earth
Come back again to Arthur on any such errand!   *470*
But I stand here alone, with only sixteen knights;
I beg you, Sir, that we may pass in safety:
If any outlaw should stop us along the way,
Within your borders, Lord, your glory would be hurt."
    "Have no fear," said the king, "your conduct is known
From Carlisle to the coast, where your ship lies waiting.
If all your coffers were full and crammed with new silver
You'd be safe under my seal for sixty miles more."
    The Romans bowed to the king and requested their leave,
Then started from Carlisle, got onto their horses;   *480*
The courteous Sir Cador pointed the way,
Conveyed them to Catterick, and commended them to Christ.

❡ The Two Kings
Prepare for War

And so they sped on spurs, made their horses spring,
   And their hired servingmen hurried along behind them;
And thus they fled for fear, and refused themselves rest
Except when they lodged under limbs, when daylight failed;

And always the senator fled by the shortest way.
When the seventh day was done they'd reached the city
And for all the joy under God, they'd never been gladder
Than now at the sound of the sea and the bells of Sandwich;   *490*
Without more delay they went up on the ship with their horses
And wearily went out at once on the wan sea;
Together with men of the wall they weighed the anchors
And fled with the first tide, and rowed towards Flanders,
And then through Flanders they fled, as seemed to them best,
To Aix-la-Chapelle and Germany, Arthur's lands;
Fled through St. Gothard's Pass, by treacherous roadways,
And so into Lombardy, beautiful to see,
And turned through Tuscany with its soaring towers.

Dressed in fine apparel, in precious robes,   *500*
They pass the Sunday in Sutri, and rest their horses,
And seek the saints of Rome, by assent of the knights;
At last they ride to the palace with its rich portals,
They bow down low to him and bring him the letters
Enclosing Arthur's credentials, and speak knightly words.
The emperor is eager, ardently enquires
And asks them soon what answer Arthur sends,
And how he arranges his realm and rules the people
And, if he is rebel to Rome, what right he claims:
"You ought to have seized his scepter and sat above him   *510*
In the name of the royal reverence due to Rome;
For surely you were my minion and senator of Rome;
He should, for ceremony, have served you himself."
"He'd never do that for a man on all this rich earth,
Save him who may win him by war, by the might of his hands;
Many, first, must be laid down fated on the battlefield,
Before he appears in this palace, attack when you like.
I tell you, Sire, King Arthur's your enemy forever,
And claims to be overlord of the empire of Rome,
Which all his ancestors owned, save Uther himself.   *520*
I carried to him myself your command this New Year—
To that ruler noble of name and nine other kings.
In the most royal place of the Round Table
I summoned him solemnly, in the sight of his knights;
Since first I was formed, in truth, I was never so afraid
In all the places on earth where I've passed among princes:

I would rather put off all my claim to position in Rome
Than ever be sent to that sovereign again on such business!
Well might he be made chieftain, and chief of all others,
Both by his fortune in arms and his noble chivalry,   *530*
As the wisest, worthiest, mightiest of hand
Of all the mortals I've met on this rich earth,
The knightliest creature I've come upon in Christendom
Of all the kings or conquerors crowned in the world—
In countenance, in courage, in cruel bearing,
The noblest of all the knights yet living under Christ.
Well may they praise his largess—a despiser of silver
Who cares no more for gold than for giant stones,
No more for wine than for water that flows from the well,
Nor for all the wealth of this world, but only for honor.   *540*
Such splendor was never yet seen in any rich country
As the conqueror commanded, there in his court;
I counted there at Christmas, of anointed kings,
No less than ten at his table, who sat with him.
He will make you war, I swear; beware if you like.
Hire your men; keep watch on your borders;
Let them be ready in array and prepared for him early;
For if Arthur reaches Rome he'll ransom it forever.
I warn you, Sire, make ready, and waste no time;
Make sure of your mercenaries, and send them to the   *550*
                                                           mountains
By the quarter of this year, and let them keep guard,
For Arthur will come on his way by force in a while."
      "By Easter," answers the emperor, "I intend
To wage war in Germany with well-armed knights
And boldly send into France, the flower of kingdoms,
To find and fetch that fellow and forfeit his lands;
And I shall set out cunning and noble keepers,
Many a Genoan giant, the best of jousters,
To meet him there in the mountains and martyr his knights,
Strike them down on the roadways and wreck them forever.   *560*
And a great tower shall be reared up at St. Gothard's,
Which shall be defended and kept by good men of arms:
And a beacon high above it shall burn when it suits them
So that no enemy with a host can invade us by the Alps;
And on Mt. Bernard I'll build me another such tower

And pack it with standard-bearers and good brave fighters;
And also at the portals of Pavia no prince shall pass
Through perilous passes, thanks to my powerful knights."
    Then Sir Lucius sends out lordly letters
At once to the Orient, with austere knights,   570
To Ambigain and Orcage and to Alexandria,
To India and Armenia, by the Euphrates;
To Asia and Africa and to all Europe,
To Irritain and Elamet and the outer isles,
To Araby and Egypt, to earls and others,
All who held any land in those eastern marches—
Damascus and Damietta, to dukes and lords.
For fear of his displeasure they prepared at once:
From Crete and Cappadocia the honorable kings
Came at his commandment, and quickly assembled;   580
Tartary and Turkey, when the tidings came,
Turned at once through Thebes, powerful tyrants,
And the flower of the mighty people of the Amazon lands:
All who failed in the field would be forfeit forever.
And from Babylon and Baghdad, noble knights,
Brilliant among their baronage, abided no longer;
From Persia and Pamphile and Prester John's lands,
Each prince with all his power in its battle gear.
The Sultan of Syria assembles his knights,
From the Nile to Nazareth, in enormous numbers,   590
They gather in haste at Gariere and Galilee.
The sultans who were the steadfast vassals of Rome
Gathered from across the Greek sea with grievous weapons
With glittering shields in their great galleys;
And by sea the king of Cyprus waits on his sovereign,
With the regal lords of Rhodes in array with himself;
They sailed with a side wind over the salt sea
Swiftly, these Saracens, as suited their pleasure.
And soon the kings had safely arrived at Corneto,
No more than sixty miles from the city of Rome.   600
By now the Greeks were gathered in great number,
The mightiest of Macedonia, with men of the marches,
Apulia and Prussia came pressing with the rest,
And the liegemen of Lithuania, with legions enough.
Thus they assemble in armies, enormous hosts,

Sultans and Saracens out of their sundry lands—
The Sultan of Syria with sixteen kings—
Assembled all together at the city of Rome.
 The emperor appears then, suitably armed,
Arrayed with his ranks of Romans, on rich steeds: *610*
Sixty giants before him, engendered by fiends,
With witches and warlocks to watch his tents
Wherever he may go, for winters and years.
No steed could carry them, those burly churls,
But covered camels with turrets, enclosed all in mail!
He set out with his allies in all their hosts
And journeyed to Germany, which Arthur had won;
He rides in by the river and riots himself,
And moves with a mighty will through all the high countries.
At Westphalia he wins the war as he wishes,   *620*
Draws in by the Danube and there dubs knights;
In the country of Cologne he besieges castles,
And he sojourns all that season with Saracens enough.
 Eight days after Hilary, Arthur himself
At his famous council commanded his lords:
"Go to your countries now and assemble your knights,
And meet me at Constantine, arrayed for war;
Await me at Barfleur, on those blithe streams,
Boldly, within your ships with the best of your men;
I shall meet you as suits my honor in those fair marches."   *630*
Swiftly then King Arthur sent sergeants at arms
To each of his mariners in order, to ready their ships;
And inside sixteen days the fleet was assembled
At Sandwich-on-the-Sea, to sail when he liked.
In the palace at York he held a parliament
Of all the peers of the realm, both prelates and others,
And after the opening prayer, in the presence of lords,
The king in his counsel came to them with these words:
"I have made it my purpose to pass down dangerous paths,
To go with my keen men to conquer those lands,   *640*
And overthrow, if Fortune chooses, my enemy
Who occupies my heritage, the empire of Rome.
I establish here a sovereign—assent if you like:
He is my kinsman, my sister's son, Sir Mordred;
Him I make my lieutenant, with lordship enough,

And lord of all my liegemen who guard my lands."
He spoke to his cousin then, in the counsel with him:
"I make you the keeper, Sir Knight, of many kingdoms,
Worshipful warden to wield and rule these lands
That I have won by war in this rich world.   *650*
I order that Guinevere my wife be held in honor,
That she want no weal or wealth she may desire;
Look that my famous castles are fully provided
With suitable servants wherever she may sojourn.
See that my forests are preserved in peace forever
And that no one troubles the wildlife but Guinevere herself,
And that in the season when meat of the deer is apportioned,
She may have at certain times what solace she pleases.
Change chancellor and chamberlain as you choose,
Ordain, yourself, the auditors and officers,   *660*
The juries, judges, and justices of the lands,
And look that you deal out justice to those who do injuries.
If I am destined to die, as God may will,
I charge you, be my executor, chief of all others,
For my soul's reward, administer my possessions
To beggars and those who are brought into painful times.
Take here my written accounts of all my great treasure,
And as I put trust in you, betray me never!
And as you must answer before that fearful Judge
Who mercifully wields the world and rules as He likes,   *670*
Look that my last will by loyally performed.
I give you entirely the care that goes with my crown,
The welfare of my wards and my wife as well;
See that you keep you so clear that no cause is found
Against you when I come home, if Christ allows it.
And if you have grace to govern yourself as is fitting,
I shall crown you with my own hand, knight, as a king."
    Then Sir Mordred most humbly replied to the king,
Kneeled to the conqueror and gave him these words:
"I beseech you, Sire, as my kinsman lord,   *680*
That for charity you choose some other man;
If you put me in this plight, the people will divide:
I haven't the power as yet for a prince's estate;
When other men proved by war are worshipped hereafter,
Then truly, I will be taken for some mere trifle.

I've therefore made it my purpose to ride in your presence
And prove my power to provide for my prized knights."
    "You're my nearest kin and foster-child of old,
Whom I have reared and chosen, a child of my chamber;
For the sake of the blood between us, forsake not this office: 690
Fail not to work my will; you know what it means."
    Now without further delay he takes his leave
Of all the lords and liegemen he leaves behind.
And afterwards the worthy man went to his chamber
To comfort the queen, whose heart was full of care.
Guinevere, weakly weeping, kissed her lord
And spoke to him tenderly, with tears enough:
"My curse on the man who moves you to make war
And robs my right to serve my wedded lord;
All that I love in life now leaves this land   700
And I am left here in sorrow—believe it forever!
Why couldn't I, dear love, have died in your arms
Before I should have to endure all alone this destiny?"
    "Guinevere, do not grieve, for God's love in heaven,
And do not regret my going; it will turn to good.
Your sorrow and your weeping wound my heart.
Yet I cannot end your grief for all this rich earth.
I've appointed a guardian for you, a knight of your own,
The sovereign to all of England, second to yourself,
The good Sir Mordred, whom many times you've praised.   710
He'll stand as your servant, my dear, to do all you desire."
Then he took his leave of the ladies in the chamber,
Kissing them kindly, commending them to Christ.
And when he asked for his sword the queen swooned,
And fell twice in a faint, for all her will.
But Arthur pressed to his palfrey, in the presence of lords,
And he rode from the palace with his prized knights:
With all the royal rout of the mighty Round Table
Struck out for Sandwich. She can see him never more.
    There the great were gathered with gallant knights,   720
Armed in the green field and in good array;
Dukes and douzeperes ride, handsome on their horses,
And earls of England, with archers enough.
Commanders call out sharply now to the soldiers
And command them, under the greats of the Round Table,

And assign each space of land to certain lords,
To the south on the sea banks, to sail when they will.
Now loading barges are brought, and they row them to the banks
And bring the horses aboard, and burly troops,
And pack in trustily harnessed steeds,   730
Tents and other tackle, and glittering shields,
Cabanes, and bundles of cloth, and noble coffers,
Hacks and riding horses and horses for battle;
Thus they stow in the gear of the many staunch knights.
      When all was shipped that should be, they stood no longer
But spread their sails to the wind, as the tide ran out:
Transport craft and wave-cutters beamed their masts
At the king's command, and all uncovered at once.
Deftly, up to the planks they weighed the anchors
By the skill of the mariners who ride the seas;   740
Men crawl out on the prow and coil the cables
On cutters, smaller craft, and Flemish freighters,
Tighten sail at the top and turn the helm,
Stand on the starboard rail and sing out sharply.
The priceless ships of the port now prove their depth
And draw with full sail over the light-flecked waves;
Without a trace of harm they haul the boats in,
And sharply then the sailors shut up the ports;
A sailor leaps to the tiller; they sound the depths;
They look to the lodestar, after the light gives out,   750
And cast their course by craft when clouds rise up,
Trusting to needle and stone on the night tides.
For dread of the dark of night they drag a little
And every craft on the current strikes oars at once.

❦ Arthur's First Dream

THE king was in a great galley, with many a knight,
      Enclosed in his royal cabin, fully appointed;
And within his splendid bed he was resting a little,
And because of the swing of the sea he fell to dreaming:
He dreamed of a dragon, dreadful to behold—
Came driving over the deep to drown his people,   760
Walking out of the western lands at dusk

And wandering fiercely over the ocean waves.
Both his head and his neck were covered all over
With wavy lines of azure, enameled and fair;
The scales on his shoulders were all of the cleanest silver
Enveloping all that snake with narrowing points;
His belly and wings were of wondrous hues,
In a marvelous coat of mail he mounted on high:
Whoever he touched was overthrown forever.
His feet were covered all over in finest sable,   770
And such a venomous flare flowed forth from his lips
That the flood seemed flashing fire from his breathing.
    Then out of the Orient and against him came
A fierce black bear with head heaved higher than the clouds
And every paw like a pillar, and monstrous palms,
And his claws were terrible, and appeared to flex,
Hateful and hating, in looks and in all else,
His hairy legs bowed and horribly matted,
Grotesquely tangled, lips all foam,
The foulest of figure that ever was formed.   780
He tumbled about and rolled his tongue and threatened,
And with flashing claws he readied himself for battle;
He howled, he roared, till he rocked the very earth,
So fiercely he struck out, to riot himself.
    At length the dragon turns against the other:
With powerful blows he drives him along the sky:
He flies like a falcon and then, fiercely, strikes,
And he fights with both his feet and his fire at once.
The bear seemed much the bigger in the battle
And bit him boldly with his baleful tusks;   790
Such vicious strokes he gave with his broad claws
The dragon's breast and neck were bloody all over.
He lunges about so wildly that all earth wheels,
Running with dark red blood like rain out of heaven.
He'd have wearied the mighty serpent by his awful strength
Were it not for the furious fire he used for defense.
    Then the dragon rises away to his heights,
Comes gliding from the clouds and swoops down even,
Pierces the bear with his talons and tears his backbone,
A rip from tail to head for ten full feet.   800
Thus did he break the bear and bring him to his grave,

23

And let him fall to the flood to float where he pleased.
They bring the brave king to the point, sleeping on shipboard,
That he nearly bursts for fear, on the bed where he lies.

    Then the wise king awakens, weary from his labor,
And calls to him two philosophers, who always follow him,
Found to be subtlest of men in the seven sciences,
And the wisest men of strange lore known under Christ;
He told them of his torment that came while he slept,
"–Harassed by a dragon, and such a dreadful beast   810
I'm weary, soul and body. Show me the meaning
Or I may soon die of it, as God is my judge."

    "Sire," they said to him then, these sage philosophers,
"The dragon you have dreamed of, so dreadful to behold,
That came driving over the deep to drown your people,
In truth and certainty, it is yourself
Who thus sails over the sea with your steadfast knights;
The colors you saw, cast on his clear wings
Are all your kingly holdings won by right;
The variegated tail with its many tongues   820
Betoken this fair host who ride in your fleet.
The bear that you saw broken, above in the clouds,
Betokens the tyrants who torment your people;
Or he may be some great giant you'll come to fight
Alone in single combat, with no man's aid;
And you, with the help of God, shall have the victory,
As you have been openly shown in this same vision.
Therefore have no more dread of this dire dream;
Fear not, O Conqueror, but comfort yourself
And all who sail on the sea with your trusty knights."   830

❨ King Arthur and the Giant

So, faithfully, on the trumpet call, all sailed,
And all that rich rout rowed across the sea;
And they caught sight soon enough of the Normandy coast
And blithely at Barfleur these bold men arrived
And there they found a fleet, and friends enough;
The flower and fairest folk of fifteen realms
For kings and captains awaited him as kindly

As Arthur had ordered himself at Carlisle on Christmas.
    And when they had taken to land and raised their tents
There came a Templar to them, and bowed to the king.   *840*
"There is a tyrant nearby who torments your people,
A great Genoan giant engendered by devils;
He has so far eaten up some five hundred folk,
And among them many an infant and freeman's child.
This has been all his food for seven winters,
And the fiend's not sated yet, he likes it so well.
In the country of Constantine he's left none alive
Outside the famous castles enclosed in walls,
But cruelly he's murdered all male children
And carried them to his crag and devoured them.   *850*
    Now today he has taken the duchess of Britain,
Near Rennes, as she rode with her strong knights,
And has carried her up to the cliff where the creature lives
To lie by that lady as long as her life lasts.
We followed far behind, five hundred or more—
Barons and burghers and noble young fighting men—
But he climbed to the crag. The lady shrieked so loud
I won't forget till I die that lady's terror.
She was flower of all France, or five such realms,
And one of the fairest that ever yet was formed;   *860*
And among the highborn, she was the noblest jewel
From Genoa to Gerone, by Jesus in heaven;
She was your own queen's cousin, know it if you please,
Born of the noblest blood to be found on earth:
As you are a righteous king, Sire, pity your people,
And see that they are avenged that are thus rebuked!"
    "Alas!" King Arthur said, "I've lived too long.
Had I known of this, I might have managed well!
It has not befallen me fair but has landed foul
Since this fair lady is destroyed by a vicious fiend.   *870*
I would gladly have given all France this fifteen winters
To be standing there, as far as a furlong off,
When he caught up that lady and carried her off to the mountains.
I'd have lost my life before letting her come to harm!
But show me the crag that cruel monster keeps:
I'll gladly go to the place and speak with him there,
To treat with that tyrant concerning his treason to lords,

And try for a time of truce until better can be done."

"Sire, do you see yonder foreland and those two fires?
There the monster lurks—seek him when you will—   880
Up on the crest of the crag, by a cold well
That closes up the cliff with its clear streams.
There you can find more dead than you can count,
More florins than you can find in the whole of France;
That traitor has got more treasure by his treachery
Than was found in Troy, I swear, when Troy was won."

Then for pity of his people, Arthur wept.
He turned at once to his tent, and he tarried no longer.
The tears ran down, and he bent and wrung his hands,
And not a man in his host knew what he intended.   890
He called for Sir Kay, the bearer of the cup,
And Sir Bedivere the bold, who bore his sword:
"Soon after evensong, see that you're suitably armed
And mounted, there by those bushes, where the river runs,
For I have decided to go in secret on a pilgrimage
At supper time, when lords are being served,
To seek a saint who lives by those salt streams,
On St. Michael's Mountain, where miracles are seen."

Then after evensong, King Arthur himself
Went into his wardrobe and changed into fighting clothes,   900
Dressed in an undercoat with splendid borders,
And over the undercoat a jerkin of Acre,
And after that a coat of gleaming mail
And a Jordan tunic, which hung in panes from the shoulders.
He puts on a visored headpiece of burnished silver,
The best to be found in all Basel, with beautiful borders—
The crest and the jeweled circlet splendidly clasped
With clips of glittering gold encrusted with stones;
Mouthplate and visor both were well adorned,
Perfect and without fault, with windows of silver;   910
His gloves were gaily gilded, engraved at the hems
With gems and gaudiwork, glorious of hue;
He buckles on a broad shield, seizes his sword,
Calls for a good strong seed and goes to the field.
He steps into the stirrup and strides aloft,
Forces the horse hard and steers him well,
Spurs the bay steed, speeds to the meeting place;

There his knights sit waiting, armed and arrayed.
    They rode along the river that ran so swift,
Where trees arched out above with regal boughs;   *920*
The roe and the reindeer ran there recklessly,
Revelling there in the thickets and wild rose trees;
The groves were all in bloom with brilliant flowers,
With falcons and cock pheasants of flaming hues;
And all the birds there flashed as they flew on their wings,
And there the cuckoos sang out clear in the groves,
And with every kind of joy they cheered themselves;
The notes of the nightingales rang sweetly there
As they struggled against the thrushes, three hundred at once,
And what with the murmur of the water and singing of birds   *930*
One might have been cured who had never been well in his life.
    The three rode on, then lit on one foot
And tied up their steeds some distance short of the slope;
And then King Arthur firmly commanded his knights
To stay here with the steeds and stir no further—
"For I will seek this saint by myself, alone,
And speak with this mighty master who lives on the mountain;
And later you shall make offerings, each in turn,
Most graciously to St. Michael, the mighty in Christ."
    The king climbs up to the crag with its high cliffs,   *940*
And up to the crest of the cliff he climbs aloft;
He casts up his visor-plate and boldly looks,
And catches cold wind to comfort himself.
He finds two fires flaming high,
And he hurries on a quarter-furlong more.
He walks alone on the path by the waterfall
To learn, concerning this warlock, where he lives;
He walks to the first fire and there he finds
A mournful widow wringing her hands,
And her dust-gray tears drop down upon a grave-mound   *950*
Newly marked on the ground, and made since midday.
He saluted the sorrowing one with gentle words
And afterward gently inquired concerning the fiend.
The woeful woman greeted him, void of joy,
Kneeling there on her knees, and clasped her hands;
She said, "Take care, Sir, you speak too loudly!
If yonder warlock hears, he'll murder us all.

Eternal doom to the man who has addled your wits
And led you to wander here in these high, wild lakes!
I warn you for your honor, you're asking for sorrow. 960
Where have you come from, Knight? You seem unblessed.
Do you dream you'll stop the fiend with your dreadful sword?
Were you greater than Wade or Gawain either,
You'd win no honor here, I warn you before!
You cross yourself in vain when you come to these mountains,
For six such men would hardly suffice against him,
For see him with your eyes and your heart will so fail you
You cannot cross yourself, he seems so huge.
    "You are freeborn and fair and still in first flower,
But by my faith you're fated to die, I fear. 970
Were fifty like you in the field, or on some fair plain,
That creature would fell you all at once with his fist.
Lo! Here lies the dear duchess—today she was taken—
Dead and buried deep and diked in clods;
He'd murdered the mild thing before midday was rung,
With never a mercy on earth. Who knows what it means?
He's forced her and defiled her and laid her to her fate,
Slew her crudely and slit her to the navel,
And here I have embalmed and afterward buried her,
From grief for this helpless one I'll never find joy. 980
Of all the friends she had, not one followed after
But I, her foster-mother this fifteen winters;
And never, now, can I leave this barren foreland,
But here I shall be found till my own fate comes."
    Then King Arthur answered the ancient woman:
"I have come from the conqueror, the courteous and noble,
As one of the noblest men among Arthur's knights,
A messenger sent to amend these wrongs for the people,
To speak with this mighty master who guards the mountain,
And treat of terms with this tyrant, by the treasure of lands, 990
To take truce for a time, until better may come."
"Ah! Your words are waste," said the woman then,
"For he sets no store by either lands or treaties,
And he cares for neither rents nor for burnished gold;
He'll rage on, outside law, for as long as he likes,
By no man's leave, with no other lord but his will.
He has a kirtle on, which he keeps for himself,

That was spun in Spain by specially chosen women
And afterward fitted together and fashioned in Greece;
It is covered over entirely with human hair   *1000*
And bordered about with the beards of stately kings,
Crisped and combed so that fighting men may know
Each king by his color, in the country where he lives.
He takes the tribute here of fifteen realms,
For on every Easter Eve—however it may happen—
They send him a beard, by their pact, for the safety of the people
And have done so every season, in the hands of knights.
A full seven winters he's sought King Arthur's beard;
It's for this he has come here, to kill King Arthur's people
Till the Britons' king has laid his two lips bare   *1010*
And sent his beard to that brute by the best of his barons;
Do not budge further unless you have brought the beard,
For it's wholly futile to offer him anything else.
The monster has more treasure to use as he likes
Than Arthur ever owned, or any of his elders.
If you've brought him the beard, the giant will be as glad
As he'd be at the gift of Burgundy or Britain;
But hold your tongue, I beg you in heaven's name,
That no words escape you, whatever the end may be;
See that your pleas are brief, and do not press him,   *1020*
For the creature's at supper, and quick to be aroused.
If you'd do as I advise, you would take off your mail
And kneel in only your kirtle, and call him your lord.
He's been eating all this season on seven male children
Chopped up in a platter of chalk-white silver
Mixed with pickles and the powder of precious spices
And plentifully flavored with Portugese wines;
Three sorrowing ladies stand turning his chimney spits
And come to his bed on command and do all he bids.
Four times as many would be dead within four hours   *1030*
Before all the filth that his flesh demands were finished."
      "Indeed, I do bring the beard," said he, "and gladly;
I'll set out at once, therefore, and bear it in person;
If you'll let me know, my lady, where the creature lives
I'll repay you well, if I live, as God preserve me."
"Walk straight to the fire," said she, "that flames so high;
There the fiend fills himself; find him when you please.

Or go seek him farther south, a little to the side,
For he may sprawl anywhere in the space of six miles."
      King Arthur strode at once to the source of the smoke,   *1040*
Signed himself carefully and said sure words;
And then, to one side of him, King Arthur saw
How filthily that foul sot supped alone.
He lay at full length, leaning, lounging obscenely,
The thigh of a man's leg lifted up by the haunch;
The back and the lower parts and the broad loins
Were roasting over that roaring fire, naked;
There were terrible roasts and sorrowful dinner meats—
Cattle and men upon one sharp spit together:
Great bowls crammed with chrismed children's bodies,   *1050*
Other corpses roasting; and the women turned them.
      And now this noble king, enraged for his people
Stands in the bending grass, and his heart bleeds.
And now he dresses his shield and stands no longer:
He brandished his blazing sword by the gleaming hilt
And stalked in all his fury toward that monster
And loudly hailed that hulk with haughty words.
"Now may great God in heaven, who gives all honor,
Give you sorrow and grief, you lout, where you lie,
The foulest, filthiest freak that was ever yet formed;   *1060*
Foully you feed yourself! The Fiend have your soul!
Here's monstrous quarry indeed you churl, I swear!
You cast-off trash of all animals, rotten-souled wretch!
Because you've killed these chrismed children,
Made them martyrs, and lifted them out of life,
Who are spitted here and broken by your hands.
I'll pay you your reward for all your service,
By the might of St. Michael, master of this mountain,
And for this fair lady forced here to her fate,
Whom you forced and fouled for the filth of your pleasure;   *1070*
Guard yourself, dog's son! may the devil get your soul,
Today is the day you die, destroyed by my hands."
      The glutton raised up in alarm and glared with rage;
He grinned like a greyhound with grizzly tusks;
His mouth gaped and he growled; his look was grim
From anger at the good king who greeted him with wrath;
The giant's mane and forelock were matted together

And out of his mouth came a half foot's breadth of foam;
The creature's forehead and face were flawed all over
And darkly splotched as the skin of a frog: *1080*
He was hooknosed as a hawk, with a hoary beard,
Haired to the very eyeholes with hanging brows;
Rough as a houndfish, as anyone could have seen,
Was the whole dark hide of that hulk, from end to end.
Enormous ears he had, and ugly to view.
And his eyes were terrible and burned like fire;
He was flat mouthed as a flounder, with flaring lips,
And the gums around his foreteeth foul as a bear's.
His beard was bristly and black and stretched to his breast.
His body fat, like the carcass of a sea pig;   *1090*
And all the fat, loose flesh of his foul lips trembled,
And every fold, like a wolf's head, writhed at once.
Bull necked the creature was, and broad of shoulder,
Badger-breasted as a boar, with big stiff bristles,
Sprawling-armed as an oak, with wrinkled sides,
Loathly of limb and loin—believe the truth!
A shovel-footed thing, and spraddle legged
With oafish shanks that shuffled his weight along;
Thick thighs like a hero's, but thickest in the haunches,
Grown to grease like a sow, grotesque on all sides;   *1100*
And whoever would truly report that wretch's length,
From forelock to foot he was five full fathoms long.
     Then sturdily up he starts on thick, stiff shanks,
And he caught up his club at once, that was all of clean iron;
He'd have killed the king with that cruel weapon,
Except that by Christ's will the churl failed;
The crest and the coronal ring, with its clasps of silver,
At one clean swipe of the club he crashed in at once.
     The king casts up his shield and keeps good guard;
With his splendid sword he strikes him a blow,   *1110*
Hits the headpan in front with his full force,
And the burnished blade of his sword runs clean to the brain;
The creature wiped at his face with his foul hands
And struck out hard in turn at Arthur's face;
Quickly the king shifts footing and ducks a little:
Had he not escaped that chop, he'd have taken it badly!
He follows in, ferocious, and lays on a stroke

High on the giant's haunch with his hard steel weapon,
And at once the sword was hidden a half foot's length;
The hot blood of that hulk ran down to the hilt, *1120*
And even into the bowels of the giant he'd hit,
And the tip hit the genitals, and cut them asunder.

    That giant roared and reared and lashed out wildly,
Eagerly after Arthur; he struck the earth
A sword's length into the sward, and he swiped again,
So that Arthur might well have swooned from the roar of his blows,
But still the king plays swiftly, nimbly with his sword,
Sweeps the sharp blade in, splits open the loins
So that both the guts and gore gush out at once,
And all the ground he stands on glitters with grease. *1130*

    The giant cast down his club, and clutched at the king;
On the crest of the crag he caught him up in his arms,
Seized him to himself, to split his ribs;
And he hugs that king so hard that his heart almost bursts;
Then the sorrowing women bent down to the earth,
Kneeling and crying, and slapped their hands together:
"Christ, defend your knight, and keep him from grief,
And never permit this fiend to pull down his life!"

    So powerful is that warlock he rolls him under,
And wrathfully they wrestle and writhe together; *1140*
They roll and wallow and twist, within those bushes,
Tumble and turn hard, and tear their clothes;
In rage at the top of that cliff they tilt together,
And one moment Arthur's above, the next moment under,
And they crash from the height of the hill to the hard rocks;
They never cease though they smash to the very seamarks.
Then Arthur stuck at him hotly with his dagger:
Again and again he rammed it home to the hilt;
The brute in his death convulsion so closed on the king
That he snapped like sticks three ribs in Arthur's side. *1150*

    The bold Sir Kay then bounded to where the king was,
Said, "Alas! we are lost! My lord is confounded—
Overthrown by a fiend, and our fate has gone foul.
We must now be forfeited, banished forever."
They lifted his hauberk and hunted for the death wound,
Probed the length of his hide from haunch to shoulders,
His flanks and loins and his fair sides,
Both his back and his chest and his gleaming arms,

They were glad they could find no wound that would let in death;
And for that day's luck those gentle knights rejoiced.   1160
    "Now surely," Sir Bedivere says, "it seems, by my Lord,
He must seek saints but seldom, to clutch them so fiercely
And so eagerly drag down their holy bones from high cliffs,
And carry home such a creature to clothe in silver.
By Michael, a man like this one, it makes you wonder
That ever our sovereign Lord would suffer him in heaven;
If all the saints are such, who serve our Lord,
I'll never become a saint, on my father's soul!"
The bold King smiled when he heard Sir Bedivere's words.
This is the saint I've sought—our Lord preserve me!   1170
    "Pull out your sword, and plunge the blade to his heart;
Make sure of the fellow; he's grieved me a good deal.
I haven't fought with his like this fifteen winters;
Except in the mountains in Wales, where I once met another,
He was the fiercest I've ever found, by far,
And if Fortune hadn't been with me, I would have been done for.
Strike off his head at once and set it on a stake
And hand it up to your squire, since he's well horsed,
Bear it to good Sir Hoel, who's been hard pressed,
And bid him be light of heart; his enemy is dead.   1180
Afterward bear it to Barfleur, and brace it in iron
And set it up on the barbican for all to see.
My sword and my broad shield are lying on the ground
On the crest of the crag where we two first encountered,
And the giant's club nearby, all of clean iron,
The killer of many a Christian in Constantine's lands.
Go to the foreland and fetch me the weapon
And let it be taken to the fleet, where it floats in the harbor;
If you wish any treasure, go take there what you please;
If I have the kirtle and the club, I covet no more."   1190
    And now these comely knights climbed up to the crag
And they brought him his broad war shield and bright steel sword,
And Sir Kay himself brought the kirtle and club
And walked with the conqueror to show the kings
King Arthur kept at his headquarters, close to himself,
While clear day climbed to the clouds overhead and was gone.
    The clamor of tidings had come into court before them,
And before King Arthur the people all kneeled at once:
"Welcome, our lord; you have kept away too long,

33

Our governor under God, most noble and able,   *1200*
To whom all grace is granted and given by His will.
But now your gracious coming brings comfort to us all:
You have wrought our vengeance for us, by your royalty;
By the might of your hand, your enemy you hurl down
Who overran your people and ravished their children;
No realm in trouble was ever so greatly relieved!"
    Then kindly the Christian conqueror spoke to his people:
"Thanks be to God," he said; "it's His grace, not mine,
It was not the work of a man but His own might
Or the miracle of His mother, mild towards all."   *1210*
And after that he assembled the shipmen quickly
To go with men of each shire, and to move down the treasure:
"All the great treasure that the traitor won
Give to the commons of the country, both clergy and others;
See it distributed justly to all my people,
And on pain of your lives, see that none need complain of their
                                              part."

Then Arthur commanded his cousin with knightly words
To build a high chapel on the crag where the corpse lay
And to make a convent within, where Christ would be served
In memory of the lady who was martyred there.   *1220*

❲ Sir Gawain and Lucius

Now after Arthur the king had killed the giant,
   He eagerly set out, at dawn, from Barfleur;
With all the breadth of his host on the brimming sea
He makes his way by ship towards Whitecastle
Through shining countryside, below chalk hills.
He tries a path across the fresh blue water,
Travels on with his fair folk, just as he pleases;
Then the stern hero steps forth, stakes his tents
On a stronghold hard by the river, there in the straitlands.
    And while the men worked, a little time past midday,   *1230*
There came two messengers riding from distant marches
From the marshall of France. They greet him fittingly
And ask King Arthur's help, and say these words:
"Milord, the marshall, your minister, asks mercy

From your great majesty, for the aid of the people
Against their border enemies, for they are assailed
And cruelly mistreated, maugre their eyes.
I come to report that the Emperor now is in France
With hosts of our enemies, horrible men and huge;
In fair Burgundy they burn your beautiful cities   1240
And break the baronage that has built them there;
By craft of arms he cruelly encroaches
On every castle or country which clings to your crown;
He's confounded all the commons, the clergy, and others,
And unless you aid them, sir, they can never recover.
He fells your many forests, forays through the lands,
Alarms the people and leaves no refuge standing,
But strikes down those who live there and seizes their goods;
It's believed that the French tongue may be fated to die.
He draws into fair France, the Germans say,   1250
With his army driving on dragons, dreadful to see;
And all that stands in their way they drive down to darkness,
Dukes and douzeperes, all those who tarry in the path;
And therefore the lords of the land—both lords and ladies—
Pray you, for love of St. Peter, apostle of Rome,
Since you have come here, quickly proffer war
To the perilous prince and repel him, in the process of time.
He is camped in those high hills, beyond the holtwoods,
Tarries there with his legions of heathen kings;
For the love of God who sits high in heaven, help us,   1260
And send sharp words to the prince who seeks to destroy us!"
     The king said to Sir Bors: "Be gone at once!
Take good Sir Beril with you, and mighty Sir Bedivere,
Sir Gawain and Sir Grun, those valiant knights,
And get to those green woods and give them my message:
Say to Sir Lucius his work is less than lordly,
Who despite all law attacks and would ransom my people;
I'll end his work before long, if my life allows,
And many a man shall drop who draws behind him.
Command him keenly, then, with cruel words   1270
To get out of my kingdom with all his infamous knights,
And if that cursed wretch should refuse to go,
Let him come, for his courtesy's sake, and encounter me once.
We shall reckon soon enough what right he claims

To riot all this realm and ransom the people;
There shall we deal out truth by dint of our hands:
Let Him who governs Doomsday deal as He pleases."
    Now they prepare to be gone, these gallant knights,
All in a glitter of gold, on great white steeds,
Riding to the green wood, with keen-ground weapons,   *1280*
Fitly to greet the great lord who was soon to be grieved.
    The noblemen paused on a hill by the edge of the wood
And beheld the high camp of the heathen kings above them—
They could hear within that forest a good many hundred
Horns of elephants, all shrieking high;
There were palaces proudly adorned and stoutly piked,
Of purple and pall, all set with precious stones;
The streamers and splendid bosses of princes' arms
Burgeoned in the open meadow for the people to see.
And then the mightly Romans had arrayed their rich tents   *1290*
In long rows by the river below the round hills,
The emperor, for his honor, in the midst of them,
With eagles all around annealed so fair;
And they saw him there with the sultan and many of his senators,
Proceeding towards his hall, with sixteen kings,
Sailing softly in, all splendor, alone,
To sup with their sovereign on all his sundry dishes.
And now King Arthur's men came over the water
And through the wood to the hall where the nobles rested
Soon after they'd washed and gone to the trestled table;   *1300*
And Sir Gawain, the worthy man spoke soberly:
"The might and majesty that gives grace to us all,
Apportioned and established by His own power,
Bring you despair on your dais, O Sultan and others
Assembled here in this hall; may dissention wreck you!
And the false heretic who calls himself Emperor,
Occupying in error the empire of Rome,
The heritage of Arthur, that honorable king,
Which all of his ancestors ruled save Uther himself,
May the curse that came on Cain for the killing of his brother   *1310*
Cleave unto you, crowned cuckold, where you sit,
Least lordly of all the men I ever looked at!
    "My lord is much amazed, man, on my oath,
To see you so murder his men who've done nothing amiss—

36

The commons of the country, the clergy, and others,
Who are culpable in nothing and take up no arms.
Therefore the true and good king, courteous and noble,
Commands you sharply to get out of his lands
Or else, for your knighthood's sake, to encounter him once.
And since you covet his crown, let your claim be declared.   *1320*
For this I have come. Come challenge me any who likes
Before all this chivalry, both chieftains and others.
Frame us an answer quickly, and fiddle no longer,
So we can be gone in good time and give it to the king."
  The Emperor answered Sir Gawain with bitter words:
"You belong to my enemy, Sir Arthur himself;
It would not serve my honor to strike at his knights,
Wrathful fools though they are who run on his errands.
But say this to your sovereign, I send him these words—
And were it not for the honor of this rich table   *1330*
You'd repent with bitter haste your high-flown talk;
How dare such a wretch as you rebuke any lord
Arrayed with his retinue, most regal and noble!—
I shall sojourn here for as long as I see fit,
And later proceed up the Seine at my own pleasure;
I besiege all the cities by the shores of the salt sea,
And then ride in by the Rhone, where it runs so fair,
And break down the battlements of his beautiful cities.
In due time, I shall not leave in Paris
His part of a haycock, prove it if he likes."   *1340*
  "Now surely," says Sir Gawain, "I'm much amazed!
That such a dwarf as you dare speak so boldly!
I'd liever than all France, the flower of kingdoms,
Fight with you faithfully, in the field by ourselves!"
  After that Sir Gayous spoke boastful words,
An earl himself, and an uncle to the emperor:
"They've always been full of braggart's talk, these Britons!
Look! How he brawls in all his pretty clothes;
As if he would butcher us all with his big rich sword!
Yet he breaks out powerful boasts, that boy, where he stands!" *1350*
  At these grim jokes, Sir Gawain was filled with rage,
And he darted toward the fellow with anger in his heart
And swiftly he struck off his head with his sword of steel,
Then started away to his steed, and rode off with his comrades.

They rushed away through the watchmen, these worshipful
                                            knights,
And found so many in their way they were fairly amazed.
Then over the water they went, by the might of their horses,
And took what wind they could by the edge of the woods.
Behind them followed on foot far more than enough
And the Roman army in array on their powerful horses,   *1360*
And through all the countryside they chased our knights
Till they came to the chief of the forests, on chalk-white steeds.
It was there that a man in fine gold, all fretted with sable,
Closed the gap on his Friesland, in clothes like fire:
He snapped his splendidly fashioned spear to its brace
And followed the heroes' heels, and howled out fiercely.
    Then Sir Gawain the good, on his steed of gray,
Gripped him a great spear and gave it flight;
He split the man through the guts and through to the gore
And the ground-steel glided smoothly clear to the heart.   *1370*
The man and the great horse lunge to the ground
Horribly groaning now for the grief of the wound.
And a pricker presses in, all proudly arrayed,
The horseskirts all of rich purple and pranked with silver:
Boldly on his brown steed, he proffers his lance.
A pagan of Persia he was, pursuing them now.
Sir Boys rode straight against him, unabashed,
And with his terrible lance he bore the man through.
The bold man and the broad shield lay on the battlefield
And he brought out the blade and bounded back to his   *1380*
                                      companions.
    Then Sir Feltemour the mighty, a man much praised,
Was moved to wrath, and he came up, menacing.
He swiftly turns to Sir Gawain to force him to battle
In vengeance for Sir Gayous, who's laid to the ground.
And Gawain's heart was glad. He rode against him
With Galuth, his good sword, and quickly he struck.
He cleaved in two that knight, still up on his courser,
Cleanly divided the corpse, straight down from its crown,
And thus he kills the knight with his well-known weapon.
    A powerful man of Rome turned round to his barons—   *1390*
"We'll live to repent it sore if we ride any farther!
These men are bold jousters and may well do us harm;

You see what has happened to those who have dared to approach
them."

And so now the powerful Romans turn their bridles,
Retreat to their tents in sorrow, report to their lords
How sir marshal of Mohammed is left on the mountain,
Jousted down that day despite all his skill.
Yet others still charged after our chivalrous knights,
Five thousand rushing men on their flashing steeds,
Firmly into the forest, beyond the deep water   *1400*
That flowed some fifty miles from the far off pale sea.
    On the hill there were Britons in ambush, with noble
bannerets,

All the chief chevaliers of the king's own chamber;
They see them chasing our men, and turning their horses
Chopping down Arthur's chief knights, those hardest pressed.
Then all the ambush of Britons broke out at once,
Hurtling forward with banners, and Bedwin's knights with them
Flew out in front of the Romans who flock through the forest,
All the noblest of the earls in Rome's allegiance;
They set on the enemy swiftly and struck out, eager,   *1410*
Earls of all England, and "Arthur!" was their cry.
Through byrnies and brilliant shields they pierce to the breast,
The boldest of all the Britons with their blazing swords.
And there were the Romans thrown down, and roughly wounded,
Arrested as rebels by Arthur's great riot of knights.
In disarray the Romans retreated at once
And they rode away in a rout, as if for sheer terror.
To the senator Peter a messenger came swiftly
And said, "Sire, truly, your soldiers are struck by surprise."
Ten thousand men this Peter assembled at once   *1420*
And went to the Britons swiftly by way of the water.
The Britons were troubled in turn, and a little hurt,
But still the standard-bearers and stout men-at-arms
Broke the foe's battle ranks with the breasts of steeds.
Sir Boys and his bold men brought bale to the enemies.
The Romans took counsel then, arrayed themselves better,
And rushed the Britons once more with their rested horses,
And checked the greatest chiefs of King Arthur's court,
Overrode the rear guard, brought them to grief.
    Then the fierce Britons could keep to the field no longer   *1430*

39

But fled away to the forest, and left the lowland.
Sir Beril was borne down, and Sir Boys was taken,
And the best of our bold men were bitterly wounded,
And still our troop in its stronghold staggered a little,
Baffled now by the buffets of Rome's bold knights,
Made sorrow for their sovereign who was captured there,
Cried to God for succour, send it when He liked.
        And then up comes Sir Idrus, armed at all points,
With five hundred fighting men upon fair steeds,
And at once they ask our people, and eagerly,   *1440*
If any allies are nearby, on the field for the fight.
Sir Gawain says to them then, "So help me God,
We've been chased about today and pushed like rabbits,
Rebuked by Romans rushing upon rich steeds,
And we've lurked under our cover like lowering wretches!
I'll never dare look at my lord all the days of my life
If we can't work better for him, who loved him so well!"
        Then fiercely all the Britons spurred their horses
And boldly rode into battle across the green fields;
In front of them they make out the fierce men   *1450*
Walking into the forest to take their rest.
The Romans quickly draw close and array themselves better
In rows on the ground clearing, and ready their weapons,
Rallying once again by the gleaming river.
And Sir Boys was held in arrest in the midst of them.
        They stand assembled at strife by the salt sea
And grimly these stalwart men address their blows;
With gleaming lances aloft they lunge together
There in lordly Loraine, with leaping steeds.
There were men enough run through with well-ground   *1460*
                                                                weapons,
Gasping, full of pain for their grievous wounds—
Great lords of the Greek host bitterly grieved.
Swiftly with their swords they swipe around them,
Striking down on the spot all fainting knights,
So that all swoon to the grass whom their swords sweep down on;
So many sway in a swoon, all falling at once!
Sir Gawain the gracious, he works on eagerly,
And greets the greatest there with grisly wounds;
With Galuth he cuts down most gallant knights,
Avenging the great lord, and grimly he strikes.   *1470*

He rides forth quickly, kinglike, after that
To where this highborn lord is held in arrest;
He cleaves their clean hard steel and pierces their byrnies,
Recaptures the worthy man and rides back to his forces.
The senator Peter went after him, hard in pursuit
Through the press of the people, with his prized knights;
Openly, close to the prisoner, proves his strength
With the proudest prickers belonging to the Roman press;
Fiercely he strikes Sir Gawain on his left hand,
And swings his battle sword and sorely hits him,   *1480*
So the back half of his byrnie was burst asunder;
Yet Gawain brought back Sir Boys, for all their brave warriors.
     Then boldly the Britons blasted on their trumpets,
And for joy that Sir Boys was brought back from imprisonment
They boldly bear down many a knight in battle:
With blades of powerful steel they break all the melee.
They stab at steeds where they stand, with hard steel weapons,
And struck with strength at all who stood against them.
Sir Idrus Fitz Ewain then cries out "Arthur!"
And rides on the senator with sixteen knights,   *1490*
Some of the surest men to be seen on our side.
Suddenly, all in a crowd, they storm in at once,
And fiercely they flay the breastplates with flaming swords
And they fight on eagerly after that, at the front.
They fell a good many on the field, on the foreigner's side,
Fated on the fair green field by the flashing strands.
But Sir Idrus Fitz Ewain breaks in himself
And goes against them singly, and eagerly strikes:
He seeks out the senator, and seizes his bridle,
And boldly he shouted to him these fitting words: *1500*
"Surrender, sir, and swiftly, to save your life;
For the ransom you may pay, remain with the living!
For I swear if you give me trouble, or try any tricks,
You're doomed to die this day by the might of my hands."
"I surrender," the senator cries, "may Christ defend me!
But let me be brought in safely before your king;
Ransom me reasonably, an amount I can pay,
As much as my rents in Rome can readily furnish."
     Then Sir Idrus answers with harsh words:
"You'll get conditions such as the king may please   *1510*
When you come into the country where he holds court.

It may be his counsel to keep you alive no longer
But kill you by his commandment before all his knights."
They led him forth in a crowd and pulled off his clothing
And left him with Lowell and Lionel, his brother.

    And now, down in that land by the quiet sea,
The loyal liegemen of Lucius are lost forever:
The senator Peter is taken a prisoner
And from Persia to far Port Joppa, many prized knights,
And many more good men have perished in the place,   *1520*
Plunged into the sea from the press of battle.
There might men see Romans ruefully wounded,
Overridden by ranks of Arthur's Round Table.
On the road to the fording place they adjust their byrnies,
The iron running with red blood streams all over;
And bringing up the rear there were royal knights
For the ransom of new red gold and regal steeds.
They pause for only a little and rest their horses
And ride all together in a rout to the greatest of kings.

    One knight rides on ahead, and he tells the king: *1530*
"Sire, your messengers come here with joy from the mountains:
They've matched today with men of the marches,
Mingled for battle in the moors with marvelous knights.
We have fought there, on my faith, by those fresh streams,
The fiercest of those who have followed your Roman foe.
Fifty thousand on the field, fierce men of arms,
Are left there to their fate, a furlong off.
We've only by heaven's chance escaped destruction
By the army of men that has marched to attack your people.
The chief chancellor of Rome, a noble chieftain,   *1540*
Will ask, himself, your charter of peace, for charity,
And the senator Peter is taken prisoner.
From Persia and Port Joppa pagans aplenty
Come riding in the press, with your prized knights,
To suffer their pains in poverty, in your prison.
I beseech you, sir, to say what your pleasure is,
Whether you'll grant them peace or give them prison.
You can get for the senator sixty horses, loaded
With silver by Saturday, all surely paid,
And for the chief chancellor, a noble chevalier,   *1550*
Chariots charged chock-full with gold;
The remnant of the Romans might be held in arrest

42

Till their rents in Rome can be rightly ascertained.
I beseech you, make known to yonder lords,
Will you send them over the sea or keep them yourself?
All your own men, in truth are believed to be sound
Except for Sir Ewain Fitz Henry, who is wounded in the side."
   "Christ be thanked," said the king, "and His holy mother
Who have aided you and helped you by heavenly wisdom;
He gives out just discomfort as suits His pleasure,   *1560*
And none can escape unscathed, twist free of His hands.
Destiny, and strength in deeds of arms
Are judged and dealt to men at God's own will!
I thank you, sir, for your message; it pleases me well.
Sir knight," says the conqueror, "as Christ is my help,
I give you for these good tidings the rich Tolouse,
The rents and all taxation, the taverns and the rest,
The town and the tenements and the lofty towers,
All that is temporal in it while my time lasts.
   "And say to the senator I send him these words: *1570*
No silver shall save his life unless Ewain recovers;
I had liever see him sink in the salty sea,
Than the man be sick who's now so sorely wounded;
As Christ is my stay, I shall scatter that company
And set them solitary in many kings' lands;
He will never again in this life see his elders in Rome
Nor sit in assembly, in the sight of his peers.
For it is not fitting for a king considered a conqueror
To communicate with his captives for his coveting of silver.
It has no knighthood in it—know it if he pleases—   *1580*
To talk about ransom terms when captives are taken;
Nor is it fitting that prisoners press lords
Or come in the presence of princes when pleas are moved.
And command my constable, who keeps the castle,
That the man be honorably kept and closely restricted;
He shall have my decision tomorrow when midday is rung
On which of my countries he'll go to, to live in grief."
   With noble men of arms they led off the captive
And turned him over to the constable, as the king bid;
Thereafter they turned back to Arthur and eagerly told him   *1590*
The answer the emperor, wrathful of deeds, had sent.
Then Arthur, noblest of all the kings on earth,
That evening, at his own table, addressed his knights:

"I am bound to honor above all others on earth
Those who in my absence defend my lands;
I shall love them all my life, as the Lord may help me,
And give them good large lands wherever they like;
If I live, they shall lose nothing in this game,
Who are hurt for love of me, here by the smooth sea."

❡ Sir Cador's Expedition to Paris

AT DAWN the following day, the king himself   *1600*
Commanded Sir Cador, together with well-born knights,
Sir Cleremus and Sir Cleremond, with good men of arms,
Sir Claudmor and Sir Clegis, to convey the prisoners;
And Sir Boys and Sir Berell, with banners in display,
Sir Bedwin, Sir Brian, and glorious Sir Bedivere,
Sir Rainalt and Sir Richer, the sons of Rolant,
To ride with the Romans in a rout, along with the others.
 "Ride out now secretly to splendid Paris,
With Peter, our prisoner, and his prized knights;
Hand them over to the provost, in the presence of lords,   *1610*
On the pain and on the peril that goes with that,
That the prisoners all be well watched and kept under guard,
Guarded and guaranteed by good strong knights;
Have him hire seasoned men, and spare no silver,
And tell the man I have warned him, beware if he likes."
 Now the Britons set out as the king has bid,
Arrange their battle gear, their banners flaring;
They chose the road towards Chartres, these chivalrous knights,
And out in the open country they cross with good luck.
 But on his side, the mighty emperor had ordered   *1620*
Sir Utolf and Sir Evander, honorable kings,
Earls of the Orient, with able knights
And among the most audacious in all his host—
Sir Sextinor of Libya and a great many senators,
The king of Assyria himself, with Saracens enough,
The senator of Sutri with great sums of men
Assigned to his royal court by assent of his peers—
To move towards Troyes and there to work their treason,
To trap with all their train our traveling knights

44

Who had vouchsafed that Sir Peter would soon be in Paris   *1630*
To endure his punishment under the provost in person.
The Romans pressed on hard with their banners in display
To ambush the Britons on the way with their big war horses;
They plant themselves in the path with their power arrayed
To take back the prisoners from our worthy knights.
  The young Sir Cador of Cornwall commands his peers,
Sir Clegis, Sir Cleremus, the noble Sir Cleremond,
"We have come to the pass of Clime with its towering cliffs.
See that the country is clear; it has many corners;
Explore the brushwood and holts, and skip over nothing,   *1640*
And see that no enemy in the thicket surprise us later.
See that you manage well, so no trouble befalls us,
For harassers hiding in the holt woods are hard men to beat."
  They ride up into the wood, these war-brave knights,
To help the convoy by hunting for men in the hills.
They find them all in their helmets and mounted on steeds,
Holding the highway, waiting by the hem of the woods.
Severely and haughtily, Sir Clegis himself
Cried to the company there and called out these words:
"Is there any valiant knight here, king or other,   *1650*
Who'll try, for the love of his king, the craft of arms?
We come here from the king of this rich country
Who is known as the conqueror, crowned here on earth,
And we are his mighty retainers, men of the Round Table,
Who ride in that royal man's ranks wherever he pleases.
We look for the jousting of battle—if battle should come—
With the mightiest men among you, whom you call lords,
If any brave man is here, among earls and others,
Who'll prove himself, for the emperor's sake, against us."
  At once an earl called back to him in anger: *1660*
"I scorn King Arthur and all his barons
Who thus unjustly occupy these realms,
Betraying the emperor, his earthly lord.
All the array of the royalty of the Round Table
Is cried against with rage in many a realm.
He holds his revels now with our Roman rents,
But soon he'll explain himself, if all goes right with us,
And many a man shall be sorry he rode with that rout
And served with a king who can rule not even himself!"

"Ah!" says Sir Clegis then, "as Christ is my help,   *1670*
I understand by your speech you're a paltry accountant;
But auditor, earl, or emperor himself,
On Arthur's behalf I'll settle with you soon.
The great and royal king who rules us all,
The rich and powerful lords of Arthur's Round Table,
Has raised up his account and has read his rolls;
He will give you a reckoning you may come to rue,
And every rich lord may repent being vassal to Rome
Before he's paid all the arrears he requires by right.
We ask of your courtesy now three courses of war   *1680*
With men who claim knighthood—take care now of your fame!
You dally with us, so far, with trifling words;
There's treachery among armed men who travel as you do.
Now soberly send out your chosen knights
Or tell me your cowardice truly, and flee if you like."

    Up speaks the king of Syria, "As the Lord save me,
Although you huff all the day, you'll not be delivered
Unless you send us your sign, by certain knights,
That the coat of arms you carry is worthy of lords,
By ancestry of arms, and appointed to lands."   *1690*
"Sir King," Sir Clegis says, "you've spoken like a knight;
I suppose it's mere cowardice that makes you ask.
My arms are of ancestry verified by lords;
We've borne them on our banners since Brutus' time.
At the city of Troy, at the time it was besieged,
My arms were seen in assault with the surest of knights,
And our line was brought from Borghte, by my bold elders,
On shipboard over the sea to the shores of Britain."

    "Sir," Sir Sextenor said, "say all you like,
Our side will suffer you, as seems to us best;   *1700*
But I'd rather you'd stow your trumpets and trifle no longer,
For though you may tarry till dark, you'll be no better off;
For never will any brave Roman who rides in my rout
Be jousted down by mere rebels while my reign lasts."

    Then Sir Clegis nodded to the enemy king
And went to the young Sir Cador and said to him, knightly,
"We've found up there in the forest, well hidden in the leaves,
The flower of the fairest folk that belong to your foe,
Fifty thousand fighters, all fierce men of arms,

With their lances braced for battle below those free boughs.   *1710*
They wait on white horses in ambush, with banners displayed,
There in the forest of beeches, beside the road.
They've cut us off from the ford of the flowing river,
And on their faith they'll be forced to fight with us;
Thus has our lot fallen, in a few words
Whether we strike or flee, decide as you like."

    "No!" said Sir Cador, "as Christ is my help,
It would be a shame if we fled from a thing so trifling!
I cannot let Lancelot laugh, back there with the king,
At my leaving the highway for any lord living on earth.   *1720*
I'll be dead and undone before any man sees me withdraw
For dread of any dog's son waiting in the thicket."
Most nobly then Sir Cador encouraged his people,
And keen with courage he called to them these words:
"Think on the valiant prince who has given us possessions,
Splendid lands and lordships, wherever we like,
Who deals out dukedoms to us and dubs us knights,
Grants us treasures and gold and many rewards,
Greyhounds and great horses and all our good sports,
All that each of us living here owns under God;   *1730*
Think on the mighty renown of the glorious Round Table:
We'll not be robbed of that for a Roman on earth!
Let no man feint or feign or strike out with no force,
But see you fight faithfully, with all your power;
I'd rather be boiled alive, or drawn and quartered,
Than fail this business, now while I feel this wrath."

    Then this doughty duke dubbed his knights,
Joneke and Ascanere, Aladuke and others,
Young men, heirs of Essex and all our east marches;
Howell and Hardelf, lucky men in arms,   *1740*
Sir Heril and Sir Herigal, high-minded fighters.
Then the leader assigned all his lords to their fields,
Sir Gawain, Sir Uriel, Sir Bedivere the mighty,
Rainalt and Richere, the royal sons of Rolant—
"Keep watch on this prince with your precious knights,
And if in the first encounter we stand successful,
Stay right here in this place, and stir no further;
But if it should chance that our forces are overthrown,
Retreat at once to some castle, and close yourselves in,

Or ride to the royal king, if they give you room,   *1750*
And beg him to rush here quickly to rescue his barons."
And then the Britons boldly braced their shields,
Let down their visors, lifted up their lances.
And thus he drew up his people and rode to the field,
Five hundred men on the front line, flank to flank.
They raised their trumpets up, on skirted steeds,
And with cornets and clarions and clear-ringing notes,
They gallop into the charge, and wait no more,
And rush to the shining passes below green leaves.
At once the Roman rout drew back a little   *1760*
And all those royal knights fell back to the rear;
So swiftly the horses rushed that the whole host rang
With plate and with rattling steel and with rich gold mail.
    Then out of the shadows came all the shining foemen
With sharp weapons of war, all shouting at once:
The king of Lebe came thundering out in the vanguard
And all his loyal liegemen leapt out beside him.
That cruel king caught his lance and clapped it to the brace,
Riding an armored steed and kept to his course,
Bearing down on Sir Beril, and brutally hits him,   *1770*
Straight through the gorger and gullet he slams his lance,
And both the man and the horse were hurled to the ground,
And Beril cried out to God, and his soul was gone.
Thus is the bold Sir Beril brought down out of life
To wait for his burial in the way he has chosen.
And then was Sir Cador of Cornwall hard grieved in his heart
To see his sweet kinsman lost, his mission miscarried;
He catches the corpse, and he kisses it time and again,
And Cador's knights rushed up in a circle to guard him.
The king of Lebe then laughed and he called aloud: *1780*
"Yon lord has alighted now; I like that better!
He'll daunt us no more today—the devil have his bones!"
"Yon king," Sir Cador cries, "crows mightly loud
Because he has killed this keen man; Christ have your soul!
He'll get his miller's pay, as Christ is my help!
Before I leave this coast we'll encounter once;
And if the wind turns right, I'll repay him by dusk,
Send him to Judgment himself, or some of his comrades."
    And then the keen Sir Cador rose up like a knight,

Cried out, "For Cornwall!", clapped his lance to the brace,   *1790*
Came riding straight through the troops on his rich steed,
And many brave men went down by the power of his rush.
When his lance was sprung awry he still sped on,
Sweeping all sides with a sword whose blade never failed him,
And he wounded sweet knights in a swath, and made him a
                                      highway;
His course in causes a good many aching sides,
And he chops the necks of the hardiest there in half
So that all the land where his horse runs blends with blood.
Thus many in armor that bold man brought out of life,
Tottering tyrants down, emptied their saddles,   *1800*
And then turned away from his toil when the time seemed right.
Then the king of Lebe cried out aloud
Against Sir Cador the keen, with cruel words:
"Great worship you have won; you wound many knights!
You think you can make all the world your own by your might.
I stand here ready at your hand, man, by my troth!
I've warned you well; beware as it may please you."
With clarions and cornets the newly dubbed knights
Galloped at Cador's call, and braced their lances,
And they hurled at the enemy line, on iron gray steeds,   *1810*
Fought down men of the first rank, fifty at once,
Shot through the enemy, shattering strong lances,
And laid out lordly byrnies in a bleeding crowd.
And thus nobly our new men now use their power.
But the sequel is a tale that is sad to tell.
    The king of Lebe has taken a horse that pleased him
And moves up, lordly under his lions of silver,
Surrounds the new knights, breaks their ranks asunder,
And many a bold man falls, brought down by his lance.
Thus he pursues young men of the king's own chamber   *1820*
And kills in that countryside those chivalrous knights,
Flies after them with his spear and strikes them down.
There was Sir Aladuke slain, and Ascanere wounded,
Sir Origge and Sir Ermingal hewn to bits;
And there Sir Lewellyn was taken, and Lewellyn's brother,
Seized by the lords of Lebe and led to their stronghold
And had not Sir Clegis come, and the noble Sir Clement,
Our new men had all gone to nought, and many another.

Then Sir Cador the keen clapped lance to brace,
A cruel lance and sharp, and rode at the king;   *1830*
He hit him high up on the helmet with his hard weapon,
And the hot blood ran down his body and flowed from his hand.
The fierce heathen king lay stretched on the heath,
And the deadly wound he had taken would never be healed.
 Then Sir Cador the keen cried out aloud:
"You have got your miller's pay; may God give you sorrow;
You killed my cousin, but now my grief is lessened.
Cool yourself in the clay now and comfort yourself.
You scorned us once at length with bitter words,
But you see how it's gone with you: your scorn has come home! *1840*
Hold what little you have won, it does us no harm,
Hate comes home to roost, whoever may use it."
 The king of Syria sorrowed much in his heart
For the sake of the splendid sovereign who was thus surprised;
He assembled his Saracens quickly, with many a senator,
And swiftly they set out in anger against Arthur's knights.
Sir Cador, lord of Cornwall, encounters them soon
With all his fair company in its full array;
There at the front of the forest, where the road went forth,
Fifty thousand fierce men were unhorsed at once. *1850*
When those two armies came crashing together, knights
Were wounded sore enough on either side;
The surest Saracens set on the roll of that draft
Were hurled behind their saddles six full feet;
They cut down there in that company shielded knights,
Pierced those princes despite all the pride of their mail,
Through chain-linked byrnies stabbed to the white of their chests,
Burst asunder the brilliantly burnished braces;
They chopped through bloody shields and bleeding horses
With their swords of gleaming steel and their prancing steeds. *1860*
The Britons killed so many so cruelly
The bending grass and the broad field brimmed with blood.
By then the keen Sir Cador had taken a captive;
Sir Clegis thunders in soon, and he seizes another,
The captain of rich Corneto, and second to the king,
Key man among the people who ruled that coast;
Young Joneke takes Utolf and Evander
With the earl of Africa and with other great lords.

And the keen old Syrian king has yielded to Cador
And the seneschal of Sotere to Sigramor.   *1870*
When the hostile chivalry saw that its chieftains were taken,
They turned their steeds at once to the deeps of the forest,
And they were so faint some fell to the ground in the groves,
Slid from their saddles exhausted and shaky with fear.
There might men see rich warriors ride through the shadows
To finish the Romans already so grimly wounded,
Shouting hard on their heels, unmerciful knights,
Hewing them down by hundreds in the eaves of the holt.
Thus our chivalrous knights pursue the foemen,
And drive back into a castle the few that escape.   *1880*
　　　Then the lords of the Round Table drew up
To search through all the woods where the duke rested,
They hunted through the trees, caught up their comrades,
Gathered survivors they'd thought were struck down in the
　　　　　　　　　　　　　　　　　　　　　　　　　fighting.

Sir Cador put them on a caisson, covered them well,
To be carried back to the king with the best of his knights;
And he passes on to Paris, himself, with the prisoners,
And he turns them over to the provost, princes and others;
Takes a quick meal in the tower, then tarries no longer
But turns back at once to the king, and tells him the story.   *1890*
　　　"Sire," Sir Cador says, "as chance would have it,
On yonder gleaming coast we encountered today
With kings and kaisers, cruel lords and courtly,
And knights and fierce men of battle in fair array.
There at the edge of the forest they blocked our road
With fierce men of arms at the fording place in the river.
We fought them faithfully, and flourished our lances   `
On the battlefield with your foemen, and ended their lives.
The king of Lebe lies dead, left there in the field,
And many of the loyal liege men belonging to him,   *1900*
And many more are captured, from many far lands.
We have led them here at last to live while you please.
Sir Utolf and Sir Evander, honorable knights,
Are taken by young Joneke, by adventure of arms,
With earls of the Orient, audacious knights,
By ancestry, the best of all that host.
The senator, Barouns, is taken by a knight,

And the captain of Corneto, famous for killing,
The seneschal of Sutere, stern man, with the others,
And the king of Syria himself with his Saracens.   *1910*
On our own side we have lost fourteen brave knights.
I'll tell you truly, sir, and hold back nothing:
Sir Beril is one, a noble banneret,
Killed at the first clash by a mightly king;
Sir Alidioke of Towell and all his attendants
Were hemmed in there by Turks, and in time they fell.
Good Sir Maurel of Maunces, and Maurin his brother,
Sir Meneduke of Mentoche, with his marvelous knights."

    Then the great king writhed, and wept with his eyes,
And he spoke to his cousin Sir Cador these words: *1920*
"Sir Cador, your courage confounds us all!
You cast down all my knights the same as a coward.
You win no praise by putting good men into peril;
The battle must first be prepared, the power arrayed.
When you saw them standing in strength, you should have stood
                       back,
Unless you'd have all my brave army destroyed at once!"

    "Sire," Sir Cador answered, "you know, yourself,
That you are king of this country, commanding as you like;
None who belong to the Round Table shall upbraid me
That I ever blanched from your bidding for any man's boast;   *1930*
When you send out the army again, supply them better,
Or they will be soon confounded and smashed on those shores.
I did my best today, dubbed knights for the battle,
And I fought at the head of all others in every skirmish;
I have won no favor from you, only fierce words;
If I'd given up my heart I'd have gotten no more."

    Then, though king Arthur was grieved, he answered him
                       kindly:
"You have done well, sir duke, with your two hands,
And you've nobly done your duty with my dear knights;
Therefore you are deemed, among dukes and earls,   *1940*
One of the doughtiest heroes that ever was dubbed;
And since I have no issue born on earth,
You stand as heir apparent, or one of your children;
You are my sister's son, and I shall not forsake you."

    The king then ordered a table in his own tent,

And those who had fought that day were summoned with
trumpets,
And they served them solemnly with all kinds of fine foods,
And came to them where they sat with silver dishes.

❧ The War in Saxony
and the Death of Lucius

W HEN the senators heard news of all that had happened,
They said to the emperor, "Your siege is suppressed;   *1950*
Your enemy, Arthur, has overthrown your lords
Who rode out hoping to rescue our valiant knights.
You only waste your time and torment your people,
And you are betrayed by the heroes you trusted most:
You will bring all your army to grief and destruction forever."
The wrathful emperor was angered in his heart
To see that our valiant soldiers had won such advantage.
And he went with his kings and kaisers into council,
With sovereigns and Saracens and senators enough.
Thus he assembles swiftly the best of his lords   *1960*
And there in that assembly he says these words:
"My heart is firmly set—assent if you like—
To drive into Saxony with my surest knights
To fight there with my foemen, if Fortune is with me,
And search him out if I can within those shores.
I'll venture forth to Augusta, seeking out battle,
And wait with my sturdy warriors within his walls;
We'll rest ourselves with revels and roam as we wish,
And dwell there in delight, with lordship enough,
And wait till Sir Leo comes with his loyal knights,   *1970*
With lords of Lombardy to clear him the way."
But Arthur learned of the plan by loyal informers,
And moved his army out by way of the woods;
He ordered his fires refurbished, flaming to the sky
Then packed all gear securely and stole away,
And thence to Saxony he sped at once,
And there at the source of the Seine dispersed his knights:
He set them over the city, on every side,
Placed them up over the walls, with seven great legions,

And down in the valley he set out a vanguard ambush;   *1980*
Sir Villiers le Valiaunt, with his valiant knights,
Who before the face of the king had made his vow
To vanquish by victory the cruel viscount of Rome.
Therefore King Arthur chose him, whatever befell,
Chieftain for the attack, with his chivalrous knights;
Then he ruled by command the men he most trusted.
He deploys the center of the army to suit himself,
Fits his footmen out as he thinks most fitting,
In front, in the first rank, all the flower of his knights,
And he ordered his archers to cover on either side   *1990*
To strike as a company, fire as soon as they choose.
And the rearguard he arrayed with royal kings,
With knights of the Round Table, of great renown,
Sir Rainalt and Sir Richere, who would run from nothing,
The powerful duke of Rouen, with riders aplenty;
The great Sir Kay, Sir Clegis, and clean men of arms,
The king decided to keep by the clear-running river.
Sir Lottex and Lancelot, those lordly knights,
Would stand on Arthur's left, with all their legions,
To move up in the morning, if there should be mist;   *2000*
Sir Cador of Cornwall, with all his keen knights,
Would keep the crossroads, closing up their flank;
And thus he plants his power, princes and earls,
That no force might slip past by privy ways.
    Now soon the emperor, with honorable knights
And earls, comes down the vale and seeks his fortune,
And there he finds King Arthur, his hosts in array,
And finds as he comes in, to add to his sorrow,
Our bold and stately king stands on his battlefield,
His army spread abroad and his banners displayed.   *2010*
He had all the city enclosed, on every side,
Both the ravines and the cliffs well stocked with men,
The mosses and marshes as well, and the mountains above,
With a multitude of men who may trouble his march.
    When Sir Lucius saw all this, he said to his lords,
"The traitor has sneaked up around us to work us treason!
He has all the city surrounded on either side,
And the cliffs and ravines are crawling with fair men of arms!
He leaves us no way of escape, and no other choice

But fight it out with our foes for we cannot flee!" 2020
Then swiftly the mighty man arrays his forces,
Gave all his Romans their orders, and royal knights;
He sends into the vanguard the viscount of Rome
With valiant knights from Viterbo to Venice;
He raises up in defiance his dragons of gold
And eagles on every side, adorned with sable;
They drew out the wine in a stream and afterward drank,
All those dukes and douzeperes dubbed as knights;
With the feverish dancing of Dutchmen and dinning of pipes,
All that was there in the valley resounded with the roar. 2030
　　　And then Sir Lucius cried out lordly words:
"Think of the great renown of your noble fathers!
And the ravagers of Rome, who reigned with lords,
Who overthrew all others that reigned on earth,
Who captured all Christendom by the craft of arms!
Wherever they've gone they've brought back victory,
In seven winters unseated the Saracen hosts,
Partitioned the world from Port Joppa to the gates of Paradise.
Though a realm be rebel to us, we do not much worry;
It is reasonable and right that the man be restrained; 2040
And so to arms! and let us sit still no longer,
For without a doubt on earth, the day shall be ours!"
　　　When the emperor had spoken, the king of Wales
Caught sight of the cruel viscount who'd worried his knights;
And boldly there in the valley he raised his voice:
"Viscount of Valence, ever contentious of deeds,
Today I'll avenge your villainy of Viterbo!
Never will I be vanquished or flee this spot."
　　　And then the valiant viscount, noble of voice,
Shouted farewell, to the vanguard turned his horse; 2050
He lifted his splendid shield, which shone with sable,
A couched dragon within it, dreadful to see,
Driving a dolphin forth with dreadful claws
As a sign that our sovereign lord should be destroyed
And that his days should be ended by dint of the sword,
For there can be nothing but death where the dragon is raised.
　　　Then the good king claps his lance to the brace
And with his powerful shaft he pierces him through
A span above the waist, among the short ribs,

So that both spleen and steel plate hung on the spear   *2060*
And the blood splashed out and spread as the steed lunged,
And he sprawls out dead, and now he speaks no more.
And thus has Valiaunt held to his former vow
And vanquished the viscount, whom men had once called victor.
    Then Sir Ewain Fitz Urien eagerly rides
At once to the emperor, to touch the eagle;
All through the breadth of the battle he rides in haste,
Swings out his sword with a smiling countenance,
Tears it down easily, and rides away;
And he galloped home with the eagle in his noble hand,   *2070*
And came back into the front line to fight with his comrades.
    And now comes Lancelot, and he gallops even
With Lucius the lord, and cruelly he hits him,
And through the plates on his paunch he pierces the mail,
And the proud pennant stuck fast in Sir Lucius' belly,
And the head haled out behind him a half-foot's length;
The hard-steel lance went straight through hauberk and haunch
And both the steed and the bold man struck hard ground;
The standard toppled, and Sir Lancelot turned back.
    "Well done, sir," laughs Sir Lottes, "yon lords are dazzled! *2080*
And now the lot falls to me, if my lord approves;
My name shall be laid low, and my life soon after
Unless some lad or two there leap from the living."
The bold man stretches forward and strains at the bridle
And strikes into the host on his splendid steed,
Jousts against a giant and jabs him through;
Then joyfully that gentle knight jousts at another,
Opens up great highways, battering knights,
And he gores whatever grim man stands in his way,
Fights with all those foemen the width of a furlong,   *2090*
And fells a good many on the field with his furious lance;
He vanquishes and overthrows fierce fighters,
And thus he rides through the valley and leaves when he likes.
    Then boldly, after that, the bowmen of Britain
Fought with the foreign footmen, brought into these lands,
With fiery feathered arrows they fired at the foemen,
And all their feathered shafts shot through their mail:
Cruel indeed was that shower that shot into flesh
And flew from afar to bite deep in the flanks of steeds;

The arrows jammed against the charging Germans,   *2100*
Striking on every side and stabbing through shields;
Bolt-head shafts beat in among all the knights
So craftily that no one can step aside.
They shrank back so, from the showers of sharp arrows,
It seemed as if all the broad army shuddered at once.
Then the rich steeds rebounded; they rushed to arms,
To fight the hundreds on the hills and upon the high ledges,
And the fiercest are still on their horses, heathens and others,
And overhead they rattle and roar to destroy;
And all the giants in front, engendered by fiends,   *2110*
Joined against Sir Jonathal, fighting with his knights,
And clubs of clean steel clattered on helmets,
Crashed down battle-crests and crushed men's brains,
Murdered mighty coursers, and skirted steeds
And chopped through chevaliers and their chalk-white horses;
There was never steel nor steed that could stand against them,
But all who stood their ground were struck down, confounded
Till Arthur the conqueror came, with his keen knights.
With a cruel countenance he cried aloud:
"I trust no Briton was ever abashed by so little   *2120*
Or feared bare-legged boys on the battlefield!"
He snaps out Caliburn, the blade polished clean,
And galloped to Golapas, who grieved them most,
And cut him in two with one clean swipe at his knees.
"Come down," said the king, "and talk with your equals!
You rear too high by half, I tell you the truth.
And yet you'll go higher still, by the help of my Lord!"
And then with his sword of steel he struck off his head.
Sternly then he turns and he strikes another,
And thus he sets upon seven with his stern knights.   *2130*
He never ceased until sixty of them had been served,
And thus when they came to Arthur the giants were destroyed
And jousted down that day by gentle lords.
        Then the Romans and the royal knights of the Round Table
Drew up again in array, both the rear and the rest,
And with heavy weapons of war they hacked through helmets
And cut with their grim steel through glittering mail;
But the Round Table fought well, those worthy barons,
Lance to brace, lunged in on iron-gray horses,

And with their shields that shone, ashiver with gold.   *2140*
So many fell to their fate there on that field
That every path in the woods ran red with blood
And all the sward was slippery with their sweat;
Steel swords snapped in two, and dying knights
Lay opened wide, hurled down from their galloping steeds;
Good men lay opened up, with aching sides;
Dead faces showed grotesque in clotted lakes,
All horribly trod down by the tramping steeds—
Faces once as fair as were any on earth—
Smashed for the length of a furlong, a thousand at once.   *2150*
By then the Romans had been driven back a little;
They drearily retreated and attacked no more;
But Arthur with all his power still pursued them,
Galloping over the proudest with prized knights.
Sir Kay and Sir Clegis, with clean men of arms,
Harass them to the cliffs and continue to drive them;
They fight on hard in the grove and hold back no strokes,
And they fell at the first attack five hundred at once.
And when they found themselves set upon by our knights,
A few against many, they are forced to more careful order;   *2160*
Fiercely they fight their foes with swords and spears,
And they make their stand against all the most mighty of France.
But the keen Sir Kay has cast his lance to the brace:
He gallops up on his courser and rides to the king;
With his Lettow lance he runs him through the sides,
And the lance slides through both the liver and the lungs:
The shaft shuddered and shot through the shining byrnie,
Struck through the shield and stayed in the body of the man.
But Kay at that encounter was cruelly struck
By a coward knight of the glorious kingdom of Rome,   *2170*
And just as he turned to ride off, the traitor hit him—
Drove through the loins and afterward through the flanks,
So that the brutal lance tore through the bowels,
Burst them open in the blow and broke them free.
Sir Kay knew well enough by that cruel wound
That the stroke would leave him a dead man and done with this life.
He whirls in his array and he rides the man down
To revenge himself on him for the unfair strike.
"Guard yourself, you coward!" Sir Kay calls out,

And with his clear sword he cuts the man in two,   *2180*
"If you'd hit me like a man, by the might of your hands,
I would have forgiven this death by Christ in heaven!"
And then he rode back to King Arthur, and greeted him:
"I'm bitterly wounded, lord; no man ever worse!
Do for me now what is just, as the world requires,
And see to my burial. I ask nothing more.
Great joy to my lady the Queen, if Fortune allows,
And to all the stately ladies belonging to her bower;
And as for my worthy wife, who never grieved me,
Bid her, for her worship, to pray for my soul."   *2190*
    The king's confessor came, with Christ in his hands,
To comfort the knight and to say last rites for him.
The knight went down on his knees, courageous of heart,
And thus he caught his Creator, who comforts us all.
    Then the rich king rode out, with grief in his heart,
And rode into the rout to revenge his death:
He pressed to the thick of the fight and met there a prince,
The heir of Egypt and all those eastern marches,
And with Caliburn he cleaved that man asunder:
He struck down through the byrnie and he split the saddle,   *2200*
And the back of the big white horse was broken to the bowels.
In his rage of melancholy he met with another,
In the midst of the mighty host and grieved him much,
Struck through the byrnie and parted the man in the middle
So that the man's torso fell to the troubled earth,
The other half still riding there high on the horse,
Wounded so badly I trust it may not soon heal!
He shot through the enemy ranks with his sharp weapon
And cut through mightly men and woven mail;
He bore down gleaming banners, split bright shields,   *2210*
And brutally with his sword worked out his wrath;
Ferociously he fought by the force of his strength,
Wounding the foreigners, now weary knights,
Lunging into the thick of them thirteen times,
Striking out fiercely in the throng and still pursuing.
    Then Sir Gawain the Good, with his noble knights,
Riding the vanguard, over by the hem of the woods,
Caught sight of Sir Lucius, on the land he was holding now
With the lords and liege men belonging to his court.

Then harshly the emperor called to the brave Sir Gawain,   2220
"What do you seek to do with your weapon, Gawain?
I judge by the way you wave it you're longing for sorrow.
I'll avenge myself on your ire, for all your proud words!"
He swept out a long sword and rushed up quickly
And fairly, there on the ground, he struck Sir Lionel—
Hit him on the head so hard the helmet burst
And it opened Sir Lionel's skull for the breadth of a hand.
Thus like a lord he lays into them all
And weakens the power of Arthur's worthy knights.
He fought with shining Florent, first among swords,   2230
And jabbed till the dark blood ran down at his wrist.

   Now the Romans rallied, who retreated before,
And tore the ranks of our men with their rested horses:
Before they will see their chieftain be sorely pressed
They'll chase and chop at the life of our chivalrous knights.
Sir Bedivere was borne down, and his breast pierced through
By a cruel battle-sword, broad at the hilt:
The keen and cutting steel runs clean to his heart
And—more's the pity!—the great man falls to earth.

   The conqueror took stock and came up with his strength   2240
To rescue the mighty warriors of the Round Table
And overcome the emperor, if Fortune would allow it;
He rode to the eagle, and "Arthur!" was his cry.
The emperor strikes out eagerly at Arthur,
Angrily, awkwardly, strikes him on the visor.
The tip of the naked sword cuts Arthur's nose
And the blood of the bold king gushes down over his breast
And splashes on the broad shield and the brilliant mail.
The bold king bows his horse by a yank at the bridle
And with his heavy sword strikes him a heavy blow   2250
Through the cuirass and the chest with his blazing weapon,
And slantwise down from the slot of the throat he slices him.
Thus came the emperor's end by Arthur's hand,
And in that instant all his host was beaten.

   They ride away to the woods, the few still remaining,
In terror of Arthur's Round Table, down by the river.
The flower of our fierce men, on iron-gray steeds,
Fly after fleeing Romans and fear nothing living.

   Then the famous conqueror cries out aloud,

"Cousin of Cornwall, take good care of yourself: 2260
See that no captain or chief be made captive for silver
Till the death of Sir Kay has been cruelly avenged!"
"Nay, my lord," says Cador, "as Christ is my shield,
There is neither kaiser nor king here alive under Christ
That I shall not strike cold dead by the craft of my hands!"
There might men see chieftains on chalk-white steeds
Chop down on that chase the noblest of the chivalry;
The richest and most royal kings of Rome
Fell broken by hard steel, their ribs asunder,
Brains smashed in within their burnished helmets,   2270
Overthrown by swords that flashed all the breadth of that land.
They hewed down heathen men with their hilted swords
By whole hundreds in a heap by the hem of the holtwood.
No silver could save their lives or succor them,
Not sultan, Saracen, or senator of Rome.
      Then the mighty men of the Round Table paused
By the gleaming river there that runs so sweetly,
And there they set up camp, by the shining streams,
These lordly barons, down on the sweeping plain.
They turned to the spoils, taking what pleased them,   2280
Camels and secadrisses and splendid coffers,
Load-horses, riding horses, and destriers,
The household goods and trappings of heathen kings;
They led out the dromedaries of diverse lords,
Milk-white mules and many another strange creature,
Llamas and Arabian horses and Elephants
Brought from the Orient by honorable kings.
      But great King Arthur goes out after a while
To stand above the emperor, with honored kings;
He raised the body gently, with the help of good knights,   2290
And brought him to the camp where the king stayed.
Then heralds went over the field, at their lords' behest,
To hunt up the rest of the heathen who lay in the hills,
The sultan of Syria and certain knights,
Sixty of the chief senators of Rome.
They carried back and embalmed them as suited their honor,
Clothed them in flowing silk, all sixty of them,
And wrapped them in leaden shrouds, lest the bodies should
Be bruised or rotted from shifting about in the caissons;

They closed them up in coffins to take them to Rome,   *2300*
Their banners flying above and their emblems below,
And in every country they pass all knights can tell
Each fallen king by his color and the land where he reigned.
  At last on the second day, as soon as it was morning,
Two senators came in with attendant knights,
Hoodless, coming from the heath beyond the holtwoods,
Barefoot over the field, for all their bright weapons,
And they bowed to the bold king and offered him the hilts;
Whether he'd hang or behead them or hold them alive
They kneeled to the conqueror in no more than their kirtles;   *2310*
And with sorrowful countenances they said these words:
"We are two senators, your Roman subjects,
Who fled to save our lives by these salt streams;
We hid ourselves in the woods, with the help of Christ.
We ask your mercy, as our sovereign and our lord;
Of your liberality, grant us life and limb
For love of Him who has lent you lordship on earth."
"I grant it," said the king, "through my own grace;
I give you life and limb and leave to pass
On condition that you carry my message to Rome—   *2320*
The same message I will give you before all my men."
"Gramercy," said the senators. "And we assure you
Truly and by our troths that we'll say what you ask.
We'll be checked by no man living in all this world,
Not pope or potentate or noblest of princes,
But we'll loyally proclaim what you wish in the land
Before both dukes and douzeperes—or die in your service."
  Then standard-bearers of Brittany brought them to the tents
Where barbers awaited them with basins aloft
And quickly wet them head to foot with warm water;   *2330*
And they pushed them about as was fitting, after that,
To show these Romans for recreants and captives,
And they shaved them shamefully, for Rome's discomfort.
They quickly chained the coffins on camels then
And on asses and Arabians—these honorable kings—
And the emperor's body, for its honor, they set alone
High on an elephant, with his eagle above it;
And then the king himself called in the captives
And before all the host of bold men he said these words:

"With all these coffins," said the king, "go over the mountains; *2340*
Let all men know that you have greatly yearned
For the tax and tribute of Rome for tenscore winters—
The same tax cruelly taken in the time of our elders.
Say to the senator who rules the city
That I send him here the sum; let him count as he pleases!
Let them never be so bold while my blood reigns
As ever again to attack or take claim of my lands
Or ask for a tribute or tax by no true title,
For this is the treasure they'll get, while my time lasts."

And now they ride to Rome by the quickest route *2350*
And kneel in the capital, and the commons are assembled,
Sovereigns and senators who rule the city;
And they beckon them up to the carnage, coffins and the rest,
As the conqueror had commanded with cruel words:
"We have loyally gone forth and have sought this tribute,
The tax and silver homage of fourscore winters,
From England and Ireland and all the outer isles,
The Occidental kingdom ruled by King Arthur.
He bids: Never again, while his blood reigns,
Be so bold as to attack or take claim of his British holdings *2360*
Or ask for a tribute or tax by no true title,
For this is the treasure you'll get, while his time lasts.
We have fought Arthur's forces in France, and evil befell us;
And all our great fair force is laid to its fate.
The chivalry could not escape, neither chieftains nor others,
But were chopped down in the chase; so chance would have it.
We advise you to draw in stones, and fortify the walls:
For wrack and ruin are upon you. Beware if you like!"

⟨ The Siege of Metz
and Gawain's Foraging Expedition

IT was in the month of May that all this happened:
The most renowned of kings, with all his Round Table, *2370*
On the coast of Constantine, by the clear-running water,
Has driven the Romans back and rebuked them forever.
After he had fought in France and had won the field
And fiercely felled his foes and finished their days,

He tarried to see to the burial rites for the heroes
Who were brought down out of life by the bitter sword.
He buried the body of Sir Bedivere at Bayone,
And the corpse of the keen Sir Kay he buried at Caen,
In a coffin covered all over with clearest crystal,
For his father had honorably conquered that kingdom by his   *2380*
                                                might.

And later he paused at Burgoine for the burial of others,
Sir Beril and Sir Baldwin and Sir Bedwar the mighty,
After Sir Kay at Caen, as his kingship required.
Then in due time King Arthur went into Autun,
Entered into Germany, hosts in array,
And encamped at Luxemburg, to heal his knights' wounds,
And he lodged there with his liege men as lord of the land.
     And on St. Christopher's Day he called up his council
With all his kings and kaisers, clerks, and others,
And commanded them solemnly to cast deep in their thought   *2390*
On how he might conquer by the craft of arms his claim.
And the conqueror Arthur, courteous and noble,
Spoke to all the council these knightly words:
"In these cliffs, closed in by hills, there is a knight
With whom I would gladly converse, because of his words;
He calls himself lord of Lorraine; I tell you the truth.
That lordship is precious enough, as people tell me.
I will carve up that dukedom and award it as I please
And in time encounter with the duke, if destiny pleases;
The man has risen as a rebel against my Round Table,   *2400*
Ready to work for the Romans and rioting my land.
We shall now determine by force, if reason is for it,
Who has true right to that rent, by God in His heaven.
     I will turn after that towards beautiful Lombardy
And establish law in that land which will last for all time;
And next I will trouble the tyrants of Turkey a little
Talk with the temporal lords, while my time may last;
I give my protection to all the wide lands of the pope
And I'll show the people my proclamation of peace.
It is rank folly to offend our father under God,   *2410*
Either Peter or Paul or the later apostles of Rome.
If we spare the spiritual lords we will speed all the better;
No holy blood shall be spilled while our power is supreme."

Now without more speech they sped on spurs,
These honorable knights, to the march of Metz,
Looked up to in Loraine as London is here,
The sovereign city within that splendid land.
The king rides at the head on a handsome steed,
With Ferrier and Feraunt and four other knights;
Around the city those seven sought, in time,   2420
Secure positions on which to set catapults.
In the city enemy bows were quickly bent
To fire at bold King Arthur their brutal shafts;
The crossbowmen fired eagerly at Arthur
To cut him down, or his horse, with cruel weapons.
The king ignored their shower and asked for no shield,
But boldly showed himself in his bright array.
And he lingered at his leisure to look at the walls
And judged where they were lowest, most easily assaulted.
"Sire," said Sir Ferrier, "this ride's sheer folly,   2430
Coming so near to their walls in all your grandeur
Dressed in only a doublet to study the city
And showing yourself to their bowmen. You'll destroy us all!
Let us be gone from here quickly, before you are killed,
For if you are hit, or your horse, we are ruined forever!"
"If you are afraid," said the king, "I advise you to flee
Before they bring you down with their rounded bows;
You're a mere child; it would be no marvel, I think,
If you were afraid of the least fly that lit on your arm;
But as God is my help, I am not afraid of them.   2440
Though the worthless may be worried, it worries me little;
They'll win no honor from me but merely waste arrows:
They'll be low enough before I leave, by heaven!
With my Lord's help, no mere lout will be so lucky
As to kill a king duly crowned and anointed with chrism!"
        Then up the first company came, courageous knights
Who would hurry to battle on the wall in no long time,
And all our ferocious fighters, from every side,
Came flying into the conflict on fervent steeds,
Riding in splendid array there, royal knights   2450
And all the men of renown of Arthur's Round Table.
The mightiest men of France came following after,
A front line handsomely fitted, and took the field.

Then the brave knights boldly advanced their steeds
To show them in all their splendor, in shining skirts;
They rushed into the battle with banners displayed,
Broad shields richly embossed, and heavy helmets
With the pinions and streamers of every prince's arms
Appareled in perfect gems and with precious stones.
The lances with all their adornment, the gleaming shields   2460
Brightened the sky like lightning and glowed on all sides.

    The great men galloped up and tested their horses
And settled into the siege upon either side;
They storm the outer suburbs after that,
Scout out the crossbow stations and skirmish a little,
Scare away the shield-bearers and sentinels,
Break down the barricades with their blazing weapons,
Beat down the barbican and win the bridge.
Had the garrison not been strong at the central gates
They might well have won the town by their own strength.   2470
Our men withdraw a little and regroup their forces,
For fear that the drawbridge may be dashed down into the moat;
They return to headquarter ground, where the king waits
With all his army in readiness, horsed and arrayed.
Every prince was ready and standing in his place,
Above them pavilions of pall and the shields of the siege.
They wait there in lordly leisure, to suit their pleasure,
And the watches in every ward, as the war chances,
Raise up—sudden and swift—the catapults,
A forest of them grown up in a single Sunday.   2480

    Now the king calls Florent, the flower of knighthood:
"The French grow somewhat feeble; it's no surprise,
For they are a moving people, in those fair marches,
And they're quick to miss the flesh and food they're used to.
But here there are splendid forests on either side
And there our liege men shall go with good light horses.
And you shall go to the moorland and hunt in the mountains.
Sir Foraunt and Floridas shall follow your bridle;
For we must refresh our people with freshly killed meat,
Who are fed now on the field, on the fruit of the earth.   2490
And I'll send along on this mission Sir Gawain himself,
One of the noblest of lords, if it suits his pleasure,
And Sir Wicher and Sir Walter, both worshipful men,

With all the shrewdest men of the western marches:
Sir Clegis, Sir Claribald, and the noble Sir Cleremond,
The Captain of Cardiff as well, in his gleaming array.
Go now, notify the knights, Sir Gawain and the rest,
And go on your way at once without more ado."
    Now they ride to the forest, these fair men of arms,
To the uninhabited moors, these honorable barons,   *2500*
Through shaded glens and valleys and over high hills,
Through holts and ancient groves and hazel thickets,
And through morass and moss and the highest of mountains,
And at last, in the mists of morning, they come to a meadow
Mowed and unharvested, untouched by man,
Swept down in wide, neat swaths and full of sweet flowers.
There the bold knights unbridled and baited their horses
In the dawning of the day, when birds begin singing
While the rising of the sun—the messenger of Christ—
Comforts all sinful things that have sight on earth.   *2510*
Then out rides the warden, Sir Gawain himself,
For he was wise and mighty, to seek out adventures.
    He soon came onto a man who was mightily armed,
Waiting on the riverbank by the woodland paths,
Dressed in a woven mailcoat bright to behold
And holding a broad shield, on a great white horse;
He had no one there beside him except for a boy
Riding his horse nearby, his spear in his hand;
On his shield, gleaming in gold, three greyhounds of sable,
Coupled together with chains of chalk-white silver,   *2520*
On the chief, a great carbuncle of changing hues;
And the knight was a man of adventure, attack who may.
Sir Gawain looks at the man with a glad will;
The man took a lance from the groom and gripped it in his hands,
And he rode across the stream on his skirted steed
To Gawain, brave in battle, waiting in his strength
And fiercely Gawain cried in English, "Arthur!"
The other gave him his answer at once, with wrath,
Lifting his loud shout in the land of Lorraine
So that any man inside a mile might hear it: *2530*
"Where are you riding, robber, roaring so loud?
Here you will poach no prey, roar all you please
Unless you can prove my better in the battle,

I'll make you my prisoner quickly, for all your proud bearing!"
"Sir," says Gawain, "as God is my salvation,
Palavering princes like you disturb me but little.
But put all your gear into action, and grief will befall you
Before you get out of this grove, for all your great words."
Then both these lordly barons lean into their lances
And lunge with their long spears on their gray steeds;   2540
They clash to the encounter, by the craft of arms,
And both those mighty lances are broken at once:
Through the shields they shot and sheared through mail
And shot through both men's shoulders the length of a span.
Thus are both knights honorably wounded,
Yet they will not even now forget their wrath.
They whirled about on the reins and rode in again:
Swiftly the two fierce men drew out their swords
And hit each other's helmets hearty strokes
And hew at the hauberks hotly with hard weapons.   2550
Stoutly both of them strike, these two stern knights,
Cruelly stab at the stomach with firm steel points,
Fighting and flourishing with their flashing swords
Till the gleam and glitter of their fire sparked up on their helmets.
　　Then Sir Gawain grew angry and worked in a rage,
And grimly he struck with his good sword Galuth,
And he cleaved the keen man's shield cleanly in half;
The horse lunged, and look at the man's left side
And you might have seen his liver by the light of the sun.
The big man groaned from the agony, getting that wound,   2560
And hurled himself at Sir Gawain as he galloped by,
And cruelly, clumsily, slashed at him in his wrath.
He clipped away an enamelled shoulder plate
And cleanly burst the back-brace with his blade,
And he cut off the elbow cup with the clean-ground edge,
And sheered away the armplate shining with silver;
Through Gawain's double layer of glowing velvet
The tip of the sword went down and it touched a vein,
And at once it bled so richly Sir Gawain's mind reeled;
The visor, the mouth-guard, and all his marvelous dress   2570
Was splatterd red at once by the proud man's blood.
And then the tyrant tightly turned on his bridle
And cried out sharply, saying, "Sir, you're struck!

We must set a blood-bond between us before you go pale,
For all the barbers of Britain can't check that flow,
For the man struck once by this sword shall never be healed."
"Never!" cried Sir Gawain. "You frighten me little;
You think you can overcome me with cruel words
And you dare imagine mere talk can tame my heart!
The time will come when you'll pay well enough in turn   2580
Unless you tell me at once, and tarry no longer,
What cure can stop this blood as it pours so thick."
"I've told you the truth, I swear it by my troth:
No surgeon in all Salerno can save you now
Unless you will allow me, for the love of Christ,
To confess myself of my sins and prepare for my death."
        "Very well then," says Gawain, "as God is my help;
I extend you grace and grant it, though you've brought me grief,
Providing you tell me, truly, what you are seeking
Alone and solitary beside this stream,   2590
And what religion you serve—but see you don't lie—
And what your allegiance and land, and where you are lord."
        "My name is Sir Priamus; my father is a prince
Highly praised among proven knights in his country;
He reigns in Rome and is known as a mighty lord;
He has stood rebellious to Rome, and has ridden those lands
Warring with crafty success for winters and years;
By his judgment and his wisdom and power at arms
He has waged an honorable war and won his own land.
He's of Alexander's blood, the overlord of kings,   2600
And his grandfather's uncle was the great lord Hector of Troy;
And this is the kindred from which I myself am come,
And Joshua and Judas Maccabeus, gentlest of knights.
I am his heir apparent, as eldest son;
[But yet I'll believe in the Lord that you believe in,
And give you for your labor lands enough!]
From Alexander to Africa and the outer isles
I stand in full possession as duly appointed.
In all the precious cities that belong to that kingdom
I have, in truth, the treasure and the lands   2610
And both the tribute and tax while my time shall last.
But I was so haughty of heart, when I lived at home,
I held no man to be equal to me under heaven;

Therefore I was sent here with sevenscore strong knights
To test myself in war, by my father's commandment;
For my swollen pride I am shamefully put down
And by the adventure of arms overthrown forever.
Now I have told, as you asked, what kin I come of;
Will you, for knighthood's sake, now tell your name?"

    "By Christ," said noble Sir Gawain, "I never was a knight;   *2620*
I serve as a chamber boy to the conqueror, Arthur,
And I've worked in the royal wardrobe for winters and years
Preparing the long suits of armor my lord loves best.
I help to stitch up the tents that belong to him
And I sew up the battle doublets for dukes and earls,
And I fashion the quilted jerkins for Arthur himself,
The ones he's used in battle these last eight winters.
He made me a yeoman this Christmas and gave me fine gifts
And a hundred pounds and a horse and a splendid harness;
If I happen, by good luck, to be of service.   *2630*
I'm speedily rewarded, that's the truth."

    "If his serving boys are such, his knights are supreme!
There is no king under Christ that can come up against him!
He'll be heir to Alexander, who's praised throughout earth,
And more able even than Hector, the honor of Troy.
Now by the chrism they gave you the day you were christened,
Tell me the truth! Are you merely a knave, or a knight?"

    "My name is Sir Gawain," he said, "I cannot deny it;
Cousin to the conqueror, as he knows well,
Known by official record as knight of his chamber   *2640*
And acknowledged the mightiest king of all the Round Table.
I am the douzepere and duke he dubbed with his hands
In due ceremony one day before all his dear lords.
Do not be grieved, good sir, though the luck has been mine;
It is wholly the gift of God; the honor is His."

    "Peter!" says Priamus, "this pleases me better
Than if I were prince of Provence and of glorious Paris!
For I would far rather be secretly struck to the heart
Than ever some proud unknown pricker had won such a prize!
But here there is harbored at hand in those huge holtwoods,   *2650*
Up in the hills, an army; take heed if you like! —
The terrible duke of Lorraine with his loyal knights,
The proudest men of all Prussia, and Germans as well,

70

The lords of all Lombardy, well known as leaders,
The garrison of Godarde, all gayly arrayed,
And the cunning men of Westual, worshipful lords,
And from Saxony and Surryland Saracens enough.
They number, by count of their rolls, to exactly the sum
Of sixty thousand and ten sure soldiers at arms;
Unless you flee from this heath we will both come to harm,   2660
And unless my side is healed I shall never recover.
Take care of your groomsman, see that he blows no horn
Or surely you will be hacked into bits in a hurry.
My retinue's there among them, who ride where I please,
And nowhere on earth are there knights more ready to strike.
Be caught by that crew up there and you'll ride no further
And not all the riches on earth will suffice for your ransom."
     Before the enemy came, Sir Gawain rode off
With the worthy prince that he had wounded sore;
They rode back into the mountains where Arthur's men waited 2670
Baiting their battle horses on a broad meadow.
The lords were leaning at their ease on their gleaming shields,
And laughed aloud with delight at the lilting birds—
Larks and linnets whose music was lovely to hear.
And some were asleep from the song of the little people
Who sang in the summer season, in the shining leaves
So sweetly in that land with soft, low notes.
     Then Sir Wicher caught sight of Sir Gawain's wound
And went up to him, weeping and wringing his hands;
And Sir Wicher and Sir Walchere, wise men in battle,   2680
Were shocked at the sight of Sir Gawain, and hurried to meet him.
They met him halfway on the path, and they were astounded
At his mastering that man, for all his might;
But by all the wealth of the world, they were never more grieved.
"All our honor," they cried, "has gone out of earth!"
"Do not grieve," said Gawain, "for God's love in heaven,
For the gift is but gossomer, mere earnest money,
For though my shoulder is split, my shield run through,
And moving my arm is a troublesome matter for me,
This prisoner Sir Priamus, perilously opened,   2690
Tells me that he has salves that can steady us both."
     Then sturdy knights stepped forward to steady his stirrup
And, lordlike, he alighted, releasing the bridle,

And he let his mighty warhorse bend to the flowers.
He lifts off his headpiece then and his gleaming mail,
Puts down his splintered shield, and bends down to earth,
And in all that bold man's body there was no blood left.
Then prized knights pressed in haste to Sir Priamus
And lifted him down in their arms from the bloody saddle;
They took off, after that, his helmet and hauberk,   2700
For his heart was failing now from the heavy wound;
They laid him down on the land and pulled off his jerkin
And they let him sprawl out full length, however he liked.
They found on his kirtle a vial of gleaming gold
And the vial was filled with the flower of the four wells
That flow out of Paradise when the flood rises
And bring forth splendid fruit that shall feed us all;
With that fair water on his flesh, where wounds are deep,
A man must be made whole within four hours.
        They uncovered the corpse with clean-washed hands   2710
And quickly a young knight cleansed their wounds with the water;
It cooled them by its nature and comforted their hearts.
And after the cuts were clean, they closed them again,
And they called for barrel-men, and brought them wine
And also bread and meat, the best of roasts.
Then later, when the two had eaten they armed themselves,
And then those errant knights cried out, "To arms!"
And now with a clarion call, they called together
The retinue for council, and told of their plight:
"Yonder is a company of strong and well-armed knights,   2720
The keenest men in contest alive under Christ;
Their battle host is arrayed in those oak woods there,
An army of fortune-seekers from outlying lands;
So Sir Priamus tells us. Peter defend us!"
Then Gawain said, "Go, men, and grope in your hearts
For which of you will clash with those lords in the grove.
If we run home, nothing won, our lord will be cross
And call us mere gadabouts, aghast over nothing.
We are here under Sir Florent today, as it happens,
The flower of all French knighthood, who never has fled;   2730
He was chosen and charged with this mission in King Arthur's
                                      chamber
As chieftain for the day, with our noble chivalry,

And whether he fights or flees, we're bound to follow;
But not for yonder foe will I forsake him."
  "By our Father," says Sir Florent, "your speech is fair,
But I am but a child, untested in arms;
If any folly results, the fault will be ours,
And we will be exiled from France forever,
If it does not displease your honor—my wit is simple—
You are our lord, indeed, and may do as you like—   *2740*
We are at most no more than a mere five hundred,
And truly, that is too few for a fight with so many,
For our serving boys and our drawers will help very little;
For all their fiery boasts, they'll fly away.
I advise you to act by reason, as wise men of arms,
And sensibly hurry away, like honorable knights."
  "I grant the point," said Gawain, "as God may save me.
But here we have veteran soldiers of many a victory,
And the grimmest of all the good men of King Arthur's chamber—
Men who boast boldly enough when we pass the cups.   *2750*
Then let us prove here today who'll win the prize."
  Now fierce front-men ride out into the forest,
And they find a fair green field and alight on foot,
Then ride on after their prey, like prized men of arms.
Florent and Floridas, with fivescore knights,
Followed the forest paths and found them at length
Riding at a fast trot, and on they drove.
And now five hundred enemies followed them hard,
Fierce warriors filling the forest and riding fresh horses.
The man at the head, on a handsome steed, was Sir Feraunt, *2760*
Fostered in Famagosta; his father was the Fiend.
He gallops up to Sir Florent and cries out at once:
"Why do you flee, false knight? The Fiend have your soul!"
  Sir Florent was eager now, and he clapped in his lance
And on Fawell of Friesland he rushed Sir Feraunt,
And he caught the reins up close on his gallant steed
And rode toward the rout and rested no longer.
Full tilt, he takes that enemy lord in the face
And horribly he disfigures the man with his weapon.
Through the bejewelled headpiece he hammered to the brains *2770*
And broke the neckbone and stopped the heart in his chest.
  Then Feraunt's cousin called out, and cried on high,

"You have killed cold dead the king of all the knights!
The man has been tested on the field in fifteen realms,
And he never till now found a man who could stand against him.
I'll see with my own dire lance that you die for your work,
And all your men as well, in the valley behind you!"

"Faw!" says Sir Floridas: "you yelping wretch,
You think your likes can flay us, you flat-mouthed fool?"
And soon with his sword, as Sir Floridas flashed by,   2780
He flicked away the flesh of the fierce man's flank,
So that all the filth of the man and the foulness of his guts
Flopped at his horse's foot as the man rode on.

And then up rides a knight to rescue that baron,
And his name was Renald of Rhodes, a rebel to Christ,
Perverted before by the pagans who press Christians hard;
He pushes in in his pride, and pursues the attack,
For he's earlier won high honor in the land of Prussia;
And therefore he places himself and proffers his lance.
But then a knight, Sir Richere of the Round Table,   2790
Mounted on a mighty steed, moves up against him,
And through the round red shield he rushes him
Until the shivering steel slides through to his heart.
The bold knight wheels in his saddle and hurtles to earth,
Roaring out aloud; and he rode no more.

Now all still whole and unfated among their five hundred
Came in against Sir Florent and his fivescore knights,
Between a pool and a river, where the land was flat,
And our people took their stand and sternly fought them.
Then loudly into the hills rang the cry "Lorraine!"   2800
When mighty men with their long spears struggled together,
And on our side, when troubles came, it was "Arthur!"

Then Sir Florent and Floridas couched their lances,
Charging on all that host, and cut through byrnies;
They felled five men at the front when first they entered,
And before they could charge any further, cut down others.
They chopped through woven byrnies, blazing shields,
And they battered and bore to the earth the best that met them;
They drove away the lords, who ruled that rout,
So cruelly these royal knights lashed out.   2810

When Sir Priamus the prince saw how they battled,
He was grieved at heart that he could not go to their aid;

74

He rode to Sir Gawain and said these words to him:
"You prized men fighting for your booty are fiercely
outnumbered—
And they're overset by seven hundred Saracens,
The loyal knights of Sultans from many lands;
If you would allow it, sir, for the sake of your Christ,
I would call my men to your side and support them a little."
    "I haven't complained," said Gawain. "The honor's their own.
They'll get rewards enough, by the gift of my lord,   *2820*
But the fighting men of France merely frighten themselves;
They haven't fought their fill these seven winters.
I'll never stir with my lance by half a steed-length
Until they are troubled by tougher encounters than that."
    And then at the side of the woods Sir Gawain caught sight
Of the men of Westphalia on mighty horses
Galloping up full tilt, along the roadway,
Armed with every weapon required for war.
The old earl of Antele was riding in the vanguard
And he brought on either side of him eight thousand knights;   *2830*
His archers and shield bearers passed any possible number
That any prince had provided before on this earth.
The duke of Lorraine came riding up behind him,
With twice as many Germans, famous for warfare,
And pagans out of Prussia, the noblest of horsemen,
Came riding up in front of Priamus' knights.
And the earl of Antele said to Algere his brother,
"It angers me indeed that King Arthur's knights
Strike back at all that host so bitterly;
But they will be overthrown before undern is rung   *2840*
But so foolishly fighting us all, here on this field.
It will be no great marvel if all of them fall to their fate.
If they would be reasonable now, and pass on their way,
Ride on home to their prince and leave off their fighting,
They might well lengthen their lives and lose very little,
And indeed it would cheer my heart, I swear to heaven."
    "Sir," says Sir Algere, "they are not much used
To their hosts being overthrown. That angers me more!
The fairest that ride in our force shall fall to their fate,
Few as those are, before they have fled this field."   *2850*
    Then the good Sir Gawain, gracious and noble,

75

With glorious pleasure gave cheer to the hearts of his men:
"Do not be dazzled, good men, by the glint of their shields
Or because yonder faint-hearts are fine on their fancy horses.
Standard-bearers of Briton, pluck up your hearts!
We meet nothing but brawling boys, for all their bright ribbons;
We shall smash down their boasts, for all their bloody noises,
And make them as meek as a lady in bed with her lord!
If we fight just a little today, the field will be ours:
The fickle faith will fail, and the false be destroyed.   *2860*
Their squadrons are all mere show, untested, it seems;
They swear their faith and creed to the Fiend himself.
We'll soon be acknowledged the victors in this battle
And vaunted by the voices of valiant men;
And we shall be praised by princes, in the presence of lords,
And loved by all the ladies alive on earth!
There was never such honor won by all our elders,
By Unwin nor Absalom nor by anyone else.
And when we are most in distress, we'll remember the Virgin,
That is our master's sign, the lady of his trust;   *2870*
Remember that mildest of queens who will comfort us all,
For he who remembers her mercy can never go wrong."

        When these words were finished, they were not far off,
No more than the length of the glade, and "Lorraine!" was the cry.
There was never such jubilant jousting on all this earth—
Even in the Vale of Jehosophat, as in stories
We hear how Julius and Joatil were jousted down—
As there was when the royal knights of the Round Table
Rushed into the rout on their royal steeds.
For so terribly they rushed with their trembling spears   *2880*
That the enemy turned in terror and tore for the groves
And were overcome by that court and known cowards forever.
"St. Peter," cries Sir Gawain, "this gladdens my heart,
That yonder fainthearts have fled, for all their numbers.
I can tell you, those timid devils will trouble us little;
They'll hide themselves in haste in the edge of the woods.
On the field they're fewer than we figured them at first—
For all their fair hosts, they're fewer by forty thousand!"

        But Jolian of Genoa, a towering giant,
Encounters with Sir Gerard, a justice of Wales;   *2890*
Through his parti-colored shield he jabs the giant,

And through his split coat-armor of shining mail
And he cuts the hinge of the joints and breaks them asunder.
It was riding a swift-footed warhorse he rode to the joust;
And thus was the giant fallen, that wandering Jew,
And Gerard is joyful enough, and cheered all the more.
  Then all the giants of Genoa join at once
And clap their lances for battle, five hundred strong;
A man called Sir Frederick, with a good many others,
Hurls into the charge and cries out anew   *2900*
To fight with Arthur's forces who now hold the field.
And then the royal knights of Arthur's Round Table
Rush forth eagerly, and they ride out against them,
And they meet in midfield, badly matched as they are;
Of such a great host it is marvelous to hear.
Soon after, at the assembly the Saracens find
The sovereign of Saxony, whom no man could save.
Our gentle knights fought hard with the Genoan giants,
And through their split mail, stabbed them to the heart.
They hacked their way through helmets and haughty byrnies *2910*
So their richly hilted swords ran through to their chests,
And then the knights of renown, of Arthur's Round Table,
Hurled at them and ran down those renegade wretches;
And thus they drove to their death both dukes and earls
Throughout the whole of the day, with mighty deeds.
  Then Sir Priamus the Prince, in the presence of lords,
Pushed to the banner of Lorraine and clipped it off cleanly,
Siezed it as if with ease, and away he rode
Back to the royal rout of Arthur's Round Table;
And swiftly Priamus' men rode after the man,   *2920*
For they'd seen his arms on the shining shield,
And out of the army they shot like sheep from a fold
And galloped swiftly to the place, and stood by their lord,
And they sent back then to the duke, and these were their words:
"We have followed you loyally six long years and more;
We forsake you today, by the sovereign right of our lord;
For in every king's lands, we follow our own liege lord.
And we here require our fees of these four winters,
For Lorraine is feeble and false, pays mere fine words;
Our hire is now due, and your war is ended,   *2930*
And we are now free in all honor to ride where we please.

We counsel you, treat for a truce, and trifle no longer,
Or you'll lose out of your total another ten thousand."
    "To hell with the devils," said the duke, "—the devil take 'em!
I'll never fear any great danger from those foul dogs!
We'll make our deal today by deeds of arms,
With my title, my dukedom, and all my most faithful knights;
Retainers like you I can easily do without,
Who suddenly leave their lord in times of danger."
The duke lifts up his shield and dallies no longer,   *2940*
But mounts a dromedary, with knights all around him,
And charges down on Sir Gawain with all his great number,
The mighty men of Granada, known to be grim.
Thus enemy hosts on fresh horses now rush the first rank
And among our fighters they unhorse some forty at once.
Our men had fought before with a full five hundred;
It might be no marvel, in truth, if now they grew faint!
Sir Gawain was filled with wrath, and he gripped his lance
And he galloped in once more with his veteran knights;
He met with the Marquis of Metz and rammed him through,   *2950*
The man on this middle-earth who had grieved him most.
But then Child Chastelain, of the king's own chamber,
Ward of Sir Gawain, the lord of the western marches,
Turns upon Sir Cheldrike, a noble chieftain,
And with his hunting lance, he lunges him through.
Such was the fortune he got by the chance of arms:
They chased that child so he couldn't escape alive,
For one called the swain of Swecy, with his sharp sword's edge
Snapped asunder the neckbone of Arthur's squire.
He fainted dead, and he stretched out on the sward,   *2960*
And the blood slid out; he would never strike again.
    Then Sir Gawain wept with his gray eyes
At the loss of so good a man, a beginner in battle.
And for that courageous boy his mood so changed
That the salty tears seared down Sir Gawain's cheeks.
"Woe is me," cried Gawain, "that ever I saw this!
I'll wage now for that squire all the power I rule
If I'm not avenged on that devil who brought down his life!"
He claps the lance in, solemn, and rides to the duke,
But another, the fierce Sir Dolphin came riding against him,   *2970*
And Sir Gawain gored him through with his grim lance

So that the hard-ground spear cut through to his heart.
And quickly he pulled it out and wounded another,
A heathen knight called Hardolf, lucky in battle;
Skillfully through the stomach he pierces him,
So that Hardolf's sailing spear flew high from his hands.
There were slain, there on that slope, by the speed of his hands,
Sixty strong men of arms, all dashed to the ground.
And though now Sir Gawain was weary, he waited his time
And at last caught sight of the man who had killed the squire,   *2980*
And with his sword he swept down hard and through him,
So that the blood burst out and he bent to the earth.
And then he rushed back to our men, and he hewed down helmets,
Rent apart rich hauberks, ruined shields,
Riding with all his force, he held to his road,
And all the length of their army he held to his way,
And there he pulled on the reins of his royal steed
And once again rode back to the men of the Round Table.
    Then all our chivalrous men reined round their horses,
To chase and to chop down those noble chieftains   *2990*
And hit out heartily at helmets and shields,
Hurting and hewing away at the heathen knights.
They cleaved the kettle-shaped helmets clear to the shoulders,
And never was there such a clamor of captains on earth!
There were kings' sons made captive, courteous and noble,
And knights of the country, known to be great and rich;
And mighty lords both of Lombardy and of Lorraine
Were captured there and brought to the hold of our knights,
And those who fought that day found fortune indeed,
For no better luck in a hunt had they ever achieved!   *3000*
    And after Sir Florent had won the field by fighting,
He galloped back to King Arthur with his fivescore knights,
And their prisoners and prizes they brought in behind him,
With shield bearers and archers and good men of arms.
Nobly now Sir Gawain leads back his knights,
And he goes by the shortest routes, as the guides suggest,
For fear lest some hostile garrison of great lords
Should seize his booty or do him some baleful harm:
And so they paused at the straits with the whole of the army
Till all his booty had passed down the path he dreaded.   *3010*
When they came in sight of the city King Arthur besieged

The city on that same day was won by assault.
    A messenger rides ahead, the best of lords,
And he comes to Arthur's camp, out of the highlands,
And turns toward the tent, and he tells the king
All the tale at once of the army's achievement:
"All your hunters are together who hunted in the hills,
Sir Florent, Sir Floridas, and all your fierce knights;
They have come to encounter and fought with a very great

                                                number,
And a great array of your foemen have gone down to earth.   *3020*
Our honorable warden Sir Gawain has won great glory,
And for his work today he's won honor forever;
He has slain the dread Sir Dolphin and taken the duke,
And many a doughty knight lies dead by his hand.
He's brought back rich prisoners, both princes and earls
Of some of the noblest blood now reigning on earth;
And all your chivalrous knights are home again safe
Except for a squire, Chastelain, who is sadly fallen."
"Valiant!" the king cries out, "my herald, by Christ,
You've bolstered up my spirits, I tell you the truth!   *3030*
I award you in Hampton a hundred pound tribute."
    The king then assembled his knights for the assault
With summer castles and miner-sheds set on all sides;
He disposes his shield bearers and scales the walls,
And every watch has his hands full with shrewd men of arms.
Then boldly they attack and they bend back their engines
Loaded heavy with stones, and they prove their casts;
Convents and hospitals they smash to the earth,
And the fairest of churches and lovely chalk-white chapels;
Huge stone steeples come smashing down into the streets   *3040*
And chambers with wide chimneys, and many chief halls;
And they smashed and pelted down those plaster walls,
And the grief of the people was a pitiful thing to hear!
Then the duchess sent down by noble damsels
And the countess of Cresyn, with her worthy maidens,
Kneeled in the castle crenels, where the king now loomed,
On a covered horse in his glorious array,
And they knew him by his look, and they called aloud:
"O, King, crowned by Nature, attend to our words!
We beseech you, sire, as a sovereign and a lord,   *3050*

That you spare our lives today, for the sake of your Christ!
And send some help to us, assure us your peace
Before the city is suddenly shattered by assault."
With a noble mien, King Arthur lifts his visor
And with virtuous countenance the valiant baron
Speaks to the lady mildly, with humble words:
"No man in my service, madam, shall do you harm.
I grant you my pledge of peace, and your ladies as well,
And the children and each of the chivalrous knights of this castle.
The duke is in danger, there can be no doubt of that;   3060
He shall pay in full, but you, you need fear no more."
        Then he sent word on each side, to certain lords,
To leave the assault, for at last the city had yielded.
The earl sent Arthur the keys by his eldest son
And surrendered that same night, by assent of his lords.
And the duke, with all his lords, was deported to Dover
To live there in danger and grief all the days of his life.
At the farther gates there fled an enormous number
For fear of Sir Florent and the fierce knights in his charge;
They emptied out of the city and rushed to the woods   3070
With food and household vessels and their fairest clothes.
Then over the broad gates up went Arthur's banner
And never, in truth, was Sir Florent more joyful of heart:
The knight, high on his hill, beheld the walls
And said, "I see by that sign the city is ours!"
And soon King Arthur entered, his hosts in array,
Just as the undern was rung, and intended to stay there.
To each of the retinues there the king cried aloud
That on pain of life and limb and the loss of their lands,
No loyal liegeman belonging to him   3080
Should lie by any fair lady or loyal virgin
Nor by any burgess's wife, either better or worse,
Nor do harm to a single soul in the captured city.

⟨ The Final Battles and the Victory over Rome

AFTER King Arthur had fully conquered
      And recovered the central castle of that rich country
By the craft of arms, all the men there, cruel and keen,

Both captains and constables, acknowledged him lord.
Arthur devised and dealt out to his diverse lords
A suitable reparation for the duchess and her children;
And he appointed wardens who would wisely rule the lands   3090
That he now had won by war with all his wise knights.
Thus he lodged in Lorraine as lord of the land
And established his laws for the kingdom as suited his pleasure.
And then on Lammass Day he went on to Lucerne
And lodged there at his leisure with pleasures enough.
There were his galleys made ready—a very great number—
And they glittered like new glass below green hills,
With covered cabins prepared for the pleasure of kings,
Containing clear gold clothing for knights and for others;
Soon they had stowed in their gear and stabled their horses   3100
And they stretched their oars to sail over into the strait-lands.
    Now Arthur moves his might with a merry heart
Over the highest of the mountains by marvelous paths,
Goes in by way of St. Gothard's, taking the tower,
And grimly he decimates the good garrison.
And when he has passed the heights, the king draws up,
While his whole battle host, and he stands looking all about
And gazes on Lombardy, and he cries aloud:
"In the lovely land below us I think I am lord."
Then he rides down into Como with anointed kings,   3110
The most famous city there, and key to the country.
Sir Florent and Floridas rode in ahead
With more than five hundred of the mightiest men of France.
They swiftly moved on the city and came up unseen
And set up an ambush that seemed to them sly enough.
Early the following morning, out came from the city
The keenest of their scouts on skirted horses:
They scattered out and they skipped along over the hills
To search out skulkers there, keep the city walls safe.
Poor people and shepherds came pouring out after that   3120
To put their pigs to pasture beyond the great gates;
And in the suburbs small boys were playing and shouting
At a loner boar as it trotted along in the field.
And then our ambush broke, and it won the bridge,
And galloped on into the city with banners displayed,
And we stabbed and struck down all who stood up in our road,

And before we stopped, four streets were entirely destroyed.
Thus the king won Como, and he called in his court
Inside the famous castle, with anointed kings,
And Arthur counseled the commons belonging to his liege   *3130*
And comforted heavy hearts with knightly words.
And he made their keenest captain a knight of his own,
And the king and all the city were soon in accord.
    The lord of Milan, meanwhile, heard the city was won
And sent at once to King Arthur certain of his lords
With great sums of gold on sixty loaded horses,
And he asked the king as his sovereign to aid the people,
And he said he would swear himself Arthur's subject forever
And stand in his service and ask him for his lands;
For Piacenza, Pallanza, and Pontremoli,   *3140*
For Pisa and Pavia he offers rich tribute —
Purple stuffs, and pall, and precious stones,
Palfreys fit for a prince and splendid steeds —
For Milan he offers the tax of a million pounds gold,
And humbly at Martinmas he'll do homage, with his lords,
And ever after, unasked, both he and his heirs
Will be homage men to Arthur as long as he lives.
The king, by assent of his council, sent him safe-conduct,
And the lord of Milan came to Como and acknowledged him lord.
    Now Arthur turns, when the time is right, to Tuscany,   *3150*
And he swiftly storms those towns with their lofty towers;
He casts down mighty walls, wounds gentle knights,
Topples towers, and torments the people,
Makes many a splendid widow sing out woe
And often sink down weary, weep, wring her hands.
He wastes all with war, whatever his force rides past,
And all their wealth and their dwellings he turns to destruction.
Thus they spring on and spread, and spare but little,
Spoil without pity and smash the vineyards down,
Spend without sparing what took long years to save.   *3160*
And they speed then to Spoleto, with spears beyond number.
From Spain into Prussia-land the report of him springs
And the tale of his destructions; despair heaps high.
    And then towards Viterbo he turns his reins.
There in that valley he feeds his warriors well
With vernage and other wines and well-baked venison,

And he chooses to stay for a time with the viscount there.
Quickly King Arthur's vanguard alight from their horses
In the valley of Vertennon, among the vineyards,
And there the sovereign sojourns to comfort his heart   3170
And to see when the senators will send him any word.
He revels with rich wine, and riots himself,
This king and all his royal ranks of the Round Table,
With mirth and with melody and with many games,
And never on earth were there merrier men ever made!
    On a Saturday, at noon, just seven days later,
The wisest of all the cardinals belonging to the court
Kneeled to King Arthur and spoke to him with words:
He asked the king's peace and afterward implored him
To have mercy on the pope, whom the Romans deposed;   3180
And he sought the king's assurance, for the sake of our Lord,
That within no more than a week they would all be assembled
And would see him, without fail, on the following Sunday
In the city of Rome as her sovereign and her lord
And the pope would crown him and duly anoint him with chrism,
And with sword and scepter make Arthur lord and sovereign.
And he had brought hostages with him in surety,
Eightscore children, the handsomest of Rome's heirs,
In togas woven at Tars, most richly attired;
And these he committed to the king and his regal knights.   3190
    After the truce was sealed, with trumpet blasts
They turned to a tent where tables were set on trestles,
And the king himself was seated with certain lords
Below a silk canopy, and the table was at peace;
And the senators were seated in a place apart
And served with all ceremony, with seldom-seen dishes.
Great was King Arthur's mirth, and with gentle words
He lifted the hearts of the Romans around his rich table
And went himself, like a true knight, to comfort the cardinal,
Thus this royal king, at his rich table,   3200
Honored the Romans, as the old romance recounts.
And when the time seemed right, these men, trained and knowing,
Took their leave of the king and turned towards home;
They made their way to the city that night with all speed,
And the hostages of Rome were left with Arthur.
    And now the king of Britain spoke these bold words:

"Now we may revel and rest, for Rome is ours!
Let us make our handsome young hostages at ease,
And let all my host take care to hold them in honor;
I shall soon be the overlord of all the earth,   *3210*
The emperor of the Germans and all eastern marches.
By Holy Cross Day we shall have taken these lands,
And on Christmas Day we'll be crowned accordingly.
I'll reign in my royalty and hold my Round Table
With the money of Roman rents, as suits my pleasure,
And then I'll go over the Great Sea with good men of arms
To avenge that knight who was murdered once on the cross."

❰ The Second Dream

THEN this noble king, as the chronicles tell us,
Turned towards his bed with a cheerful heart;
He threw his robes down lightly and slackened his waistband,   *3220*
And soon he had slipped away into heavy slumber.
But soon after midnight, at one, his mood was changed:
He dreamt in that morning hour a marvelous dream,
And when that dreadful dream had been driven to the end,
The great king stared in terror, as though he should die,
And he sent for philosophers quickly to tell them his fear.
      "Since first I was formed, I swear, I was never so frightened!
Therefore ransack your wits and tell me the meaning,
And I will tell you this nightmare exactly and truly.
I thought I was deep in a wood, by my own will,   *3230*
And didn't know what the path was or where to turn
Except through wolves and swine and wicked beasts,
And so I walked in that wasteland, watching for dangers.
There great, loathsome lions licked their teeth
As they lapped up the glowing blood of my loyal knights.
Through all that forest where flowers grew tall I fled
For the terrible fear I had of those foul creatures.
I made my way to a meadow closed in by mountains,
The fairest a man might find on this middle-earth.
And the clearing was encompassed and closed around   *3240*
And evenly covered on all sides with clover and clevewort;
And all around that valley were vines of silver,

And on them grapes of gold—no greater on earth—
Surrounded by shrubs and by every kind of tree,
Handsome arbors, and herdsmen lying beneath them.
And all the fruits that flourish on earth were there,
Hanging on all the boughs and sheltered by hedges;
Even in shadows I saw no harmful dew,
But every flower was dry from the drying of daylight.

    "And then down out of the clouds there came to the dale   *3250*
A duchess preciously dressed in the finest of garments,
A surcoat made of silk, of strange, rich hues,
And all overlaid to the lowest hems with ermine
And ladylike lappets to the length of one full yard,
And all of them lightly turned back with ribbons of gold,
With broaches and bezants and other bright stones
She was splendidly adorned, both her back and breast;
And her head was arrayed in a caul and a coronal
So lovely with color no finer has ever been known.

    "And she whirled a wheel around with   *3260*
                       her two white hands,
And she turned that wheel as deftly as ever she pleased.
The rim was of yellow gold, with royal stones
Arrayed in wonderful wealth, and rubies aplenty;
The spokes of the wheel were resplendent with splinters of silver
Springing out, all dazzling, the space of a spear-length.
On the wheel there flew a chair of chalk-white hues;
To the outer rim there clung six kings in a row,
Their crowns of clearest gold all cracked asunder;
Six from that splendid seat had suddenly fallen,
Each man after the other, and said these words: *3270*

    " 'I rue forever that ever I reigned on this wheel!
There was never a king so rich that has reigned on earth!
When I rode my joyful way I did nothing else
But hunt with my hawks and revel and tax the people;
Thus now I drive down my days, as long as I last,
And therefore to agony I'm condemned forever.'

    "The last was a little man that was laid beneath;
His loins lay very lean and loathsome to look at,
And his locks were gray and long, the length of a yard,
And all his flesh and body were horribly maimed;   *3280*
One eye of the man was as bright as any silver,

The other eye more yellow than the yolk of an egg.
'I was once lord,' he said, 'of lands aplenty,
And all bowed low to me, who lived on this earth;
But now there is left me no rag that will cover my body,
And lightly I am lost. Let all men believe it.'
    "The second I saw before me, who followed soon after,
Seemed stronger, to my eye, and surer in arms;
But heavily he sighed, and he spoke these words:
'On yonder seat I was seated as sovereign and lord,   3290
And loved by ladies, who held me in their arms:
But now my lordship is lost and laid by forever!'
    "The third man there was massive and thick in the shoulders,
A man too fierce for thirty men to threaten;
His diadem had fallen, adorned with stones,
All indented with diamonds, designed for the time.
'I was dreaded in my days in diverse realms,
But now I am dead and damned, and my grief is the greater.'
    "The fourth I saw was a fair man, forceful in arms,
And in figure the fairest man that was ever yet formed.   3300
'I was fierce in my faith,' he said, 'while I reigned on earth,
Famous in far-off lands, and the flower of kings;
Now my face is faded, my fortune gone foul,
For I'm fallen from afar, and find myself friendless.'
    "The fifth was a fairer man than many of the others,
A forceful man and fierce, with foaming lips;
He clung fast to the felly and gripped it in his arms,
Yet still he failed, and he fell some fifty feet;
But still he sprang up and leapt and he spread out his arms,
And on those spear-length spokes he said these words: 3310
'I was a sire in Syria, seated alone
As sovereign and suzerain over sundry kingdoms;
Now out of all my joy I am suddenly fallen,
And because of my sins my throne is lost to me.'
    "The sixth one had a psalter most handsomely bound
And a surplice of silk that was elegantly sewn,
And he had a harp and a hand-sling, with hard flint stones;
And what harms he has known he tells at once:
'For deeds of arms I was judged in my day,' he says,
'The doughtiest of all kings down here on earth;   3320
But I, for all my strength, was made to bend

By the mild maiden of the wheel, who moves us all.'

    "Two kings were climbing and clambering aloft,
And with all their hearts they covet the crest of the compass.
'This chair of carbuncle,' they said, 'we claim henceforth,
As two men chiefly chosen, above all the earth.'
Those nobles were chalky-white, both cheeks and faces,
Yet never might they achieve the chair above them.
The furthermost was handsome and broad of forehead,
The fairest man in figure that ever was formed;   *3330*
He was clad in a splendid coat of royal blue,
Flecked all over with fleurs-de-lis of gold;
And the other prince was dressed in a coat of pure silver,
And on it a comely cross that was carved of fine gold,
And by that cross four smaller crosses rested,
And by those signs I knew him a christened king.

    "Then up I went to that fair one and fondly hailed her,
And she said, 'Welcome, in truth, you are well met.
Well may you worship my will, as you know well,
And more than all other great men that were ever on earth;   *3340*
All your worship in war you've won by my will,
For I have been friendly, man, and helped against others;
You've found that out, in truth, as well as your warriors,
For I brought down Sir Frolle by cruel knights
So all the fruits of France might freely be yours.
And you shall achieve the chair, I choose you myself
Before all the kings to be chosen here on earth.'

    "Lightly she lifted me up with her slender hands
And she set me soft in that seat and reached me the scepter;
Then carefully with her comb she combed my head   *3350*
So that the crisping curl came to my crown;
She dressed me up in a diadem beautifully jewelled
And she handed me an apple set full of fair stones,
Enameled over with azure, the earth painted on it,
Circled by the salty sea upon every side,
In sign that I surely was sovereign of all the earth.
Then she brought me a sword with a shining hilt,
And she told me to brandish it: 'The sword is my own;
Its swing has let out the lifeblood of many a swain,
For while you worked with this sword it never failed you.'   *3360*
    "Then she departed in peace, all mild, when it pleased her,

And went to the trees of a forest—no holt ever richer!
No orchard was ever made fairer for princes on earth,
Or could boast such proud appointments, save Paradise.
And she bade the boughs to bend down and bring to my hands
The best of the fruit they bore on their highest branches,
And all the boughs together obeyed her command,
The highest on every tree: I tell you the truth!
She bade me spare no fruit but pluck all I pleased:
'Take all the finest here, O noble warrior,   3370
And reach toward the ripest! Refresh yourself!
And rest, O royal King, for Rome is yours,
And I shall be ready to bring you rest most swiftly
And bring rich vine to you in cups rinsed clean.'
      "Then she went up to the well, by the hem of the wood,
Which bubbled up with wine and marvelously ran,
And she caught a cupful up and covered it well
And she kindly bade me draw in, and drink to herself,
And thus she led me about for the length of an hour,
With all the sweetness and love that a man could long for.   3380
      "But then at high noon exactly her whole mood changed,
And she turned and menaced me with marvelous words.
When I cried for mercy she lowered her mighty brows:
'Sir King, you speak in vain, by Christ that made me!
For now you shall lose this game, and your life soon after;
You have lived in all delight and lordship too long.'
      "Then round she whirls that wheel, and rolls me under,
Till both my legs at once were crushed to pieces
And my backbone chopped in two by the reeling chair;
I've lain and shivered with chills since all this happened   3390
And since I awakened again, all weary and spent.
You know my trouble now. Say all you think."
      "Friend," the philosopher said, "your fortune has passed,
For ask whenever you like, you'll find her your foe.
You stand at your highest point: I speak the truth.
Complain now all you choose, you'll achieve no more.
You've shed much blood and have mowed down innocent knights
For nought but pride in many a proud king's land;
Confess yourself of your sins and prepare for your end.
You've seen the foreshadowing, sire. Take care if you like.   3400
For fiercely you shall fall within five winters.

Go found abbeys in France—the fruits are your own—
For Frolle and for Feraunt and for all their fierce knights
Whom fiercely there in France you fought and killed.
Remember the other great kings, and cast in your heart;
Consider the greatest of conquerors crowned on this earth.

"The eldest was Alexander, to whom all earth bowed;
The second was Hector of Troy, that chivalrous man;
The third was Julius Caesar, a giant among men
On each of his famous campaigns, attended by lords.   3410
The fourth was Maccabeus, a most noble jouster,
The masterful Sir Judas, mighty in his strength;
The fifth was Joshua, joyful man in arms,
To whom joy came in an inn once, in Jerusalem.
The sixth was the valiant David, judged among kings
One of the doughtiest men that was ever yet dubbed,
For he slew with only a sling and the speed of his hands,
Goliath the greatest of giants and grimmest on earth.
And he was the prince who composed the precious psalms
That are set forth in the Psalter, in peerless lyrics.   3420

"The first of the climbing kings, I know in truth,
Shall be King Charles, the son of the king of France;
And he shall be cruel and keen and held a conqueror,
And in time will recover by conquests many a country;
He'll acquire the crown that Christ Himself once bore,
And the splendid lance that once leapt to his heart,
When Christ was crucified, and all the keen nails
Shall Charles the Great win back for Christendom.

"The second, then, shall be Godfrey, whom God shall revenge
For that Good Friday, with all His gallant knights;   3430
And he shall be lord of Lorraine, by leave of his father;
And then in Jerusalem much joy shall befall him,
For he shall recover the cross, by craft of arms,
And then be crowned as king and anointed with chrism.
No duke of his day shall achieve such destiny,
Nor suffer such great misfortune, when all is known.
And you, sire, Fortune brings to fill out the number
As ninth among the noblest men named upon earth;
Your work shall be read in romances by noble knights,
And reckoned and revered by reveling kings;   3440
Your deeds of arms shall be judged when Doomsday comes

The mightiest deeds that were done in the days of earth.
Thus many a clerk and king shall proclaim your feats
And keep all the chronicle of your conquests forever.
    "But the wolves out in the wood, and the wild beasts,
Are certain wicked men who riot your kingdom
And enter while you are away to attack your people,
And they're aliens and hosts from barbaric lands.
You'll hear of them, I trust, within ten days,
And know what trouble has come since you turned from home;   *3450*
I urge you, recall and count up all your cruel deeds
And repent at once, my lord, of your rueful works.
Man, amend your heart before any misfortune,
And meekly ask for mercy and help for your soul."
    Then up King Arthur arose and put on his array,
A jacket as red as a rose, the richest of flowers,
Chest-plates, and belly-plates, and a precious girdle;
On his head he puts a hood of magnificent hue,
And on that a pillion-hat that was richly set
With pearls of the Orient, and precious stones;   *3460*
His gloves were gaily gilt and embroidered at the hems
And sprinkled all over with rubies, splendid to look at;
And then with his greyhound and sword, and with no one with
                                   him,
He walked out over a meadow with woe in his heart;
He stalks along a path by the silent wood-eaves,
And stops at a wide highway, and stands deep in thought.
And when the sun came up he saw there, coming,
Rushing along towards Rome by the shortest route
A man in a round cloak and with heavy clothes.
In a hat and in high shoes, homely and round,   *3470*
Flat farthings fixed to his coat, one would have said,
And shreds and tatters swung to the road from his skirts,
And the man had scrip and mantle and pilgrimage badges
And pike and palm, the sort a pilgrim has.
    The traveler greeted him quickly and bade him good morning:
The king himself, like a lord, in the language of Rome,
But Latin quite corrupt, spoke courteously:
"Where would you go, man, walking all alone?
It seems hardly safe, when the country stands at war.
There's an enemy camped with his army beyond those vines;   *3480*

If they see you, in truth, it will mean great trouble for you,
Unless you've been given safe-conduct by the king.
Outlaws will come and they'll kill you and keep what you have;
And hold to the highway, they'll seize you even so,
Unless you get help at once from friendly knights."
　　Then Sir Craddock replies to the king himself:
"If so, I'll forgive my death, so help me God,
And any groom under God that I find on this ground;
Let the keenest man that belongs to the king come up,
I'll encounter the man like a knight and Christ have my soul!　　*3490*
For not even you can reach me, sir, or arrest me,
However rich your clothes and your fine array;
No war on earth can prevent me from passing as I please,
Nor can any mortal man that is made on this earth.
But I'll pass in pilgrimage down this path to Rome
To procure my holy pardon of the pope himself
And thus be absolved in full from the pains of Purgatory.
Then after that I shall seek my sovereign lord,
King Arthur of England, the greatest of errant knights,
For he is somewhere in this empire, as valiant men tell me,　　*3500*
Campaigning in the Orient with awesome men."
　　"And where do you come from, keen man?" the king
　　　　　　　　　　　　　　　　　　　　　　　　　　said then,
　　"And where do you come from, keen man?" the king
Were you ever in his court while he dwelt at home?
Your tongue is familiar to me and comforts my heart;
You've come a long way, and wise indeed your quest,
For by your broad speech you seem a British soldier."
　　"Well might I know him! The king's my own vowed lord,
And I was called in his court a knight of his chamber;
Sir Craddock I was called in his royal court,　　*3510*
The keeper of Caerleon, and second to the king.
But now I am driven from the country with care in my heart,
And the castle Caerleon is captured by strangers."
　　Then quickly the handsome king caught Craddock in his arms,
Cast off his kettle-hat and kissed him at once,
And said, "Welcome, Sir Craddock, as Christ defend me!
Dear cousin and kinsman, you make my heart turn cold.
What has become of fair Briton and all my bold men?
Are they beaten down or burnt or brought out of life?

Come, let me know at once what fortune has fallen;   3520
I ask no assurances of you; I know you are true."
    "Sire, your warden is wicked and wild in his deeds,
And he's caused great sorrow while you have been gone.
He's captured castles and crowned himself king,
And he's taken in all the rent of the Round Table;
He's divided the realm and has dealt it out as he likes;
Dubbed men out of Denmark dukes and earls,
Sent them out on all sides, sacked your cities;
And Saracens and Saxons of every shore
He's set up as an army of foreign soldiers—   3530
Sovereigns of Surgenale, and mercenaries,
Picts and pagan peoples and proven knights
Of Ireland and Argyle, whom you have outlawed;
All those highland outlaws now are knights
And lead and hold what lordship pleases them.
And now Sir Childeric is held a chief in Britain,
And the old chivalric marauder afflicts your people.
They rob your religious men and ravish your nuns,
And he rides with his eager rout to ransack the poor.
He holds as his own all the land from Humber to Hawick   3540
And all the country of Kent, and claims as his
The splendid castles that once were kept by his crown,
The holts and ancient woods and the hard cliffs
And all that Hengist and Horsa held in their time.
And sevenscore ships at Southampton-on-the-Sea
Are freighted with the fiercest men from far off lands
To fight with your forces whenever you come to assail them.
Yet one word more, for you do not know yet the worst:
He has wedded Guinevere and he calls her his wife
And they live in the wildest reach of the western marches,   3550
And he's got her with child, as witnesses have told us.
May more grief meet that man than any other,
The warden most unworthy to look after women!
Thus has the vicious Sir Mordred defiled us all!
And therefore I've crossed these mountains to bring you the truth."
    Then the boarlike Arthur, with anger in his heart,
Changed all his hue for this injury past cure.
"By the cross," the king cried out, "I will revenge it!
I'll make him repent at once his monstrous work!"

Then, weeping for woe, he went to his tents;   *3560*
Joylessly the wise king awakens his barons,
Summons in by trumpet-call kings and others,
Gathers them to council and gives them this news;
"I am betrayed by treason, for all my true deeds,
And all my work is wasted; thus falls my fortune;
Grief shall howl him down who did this treason
If I am still true lord, and still can take him.
So this is Mordred, the man whom I most trusted! —
He has captured my castles and crowned himself king
With the rents and riches of the Round Table;   *3570*
And he's made him a retinue out of renegade wretches,
And dealt my kingdom out to diverse lords,
To soldiers and Saracens brought out of sundry lands.
And wedded the queen, you say, and calls her his wife.
And a child begotten, my chance is no better than that!
And now they've assembled on the sea their sevenscore ships,
Freighted with fierce men who will fight with my own.
Then I must set out at once, go back to Britain
And break that bold man down who's brought us this grief.
No fierce man shall I take there except with fresh horses,   *3580*
And veterans in battle, the flower of my knights.
Sir Howell and Sir Hardolf shall wait for me here
To be lords to the people here who belong to me;
They shall look after Lombardy, so none there change heart,
And take care of Tuscany too, as I shall bid them,
And receive the rents of Rome, when they have been reckoned,
And take seisin the same day as the date assigned,
Or else outside the walls our hostages
Shall all be hanged on high, the whole lot as one."

    Now the bold king, with his bravest knights, makes ready: *3590*
Sounds trumpets, loads for travel, starts at once;
He turns through Tuscany, and he tarries little,
In Lombardy hardly dismounts except when the light fails;
He marches over the mountains on marvelous passes
And journeys through Germany by the shortest route,
And so with his fiercest knights he arrives in Flanders.
There within fifteen days his fleet is assembled
And he moves his men on shipboard, stalls no longer.
He steers with the sharp wind over sheer waters

And soon ties up by the rocks and rides at anchor.   3600
    There the false men floated and lingered on the flood
Big ships linked together by cargo chains
And charged from wall to wall with chivalrous knights,
And piled up high, to aft, were helmets and crests,
And the covered hatches below were crawling with heathens.
Above each ship, on boldly painted cloths
Made piece by piece, and each piece fastened to the other,
Hung shielding camouflage of double thickness;
And thus had those sharp Danes dressed all their ships:
No arrow's blow could do them cruel damage.   3610
    Then the king and the regal knights of the Round Table
Arrayed their ships all royally in red.
That day he dealt out dukedoms, dubbed new knights,
And fixed dromons and drags, and they drew up stones;
Top-castles he armed with battle-tools as it pleased him,
And bent crossbows to the screws soon after that;
The weaponsmiths work carefully with their tackle,
Mount great broad brazen heads on arrow-shafts;
And then, all ready for defense, they draw up their men
With grim steel gads and fetters of iron;   3620
Station strong men on the stern, with stout men of arms,
And many a lovely lance stands up aloft;
And men upon the leeboard, lords and others,
Place pavises on the port, great painted shields;
And high on the rearward hurdles stand helmeted knights.
Thus they ready their shots toward those sheer strands,
Each man there in his mantle, and splendid to see.
    The bold king takes to his barge, and they row him about,
An active man, bareheaded, with beaver-brown locks,
And a soldier carries his sword and an inlaid helmet,   3630
And attached to that a mantle of silver mail,
Crowned with a coronet, and splendidly covered;
He works his way to each warship to sheer on his knights.
To Clegis and Cleremond he cries aloud,
And Gawain and Galyron, both mighty men,
And to Lottes and Lionel he cries out his love,
And to Lancelot of the Lake, in lordly words:
"Let us recover the country! the coast is our own!
We'll make them blench in haste, those yawling bloodhounds!

Break them down where they sit, and burn them later;   3640
Hew down with all your hearts those heathen beasts;
They're on that traitor's side, I'll bet my right hand."
        Then he comes back to his warship and catches up anchor
And pulls on his splendid helmet and shining mail.
He runs up banners aloft, embroidered with gules,
With crowns of clearest gold in careful array,
And high there, up on the banner, a chalk-white Maiden,
And a Child in her arms, the Chief and King of Heaven;
These were the royal arms, and never changed,
Of Arthur, adventurer, while his time on earth lasted.   3650
        And then all the sailors cried out, and the masters of ships,
Merrily every mate shouted out to the other
In the jargon of their trade, as chance befalls:
They tow furled sheet to the wind, and truss up sails,
Beat all the bonnets abroad, and batten down hatches;
And they brandish their brown steel and blast on their trumpets,
And standing stiff on the stem, they steer ahead
And streak along the stream; and the strife begins.
And swiftly a raging wind rose out of the west
And fiercely swept with its blast those warriors' sails,   3660
And the heavy warships hurl to the walls of their foemen
And both the bilge and the beam are burst asunder;
So stoutly that forestem rams into the stem
The stocks of the steerboard shatter away in pieces.
At that, warship on warship, craft on craft,
They cast their creepers across, by mariners' craft;
They hacked away the headropes that held up the masts,
And there there was conflict keen and the crashing of ships,
Great dead-weight ships of battle dashed into splinters,
Many a rich cabin cleaved, and cables destroyed,   3670
And knights and keen men killing all who fought them,
Splendid castles carved by cruel weapons—
Handsome castles, and gloriously painted!
And they cut in afterwards, with upward glances,
With the swing of the sword the heavy sways of the mast;
At the first encounter, down fall fighters and others,
And many a man in the foreship is fallen to his fate.
Then sternly they turn about with their savage tackle,
And boldly byrnied knights there push aboard;

From the deck of every boat they attack with stones, 3680
Beat down the best, and burst the heavy hatches;
And some men are gored through with gads of iron—
Good soldiers gaily dressed, with bloody weapons.
The archers of Ireland all shoot now eagerly
And drive through hard steel many a mortal dart.
But there in the hull the heathen knights soon stagger,
So hurt by the hard steel they will never be whole.
Then the British fall to the fight with fiercer spears,
The fiercest men in front, as is fitting in battle,
And each one there puts forth his strength afresh 3690
To fight the war of the fleet with ferocious weapons.
Thus they worked that day, these anointed knights,
Till all the Danes were dead and hurled to the deep.
And the Britons breathing wrath hacked with their swords
Leaping there aloft, like lordly fighters;
And when those foreign swordsmen leaped to the water
Our British lords all laughed aloud together.
And spears were sprung, and mighty ships were splintered,
And Spaniards sprinted swiftly over the side;
All the brave enemy soon—both knights and others— 3700
Are laid cold dead, and cast into the sea.
And swiftly all their squires shed their lifeblood,
Climb to the hatches, rise to the bordered platforms,
Sink to the salty sea seven hundred at once.
And now Sir Gawain the Good has gained his desire,
And all the worthy warships he gave to his knights;
Sir Geryn and Sir Griswold, and other great lords,
By Galuth, his good sword, had given their heads.
Such was the false fleet's fortune there on the flood,
And thus the foreign folk are left there fated. 3710
　　　But the traitor is still on land with his trusty knights,
And with all their trumpets they ride on their skirted steeds
And they show themselves under shields on the shining banks:
No shame dismays him: he shows himself on high.
Arthur and Gawain started, both of them,
Towards the sixty thousand who showed themselves;
But after the fleet was beaten, the tide was out,
And the shore was like a mire, with great banks of mud,
And the king was kept from the landing by low water;

Therefore he lingered awhile, lest he lose his horses,   3720
To look over wounded liege men and loyal knights
To learn who was lamed or lost and who would live.
    But then Sir Gawain the Good, he takes a galley
And glides up into an inlet with good men of arms;
After he's grounded, he springs in grief to the water
And goes in up to his waistband, for all his fine weeds;
He runs up onto the sand, in the sight of the lords,
With no more men than his own—my sorrow's the greater!
With all the banners of his emblems, the best of his arms,
He hurls up onto the bank in his blazing array.   3730
He cries to his standard-bearer, "Forward, swiftly,
And ride to that broad battalion that waits on the bank;
And I can assure you truly I'll ride on your heels.
See that you shrink for no swordsman or any sharp weapon,
But bear down hard on the best, and rob them of daylight.
Do not be abashed by their boasts! Live on on earth!
You've borne my banners through many a bitter battle;
We'll fell those false ones too—the Fiend have their souls!
Fight hard against that host and the field will be ours.
If I overtake that traitor, foul fortune take him!—   3740
The man who has turned this treason against my true lord;
From bastard unions little joy can follow:
That we will prove today past all denial!"
    They seek them over the sand at the best point,
Meet with the enemy, make their shields ring out,
Through glittering shields they crash to touch their man
With the briefly shivering shafts of shining lances;
Great, cruel wounds they carve with their cutting spears,
And in the dank dew many a dead man lies,
Mighty dukes and douzeperes, rightly dubbed knights,   3750
The doughtiest men of Denmark, undone forever.
Thus these British brutally break through byrnies
And take from the strongest blows that they scarcely feel;
They fight in the thick of them, and thrust to the earth
The stoutest of all their men, three hundred at once.
    But Gawain, full of anger, could not hold back:
He claps his lance and gallops towards a man
Whose arms bore splendid gules with teardrops of silver;
He thrust him through at the throat with his thirsty lance

So that the well-ground point is shattered asunder,   3760
And with that mighty jolt he is jarred to his death:
The king of Gothland it was, and a good man of arms.
The vanguard after this all fled in retreat,
Vanquished utterly by our valiant warriors.
And now they meet with the middle guard, led by Sir Mordred.
Our men sweep down on them, for their misfortune;
For had Gawain had the grace to hold that green hill,
He'd have won indeed high worship for ever and ever.

    But now, in truth, Sir Gawain watches well
To avenge himself on this traitor who started the war,   3770
And he makes his way to Sir Mordred among all his fighters,
The Montagues beside him, and other great lords.

    Then fierce was Gawain's wrath, and with great will
He claps a fair lance in and lifts his challenge:
"Falsely fathered filth, the Fiend have your bones!
My curse is on you, thief, and your rueful works!
I'll see you dead and undone for your violent deeds
Or else I'll die this day, as destiny wills."

    Then Mordred with his host of outlawed barons
Circles on every side our excellent knights,   3780
As the traitor in his treason had plotted before;
The dukes of Denmark close up one side quickly,
And the mighty leaders of Lettow with legions aplenty,
And thus their shining lances surround our men;
Hirelings and Saracens brought out of sundry lands,
Sixty thousand men, in suitable array,
Solemnly close in around sevenscore knights
By a sudden trick beside that salty sea.

    And then Sir Gawain wept with his gray eyes
For grief over those good men he had guided;   3790
For he knew well they were wounded, weary, and spent;
And for wonder and for woe, his wit now failed.
With gasping sighs he said, tears sliding down:
"We're circled on all sides by Saracens!
I do not sigh for myself, as Christ is my Lord,
But for letting them surprise us, my sorrow's the more.
Be dauntless today and these dukes shall all be yours!
For our dear Lord today dread no man's weapons!
And we shall end this day as peerless knights

And fly to endless joy with flawless angels.   *3800*
And though we have wasted ourselves unwittingly,
We'll work like loyal men for the court of Christ,
And for yonder Saracens, I swear on my troth,
We'll sup with our Savior in ceremony, in heaven,
In the presence of the King of Kings and Prince of all others,
With prophets and patriarchs and the noble apostles,
Before His gracious face, who formed us all!
Now on to yonder jades' sons: he who yields
While quick and still in health, unkilled by their hands,
May he never more be saved, nor succored by Christ, *3810*
But Satan sink his soul deep down in hell!"
  Now most grimly Gawain grips his weapon,
And claps his lance against that great battalion,
Hastily straightens the chains on his blazing sword
And brandishes his shield, holds back no longer.
Unwisely, like a madman, he charges the closest,
And the wounds of his enemies, where Gawain swings
Are wells of blood wherever he passes by;
And though he rode half-mad, he held his course
And works out, to his worship, the wrath of his lord. *3820*
He strikes in his rush both steeds and stern-faced knights,
And strong men in their stirrups sit stone dead.
He hurls the hard steel, rips through coats of mail,
And no man there could restrain him, his reason was gone.
In the fierceness of his heart he fell into frenzy
And fought and struck down all who would stand before him;
There never befell a doomed man such misfortune on earth!
Through all their ranks he rushes himself headlong
And hurts the hardiest men that move on the earth,
And raging like a lion he lunges through them, *3830*
All the lords and leaders who hold that land.
And still for all his woe he wavers but little,
But wounds on every side with wonderful strokes
As if by his own will he would waste himself;
From pain and the power of his will his wits all failed him,
And mad as some wild beast he rushed at the nearest,
And all where he passed by must wallow in blood;
Let each beware by his vengeance on the others!
  And he moved towards Sir Mordred among all his knights

And he met him in the midshield and hammered in through it;   *3840*
But Mordred at that jolt shrank back a little,
And Gawain shore him in the shortribs and hand's breadth wide.
The shaft shuddered and glanced off the gleaming warrior
So that the blood washed out and slid down his shanks
And shone clean red on the brightly burnished shinplates
As they shifted and lurched; and Mordred shot to the ground.
From the lunge of the lance he landed on his shoulders,
Stretched full length on the grass, with loathsome wounds.
Then Gawain leapt at the man, fell groveling,
For although his anger was wild, his luck was bad.   *3850*
He swiftly pulled out a short knife sheathed in silver
And meant to stab his throat—but no stab came:
His hand slipped low, slid slantways on the mail;
And slyly the other man slipped under him
And with his trenchant knife the traitor hit him
Through both helmet and head, high up in the brain.
And thus is Sir Gawain gone, that good man of arms,
Unsaved by any mortal, and more's the pity!
Thus is Sir Gawain gone, the guide of great men!
From Gower even to Guernsey, all the great lords   *3860*
Of Glamorgan and of Wales, those gallant knights,
Will never escape their sudden assaults of grief!
     King Frederick of Friesland, cautiously, after that,
Asks of the false Sir Mordred concerning the knight:
"Did you ever know this knight before in your kingdom?
Of what line did he come? Let me know the truth.
And what man was he, the one with the gay arms,
With his fiery griffen of gold, who is fallen face down?
He has greatly grieved our host, as God is my help!
He's struck down many good men and grieved us sorely.   *3870*
The man was the sternest in battle that ever wore steel,
For look, he has stunned our host and destroyed us forever!"
     Then Sir Mordred spoke and answered with honor:
"He was matchless here on earth, man, by my troth.
This was Sir Gawain the Good, the gladdest of warriors,
And the man most gracious of all that have lived under God,
And the hardiest of hand, and happiest in arms,
And most courteous in the court under heaven's kingdom,
And the lordliest of leaders as long as he lived.

For the man was renowned as a lion in many a land,   3880
And had you known him, king, in the land he belonged to,
His knowledge, his perfect knighthood, his kindly works,
His doings, his doughtiness, his deeds of arms,
You'd grieve for dole at his death all the days of your life."
        Then Mordred wept, and tears fell on his face,
And he turned himself away and would talk no more,
And weeping, he went away, and cursed the hour
That fate had fashioned him for such destruction;
And when he thought on the thing, it pierced his heart.
Sighing for his kinsman's sake, he rides away.   3890
And when the renegade wretch remembered within him
The reverence and the revelry of the Round Table,
He cried aloud and repented his rueful works,
And he rode away with his rout and would rest there no longer
For fear of our rich king, who would soon arrive.
He turns to Cornwall, heavy with care in his heart
Because of his kinsman who lies there on the coast;
And there he waits, and trembles, and listens for news.
        Then the following Tuesday the traitor crept out
And went to work more treason by a trick,   3900
And by the Tamar River he raised his tents
And then in a short while sent off a messenger
And he wrote to Guinevere how the world was changed
And to what convenient coast the king had come,
And how he had fought with the fleet and had felled them all,
And he bade her go far away and flee with her children.
Meanwhile, he'd slip away, and would come to her,
Withdraw into Ireland, and into those outer mountains,
To live there in wilderness within the wastelands.
        Then Guinevere weeps and cries in her chamber at York 3910
And groans most grievously, with dropping tears,
And she leaves the palace, with all her peerless maidens;
They take the road towards Chester in a chariot
And the queen makes ready to die for the grief in her heart.
She goes to Caerleon and takes up a veil
And asks there for a habit in the honor of Christ,
But all was falsehood and fraud, and fear of her lord.
        But when King Arthur learned that Gawain had landed,
He writhed for woe and, wringing his two hands,

Ordered his boats to be launched upon low water, 3920
And soon he lands like a lion with lordly knights,
Slips in the sliding water aslant to his belt
And sweeps up, swift, to the sand, with his sword drawn,
He makes his battalion ready, with banners in display,
And moves across broad sands with rage in his heart.
He fiercely stalks to the field where the fallen lie:
And of Sir Mordred's men on skirted steeds
Ten thousand had been lost, by true account,
And on our own side, certainly, sevenscore knights,
In company with their leader, left there dead. 3930
     The king looked down from aloft and knights and others,
Earls out of Africa and Austrian warriors,
The Irish kings from Argyle and from Orkney,
The noblest men of Norway in numbers enough,
Mighty dukes of Denmark, anointed knights;
And the king of Gothland in all his gay apparel
Lies groaning on the ground, pierced through and through.
The great king searches about with sorrow in his heart
And he searches out the royal ranks of the Round Table;
He sees them all in a band, together by themselves, 3940
With the dying Saracens in a circle around them,
And he sees Sir Gawain the Good in his splendid armor,
Fists closed on the grass, and fallen face downward,
His beautiful banner down, adorned with gules,
His sword and his wide shield both wet with blood.
Our king was never so sorrowful in his heart,
And nothing so filled him with grief as that sight alone.
     Then the good king stared and grieved in his heart,
Groaned out most grievously, with falling tears.
He kneeled down by the corpse and caught it in his arms 3950
And he cast the visor up and kissed the face,
And Arthur looked at the eyelids, closely shut,
And the lips now like to lead, and the cheeks gone fallow.
     Then the crowned King Arthur cried out loud,
"Dearest cousin in kingship, I'm left here in care,
For now my worship has turned and my war is ended;
Here lies the hope of my welfare, my might in arms;
My heart and my hardiness were wholly his work,
My counsel and my comfort that kept up my heart!

Of all the knights alive under Christ, the king; 3960
You were worthy to be king, though I wore the crown.
My happiness and my honor in all this rich world
Were won through Gawain, and through his wisdom alone.
Alas!" the king cries out, "my sorrow's the more!
Within my own lands I am utterly undone;
O death, mighty and dreadful, you've waited too long!
Why do you draw on so slowly? You drown my heart!"

    And then that sweet king faints and falls in a swoon,
But at once he starts up, and he lovingly kisses the corpse
Till all his heavy beard was shiny with blood 3970
As though he had fought some beast and had bit out its life.
Had not Sir Ewain come, and other great lords,
His bold heart might have burst from the bale of that moment.
"Enough," these bold men say, "you harm yourself;
Now grief is hopeless, for nothing can make it better.
There can be no honor, truly, in wringing your hands,
And weeping like a woman is not for wise men.
Be knightly of countenance, as a king should be,
And leave off all your clamor, for Christ's love in heaven!"

    "God's blood!" the bold king cried, "I'll never cease 3980
Till my brain has burst in two and my breast as well.
There was never yet such sorrow as sinks to my heart;
And he was close kin to me—my sorrow's the more!
I've never seen a more sorrowful sight with my eyes:
He was taken without any guilt, for the sin was my own."

    Down kneels the king, and he cries out aloud
And with sorrowful countenance he cries these words:
"O righteous, almighty God, look down at this sorrow!
This royal red blood running out over the earth!
Such blood would be worthy to take and enshrine in gold, 3990
For it's guiltless of any sin, as my Lord may save me!"
And down the king kneels, care heaped high in his heart,
And he caught it up reverently with his two clean hands,
And he stored it in his helmet, and covered it fairly,
And he went away with the corpse toward the land where he
                                 dwelled.

    And then the king said, "Here I make my vow
To the Messiah and to Mary, the mild Queen of Heaven,
I shall never hunt, or uncouple hunting dogs,

For any roe or reindeer that run upon earth,
Nor let my greyhounds glide or my goshawk fly   *4000*
And never see any bird felled that flies on wings;
And I'll take no falcon or formel on my fist,
Nor fare over the ground with my gyrfalcon,
Nor reign in my royalty, nor hold my Round Table
Till your death, dear knight, is duly avenged;
But I'll droop in darkness all the days of my life
Till God or grim death have done whatever they like."
    Then they caught up the corpse with care in their hearts
And carried it off on a horse, and the king beside it.
They went by the quickest route away to Winchester   *4010*
In weary and wan procession with the wounded knights.
Down came the prior of the place, and professed monks,
Solemnly in procession, and met the prince;
He led them all to the corpse of the noble knight.
"See that this body is kept and maintained in the church,
And dirges sung over it, as is right for the dead,
And honor the body with masses to speed the soul.
See that it lacks no candles or anything else,
And then let the body be embalmed and placed on a bier;
If you keep your covenant with me, ask all you wish   *4020*
When I come to you again, if Christ allows it.
But stay the burial until I have brought down those
Who have brought this grief upon us and caused this war."
    Then spoke Sir Richer the Mighty, prudent in arms:
"I counsel you, be wary and work for your safety;
Stay here in this city and assemble again your barons
And wait with your mighty men within these walls.
Call for the knights of the country, who keep your castles,
And call from your garrisons good men of arms,
For in truth, we are too few to fight with all those   *4030*
We see drawn up against us there on the sea banks."
    But the king, with a cruel countenance, said these words:
"I pray you, knight, fear not, and give up your dread.
Had I no men but myself here under the sun,
If I might see him with sight, set hands upon him,
I would among all his men maul him to death
Before I'd stir from him by half a steed-length.
I shall strike him on this ground and destroy him forever,

And on that I take my vow most devoutly to Christ
And to his mother Mary, the mild Queen of Heaven.   *4040*
I shall never sojourn in health nor ease my heart
In any city or suburb that stands on earth,
Nor sit in slumber, nor close my eyes in sleep
Till the man is slain who slew him, if I have the craft,
And I'll drive out forever the pagans who've slain my people.
While I live to give pain to those people, whatever the place."
No man of all the Round Table dared disagree
Yet none delighted their prince with pleasing words
And none of his liege men would look King Arthur in the eye,
So fiery was his look at the loss of his knights.   *4050*
      Then he draws to Dorset, delays no longer,
Full of grief, fearless, with falling tears,
And comes into Cornwall with care in his heart.
He follows on, steadily, the tracks of the traitor
And turns in by the Trent to hunt the betrayer,
And finds him hidden in a forest the Friday after.
The king alights on foot, takes the lay of the land,
And now with his fierce host he has taken the field.
      And now the enemy comes from the eaves of the wood
With hosts of aliens horrible to look at.   *4060*
Sir Mordred the Malebranche with his many people
Advances out of the forest from many sides
In seven great battalions in splendid array,
Sixty thousand men, a marvelous sight,
All fierce fighting men out of faraway lands;
And there by those fresh strands they formed their front.
And Arthur's host of knights was made up
Of eighteen hundred, no more, as entered on the rolls:
They were no match, without the might of Christ,
To fight with that multitude in those great meadows.   *4070*
      Then the royal king of the Round Table,
Riding a mighty steed, arrayed his barons:
He would ride with the van himself, as it suited him;
Sir Ewain and Sir Errake, and other great lords,
Would bring up the middle in mighty array,
With Merrake and Menyduke, mighty in battle;
Idorus and Alimere, their handsome sons,
Would ride with Arthur, with sevenscore strong knights:

He arranged the rearguard quickly, after that,
The mightiest, readiest fighters of all the Round Table;   *4080*
And thus he prepares his host, and he cries anew
And once more comforts his men with knightly words:
"I beseech you, sirs, for the sake of our Lord,
That you do your best today, and dread no weapon;
Fight your fiercest now, and defend yourselves;
Fell that fated host and the field shall be ours;
They are Saracens in that army; may we see them dead!
Set on them with fury, for the sake of our Lord.
If it is our destiny to die today,
We'll be raised to the gates of heaven before we're half cold.   *4090*
Look that you let no man there hold back your labor
But lay that host at the end of the lake down dead.
Take no account of my welfare, nor ask how I do,
But battle below my banners with all your bright weapons.
See that my ranks are staffed by the stoutest of knights
And hold your standards high, so that all can see them.
If any man there snatch them, rescue them quickly.
Work now for my honor: today my war ends.
You know my weal and my woe. Work as you like.
May Christ in his crown bring comfort to you all,   *4100*
The fairest creatures a king ever ruled on this earth.
I give you my blessing with all my heart,
And I say to all Britons, may all be well with you!"
      At prime the trumpet sang, and the host drew nearer;
Mighty men and swift now prove themselves;
Boldly the trumpeters gave trumpet blasts
With their gleaming horns, when all the knights were assembled;
Then jubilantly those gentle knights rode to joust;
A more joyful day's work was never known
When Arthur's Britons boldly dressed their shields   *4110*
And Christians crossed themselves and clapped in the lance.
      Then King Arthur cried out the charge on that host
And in they rushed with their shields, and stalled no longer;
They shot to the enemy army and shouted on high
And burst through their gleaming shields and slashed through flesh.
Swiftly those ready knights of the Round Table
Cut through blazing mail with bitter steel,
Burst through woven byrnies and burnished helmets,

Hewed down heathen men, hacked through their necks,
Fighting with fine steel; the fated blood   *4120*
Runs from the fiercest of front men, robs them of force.
Ethan of Argyle, and the Irish kings,
Surround our steady van with venomous barons;
Picts and pagans with perilous weapons
And pitiless long spears despoil our knights
And hew down even the noblest by deadly blows;
Through all the length of the battle they battered their way.
And thus they fought on, fierce, from either side,
So the brave-hearted Britons spill so much blood
That none can be rescued for all the riches on earth,   *4130*
The foes were so fierce and steady and so well reinforced.

    He dared not stir a step but stood his ground
Till three divisions were wrecked by the king's own hand.
"Idorus," Arthur cries, "it behoves you to hurry!
Sir Ewain is overset by Saracens!
Ready yourself for the rescue, and array yourself!
Ride up with hardy men and recover your father!
Lay into them from the side, and give help to our lords,
For unless they are helped, I'm your enemy forever!"

    Idorus answers him quickly after that: *4140*
"He is my father, in truth, and I'll never forsake him;
He has fostered me and fed me and all my fair brothers;
But if I forsake this ground, as God is my shield,
I abandon all kinship except to yourself alone.
I would never break his command for a man on earth,
But always battle like a beast to bring him joy.
And he has commanded me, truly, with knightly words,
That I loyally stand beside you and no other man,
And I shall obey his command, if Christ will allow it.
He is my elder, and we both must come to our end: *4150*
He shall ride before, and I shall come after.
If his destiny is to die on this field today,
May Christ in his crown give comfort to his soul!"

    Then rich King Arthur whirls, with wrath in his heart,
And he hurls his hands on high, and he looks to heaven:
"Would that God on high would destine by his will
That I should be judged today and should die for you all!
I would liever do that than be lord all the rest of my days

Of all Alexander owned while he lived on this earth!"
    Sir Ewain and Sir Errake, excellent warriors,   *4160*
Encounter the enemy host and eagerly strike;
The giants out of Orkney and the Irish kings
They strike with their ground swords in all their grimness:
They hew with their hard weapons at those hulks
And bend down those barons with brutal blows;
They split their shields and shoulders to the haunches,
And through their mail coats break their bellies open.
No earthly kings have ever won such honor
On their last day save only King Arthur himself.
And the searing drought of the day so dried their hearts   *4170*
Men died for lack of drink—and more's the pity!
Now our main force moves in, mingling with them.
    Sir Mordred the Malebranche with his many men,
Had hid himself behind, in the eaves of the wood,
With a whole battalion on the heath, to make things worse.
He'd watched the conflict clear to the end,
How our chivalry had managed by the chance of arms,
And he knew they were fought out and left there fated;
And he quickly judged it was time to encounter the king.
But the churlish Mordred had changed his arms: *4180*
Had forsaken entirely the saltire engrailed
And caught up instead three lions of light silver,
Passant on purple, with many precious stones,
So that the king could not know the crafty wretch;
And because of his cowardice he cast off his arms,
But nevertheless, the king knew him very well,
And he called out to Sir Cador these keen words:
"I see the traitor coming, moving in eagerly;
The lad with the lions is very like himself.
If I may touch him, misfortune shall be his   *4190*
For all his treason and treachery, as I'm true lord!
Today Clarent and Caliburn shall contest
Which is the keener in carving or harder of edge,
And we shall test fine steel on fair attire!
That sword was once my darling, and held most sweet,
And kept for the coronation of chrismed kings:
And on days when I dubbed my dukes and earls
It was gravely borne aloft by the beaming hilts.

I never dared to draw it for deeds of arms
But kept it forever clean for my finest cause.   4200
But since I see Clarent unsheathed, the crown of swords,
I know my wardrobe at Wallingford is destroyed;
There no one knew of its place but Guinevere herself:
She had, herself, the keeping of that choice weapon,
Enclosed in coffers belonging to the crown,
Along with rings and relics and regalia of France
That were found upon Sir Frolle, when he was left dead."
        Then Sir Marroke, grieving, came against Mordred,
And with a hammered mace he mightily struck him;
The border of his basinet was burst open   4210
And sheer red blood ran out and over his byrnie.
Sir Mordred paled with pain, and his color changed,
But he waited like a boar and returned the blow:
He brings out a sword as bright as any silver,
And the sword was Arthur's own, and Sir Uther's, his father's,
And long had been kept in the wardrobe at Wallingford.
With it that dangerous dog dealt out such blows
That the other was driven aside and dared do no more,
For Sir Marroke was a man marred by old age,
And Mordred was mighty and still in the prime of his strength;   4220
None came within his compass, knight or other,
Within the swing of his sword, without losing his life.
        This our prince soon saw, and he pressed towards him,
Struck into the struggle by the strength of his hands,
And when he met Sir Mordred he cried out, stern:
"Turn, false traitor! Dark trouble is upon you!
By great God, you shall die by the power of my hand,
And no man shall rescue you, nor reach you on earth!"
        The king with Caliburn comes down like a knight,
And the cantle of the bright shield he carves asunder   4230
And into the shoulder of the man, a hand's breadth wide,
So that the shining blood showed red on his mail.
Now Mordred shudders and flinches and shrinks a little;
But now, in his fine attire, he shoves in hard,
That thief with the gleaming sword, and grimly strikes,
And the flesh on the far side he flaps away
Through tunic and jesseraunt of noble mail.
The man cut out a half foot's breadth of flesh,

And Arthur knew he must die; then more's the pity
That ever that hero should fall, through heaven's will!   *4240*
And yet with Caliburn he cruelly strikes,
Casts up his shining shield and covers himself,
Swipes off the sword hand, sweeping past—
Severed it clean, an inch below the elbow,
So that Sir Mordred swoons on the sward in a faint,
And he cut through brown steel bracer and bright mail
So that both hilt and hand lie flat on the heath.
Then fiercely Arthur raises up the shield
And bears down with his sword to the beaming hilts,
And Mordred screamed and settled down toward death.   *4250*
    "In faith," said the dying king, "it gives me grief
That such a false thief find so fair an end."
    When these two finished the fight, the field was won,
And the false host on the field were left as fated.
They fled away to a forest and fell in the thicket
And the fiercely fighting British flew after them;
They hunted and hewed down the heathen men
And murdered in the mountains Mordred's knights;
And none escaped, neither noble youth nor chieftain,
But they chopped them down in the chase, and it cost them but   *4260*
                                          little.

    But then King Arthur came on the body of Ewain,
And Errake the affable, and other great lords,
And he caught Sir Cador up with care in his heart,
And Clergis and Cleremonde, those famous knights,
Sir Lottes and Sir Lionel, Sir Lancelot and Lowes,
Marroke and Menyduke, who had always been mighty,
And in sorrow he stretched them out on the heath together;
And he looked down over their bodies, and gave a loud moan,
Like a man who might not live and had lost all mirth.
He staggers like a madman, all his strength fails him,   *4270*
And he looks aloft, and all his color changes;
Down he sways heavily, and falls in a swoon,
Comes up on his knees again, and cries aloud:
"O King, splendidly crowned, I am left here in care,
All my lordship now laid low on the land,
All who gave me the guerdons of their grace
And ever maintained my manhood by the might of their hands

And made me mighty in the world, and master of earth.
But now in a sorrowful time misfortune is upon me,
And my loyal lords are lost because of a traitor.   4280
Here rests the royal blood of all my Round Table,
Struck down by a scoundrel, more's the pity!
Now, helpless on the heath, I must live alone
Like some young woeful widow who lacks her lord;
I must lie weary, and weep, and wring my hands,
For my wisdom and worship are stolen from me forever.
Now at my end, I take my leave of lordship.
Here is the British blood brought down from life.
And all my joy is done with this day's work."

    Then the men of the Round Table return,   4290
And to that lordly king they ride together;
There they quickly assemble, sevenscore knights,
In the sight of their sovereign, now sorely wounded.

    Then the crowned king kneels and cries out aloud:
"I thank thee, God, for thy grace, with a good will,
Who gave us the virtue and wisdom to vanquish these warriors
And hast granted the victory to us against these lords.
He never sent us shame or disgrace on earth,
But gave us the upper hand over all other kings.
We have no leisure now to seek far lands,   4300
For the loathesome lad over there has hurt me sorely;
We'll go to Glastonbury: we're given no choice.
There we may rest in peace and empty our wounds.
For the work of this special day the Lord be praised,
Who has destined us to die in the midst of our own."

    Then they did as he told them, all together,
And went towards Glastonbury by the quickest way:
At the Isle of Avalon, King Arthur alights
And goes to a manor, for he could not ride on further.
A surgeon from Salerno examines his wounds,   4310
And the king discovers with questions that death is near.
Soon to his surest men he said these words:

    "Call me my confessor, with Christ in his arms;
I'll take the sacrament quickly, whatever may come.
My cousin Constantine shall bear the crown,
As suits his nature, assuming Christ allows it.
Cousin, for my blessing, bury yon lords

Who are brought down from life in battle, by the sword;
And afterward make your way to Mordred's children,
And see them duly slain and slung to the waters,   *4320*
And let no wicked weed wax mighty on earth;
I warn you for your honor, do as I bid you!
And for God's love in heaven, I give up my wrath:
If Guinevere is well, may peace be with her."
He said, on the land where he lay, "*In manus tuas*,"
And thus his spirit passed and he spoke no more.

    Then the baronage of Britain, bishops and others,
Go on to Glastonbury with grieving hearts,
To bury that boldest of kings and bring him to earth
With all the splendor and pomp that a man should have.   *4330*
Sadly they toll the bells and sing the requiem
Say the masses and matins, and chant songs of mourning;
The religious vest themselves in their gleaming cloaks,
Pontiffs and prelates both in precious vestments;
Dukes and douzeperes come, in their coats of mourning,
And countesses kneel down and clasp their hands,
Solemn ladies languishing, sorrow in their hearts.
All were clad in black, both brides and others,
And stood at the burial with streaming tears.
And never a sight more sad was seen in their time.   *4340*

    And thus came Arthur's end, as the chronicles tell,
Who was of Hector's kin, king's son of Troy,
And of Sir Priam the prince, much praised on earth;
From thence came those bold ancesters of Britain
To Britain's banks, as the *Brut* tells.

Winner and Waster

Winner and Waster

―――――――――――――――――――――

◖ *Here begins a treatise and a good short debate between winner and waster.*

Since Britain first was built and Brutus owned it,
After the taking of Troy by treason from within,
Many strange sights have been seen in many kings' times,
But never a ninth so many as now are seen;
For now all our dealings are willfulness and craft,
All sly and wily words, each tricking the other;
And there is no friendship, but only faintheartedness;
While this world lasts no man of the West would dare
To send his son to the South to see and hear,
For the son, when his father grew feeble, would quickly forget   *10*
                                          him.

And therefore the prophecy spoken by wise King Solomon
Draws near at hand—what else can I believe?
When waves grow wild and mighty walls fall down
And the hares huddles to the hearthstone for her nest,
And bloody-hearted boys with boasts and pride
Wed highborn ladies in the land and lead them at will,
Doomsday in all its dread will dawn soon after.
Whoever will solemnly look, and will speak the truth,
Must grant that it's close upon us, or already here
     Oh, once there were lords in the land who loved in their   *20*
                                         hearts

117

To listen to men of mirth who could find good matter
Set in the wisest of words, never written before
And never before read or heard of in any romance;
But now any child to art, no hair on his chin,
Who never worked out by his wit three words together,
As soon as he jangles like a jay, or can tell some joke,
He'll be believed and loved and lauded to the heavens
Far more than the man who can make new songs of his own.
But nevertheless, in the end, when all things are known,
Work shall bear witness on what man's work is best.   *30*

Bᴜᴛ I shall tell you a tale of what happened once
    As I walked out in the west country, alone,
By the bank of a river—bright was the sun—
And below was a noble old wood and a splendid valley,
And every step of my foot bent many fair flowers.
I laid my head on a hill, in the shade of a hawthorn,
And thrustlecocks argued there eagerly together,
And the woodpeckers clinging to hazels called up to those higher,
Their bills ringing out on the barnacles raised on the bark,
And the bluejay chattered on high amid all that cheer,   *40*
And boldly the river rushed on between its banks.
So wildly the rough stream rattled, and the waves reached so high,
It was almost night by the time I was able to sleep,
For the noise of the fast, deep water and the chattering of birds;
But at last as I lay there my eyelids locked,
And swiftly my spirit was swept away in a dream.
I dreamed I was standing—I know not where in this world—
On a fair lawn, the grass all equally green,
With mountains a mile away on every side.
In the woods on either hand there were hosts in bright hauberks,   *50*
With splendid crested helmets on their heads.
Their banners were all unfurled, and they stirred to the charge,
And shoving out of the shadows they fell into squadrons,
And only the length of the green lawn lay between them.
And as I was praying for peace till the prince might come—
For he was more wise and more worthy than anyone else
To part them and counsel them wisely and to rule the wrath
That each side felt at the sight of the other on that heath—

At the crest of a cliff a pavilion was lifted up,
The roof and sides arrayed in red   60
With brilliant English besants embossed in gold
And each one gaily surrounded by a garter of blue
And each of the garters embellished with golden trim;
And then in the tapestry above, these words appeared,
Painted in grayish blue, with points between them,
The words all handsomely formed, the letters fresh-hued,
And the words, one saw, were written in the English tongue:
Evil to every man who thinks on evil!
Now the king of this country is coming! May God preserve him!
And now, high on that hill, his servant appears   70
Dressed like a wight of the woods, with curling locks,
A helmet on his head, and a helmet cover,
And high on the helmet cover a terrible beast,
A leopard light and long and cruel looking,
The figure beautifully fashioned of yellow gold.
And the veil of the helmet, which covered the back of the neck,
Was cleanly cast into four heraldic quarters—
Two with the French fleurs-de-lys, the first and the last,
And also two of England, with six angry beasts,
Three leopards courant above, and three quartered third,   80
At each of the corners a cluster of clearest pearl,
Tile-red silk tassels splendidly protruding.
And by the pavilion I knew what knight must own it,
And knew I'd see wonders enough before I withdrew.
And as I looked inside I caught sight, at last,
Of a handsome king in a golden crown,
Seated on a silken bench, with scepter in hand,
To those who love him, one of the loveliest lords
A subject beneath the sun ever saw with his eyes.
The king was beautifully clad in a kirtle and mantle   90
As berry-brown as his beard and embroidered with birds,
Falcons of excellent gold, with extended wings,
Each bearing emblazonry—blue, as I thought:
A great garter of blue that was richly adorned.
The great lord's mantle was gaily gathered in the middle
By a belt of blazing color, embroidered with birds,
Ducks and drakes that indeed seemed terrified
For fear of the falcons' claws which might hold them fast.
And I said to myself, "It would surely be strange indeed

If the man did not hunt by the river from time to time!"   *100*
The king now speaks to a baron who stands beside him,
One of the finest of his men, who had never failed him:
"Remember I dubbed you knight to serve me in battle;
Now quickly go your way to make known my will:
Go bid those men down there on the battlefield
To draw no nearer to one another than now;
For if they strike one stroke, they'll never be stopped."
"Your servant, milord," said the man, "while my life lasts."
He goes from the bank at once and is gone for a while
Until he is dressed and bound up in the bravest array.   *110*
He covered the lower bones of his legs with iron
And put on polished chest and body armor
With braces of burnished steel tight-braided with rings,
And great plates buckled behind to guard the body,
And he put on a good short doublet, joined at the sides,
A broad scutcheon in back and another on the breast,
Within the scutcheon three wings well copied from Nature,
Encircled with golden wire. When I looked at him,
The man was the youngest in years and the keenest in wits
That any man of this world ever saw in his time.   *120*
He broke off a branch in his hand and brandished it aloft,
Set off at a fast trot, and took his way
To where the two hosts were waiting, down the field.

    He said, "Lo, the king of this country—the Lord preserve
                                     him!—
Sends word to you by me, as suits his pleasure,
That none, on pain of blinding, be so bold
As to strike a single stroke or to move any nearer
To lead his host, or think himself so regal
That he may by his prowess disturb the king's peace.
For this is the custom here, and always shall be: *130*
If a baron is so bold as to ride with his banner
Within the bounds of the kingdom, save only the king,
That man shall lose his land and later his life.
But for ignorance of the custom and the king's right,
The king will forgive you, this once, by his grace alone.
    "I've walked on this world widely, up and down,
But never, sirs, have I seen such a sight before;
For all the fair people of France are gathered together,
And Lorraine and Lombardy, and the people of Spain,

And the men of Westphalia, that are always in battle,   *140*
And many an Eastern man in England and Ireland,
Stuffed into steel armor to deal out strokes.
     "And there on the battlefield rises a banner of black
Blazoned with three white bulls embroidered within,
And hanging from each a cord of hemp
With a solid lead seal. I will say what I think:
He who stands here at the head of the holy church,
With the host he leads, is eagerly spoiling for a fight.
Now a second banner rises, with a bend of green
And three white-haired heads, with hoods on them,   *150*
The hair curled craftily, combed in at the neck.
These are the liege men of the land who should guard our laws,
But today it is their intention to deal out blows.
But surely battle is mad when debate may help
And the man has found that friend who never fails him!
The third banner on the field is of bleached white
And I see three boots upon it, with sable inside,
Each with a brown strap and two great buckles:
The hosts of St. Francis, who say soon flesh shall pass.
They are fierce and fresh; no doubt they have not fought   *160*
                                                                    often;
One sees that they came from their homes for what they might
                                                                    win;
And whoever has won them here has a weighty purse!
Now the fourth banner is borne aloft in the field,
Two borderlines of black, a ball in the center
That glitters as does the sun in the summertime,
When midsummer madness is greatest, at Midsummer Eve.
The Dominicans too are determined to strike out with blows,
And many a brilliant brother has hoisted his banner;
And since the pope is so prompt to support these preachers,
And Francis with all his host gives additional force,   *170*
And the pope by his counsel leads every liege man in the land,
There is not a man on earth who's a match for them,
Under God Himself, at winning honor in the battle.
And yet the fifth on the field is the fairest of all,
A bright banner of white with three boar-heads upon it:
If I am not much mistaken, they're Carmelites,
And they are the liege men who love to serve our Lady.
If I tell the truth, it seems there can be no outcome

But that the friars and their forces must win the field.
The sixth I see is sendal, and so are the men,   *180*
As white as whale's bone, as all who speak truly will say,
And the belts they wear are black and buckled up neatly,
The buckle-points rounded, the standard pendants streaming,
And all the leather above, where it dangles down,
Gleams and shines from the sharpening of their razors:
The Order of Augustinians, I would imagine,
For by just one glimpse of the belt I know their banner.
And I see here other emblems are lifted on high,
And some of them speak of wool and some of the wine tun—
So many merchants' emblems in a throng together   *190*
I cannot call up in my mind, for all rich creation,
What lord here under the sun could sum up the total!
And over on the other side stand strong men of arms,
Bold-blooded squires and many a bowman
Who, if they strike one stroke, will never be stopped
Till one of these hosts on the heath has been hacked to bits.
     "Therefore I bid you two that have brought them together
That you come with me, before any harm can come,
To our noble king, the ruler of all this country;
And when he has justly determined which side's in the wrong,   *200*
Neither one will have reason to regret having asked for his ruling."
     I dreamed that out of each army a rider went,
Knights in handsome array, on splendid horses,
Saying, "Sir Bringer-of-News, all bliss be with you!
We know that good king well; he clothes us both,
And he's fostered and fed us these five and twenty winters.
Therefore go on before, we'll follow behind you."
And now, their bridles taut, they bound on their way,
And out on the lawn they alight and, leaving their steeds,
Come up to the crest of the cliff and fall on their knees.   *210*
The king now takes them by the hands and tells them to rise;
"Welcome, sirs," he said, "both servants of our house."
The king then glanced to one side and called for wine,
And soon men brought it in, in bowls of silver,
And I dreamed I drank so deep it seared my eyes.

Let any who wish to hear anything more of this work
Fill up his cup and quickly, for here ends Fitt One.

THEN up spoke the king and said: "Declare your names,
And tell why such hot hatred has filled your hearts.
If I am to judge you today, I must now hear all."   *220*
    "Gladly," replied the first. "I will tell you the truth:
I am known as Winner, and one who helps all the world,
For people can learn from me to be led by Reason;
All those who live cautiously and keep hold of their money
And live upon little—all those are the men I love.
And Reason is my friend and teaches me wisely,
And when I gather my goods, my heart is glad.
But this false thief who stands before you here
Desires to strike out at me and destroy me forever.
All that I win by wisdom, he wastes by pride;   *230*
I gather, I glean, and quickly he hurls it away;
I pin up my purse and pinch it, he cuts it apart!
How dare this wretch have no interest in how men sell grain!
His lands lie fallow and all of his tools are sold,
His dovecots tumble down, his pools are dry,
And the Devil himself might wonder at the wealth he wields—
Nothing but hunger, big horses, and well kept hounds!
Besides a spear and a halberd hidden in the corner
And a blade at the head of his bed, he asks for nothing
But a good fast gelding to gallop with his friends: *240*
He'll boast and flash his blade and bluster around,
This wicked wretch—and Waster's what they call him—
And if he lives for long he'll leave the land ruined.
And therefore judge us today, for the dear Lord's love,
And let us attack with our hosts until one of us falls."
    "Ah yes, Winner," said Waster, "your words are grand;
But I will tell you a thing that will trouble you plenty!
After you've tossed and turned and have sweated all night,
You and every last servant that sleeps in your house,
And after you've stocked your wide barns with bursting   *250*
                                                            woolsacks—
And the beams of your roofs all bend from the weight of your
                                                                bacon,
And all your pounds sterling are stuffed in your great steel chests—
What could that great wealth win if no waste were to come?

Some would rot, some rust, some feed the rats!
Leave off all your cramming of coffers, for Christ's love in heaven!
Let the common people and the poor have some part in your silver;
For walk abroad just once, and watch what you see there,
You'd weep for grief at how rich all the world is with poor men!
Live on much longer as you do, and believe me well,
Your soul will be hanged in hell for all your saving!   260
For by this sin you have sold off your soul to the Devil,
Where grief wells up forevermore, world without end."
    Rich Winner cried, "Leave off your vain talk, Waster!
You talk of a trouble that you yourself created!
With all your stirrings and strife you destroy my goods
With wild wrestling and staying awake winter nights,
With excess and profligate spending and arrogant pride.
There's not in this world the wealth to wash your hands with
That was not given and ground before ever you touched it.
You lead around roisterers in rich attire,   270
Some with girdles of gold that have cost more goods
Than all the fair free land that was yours before.
You forget the words of your fathers who fostered you,
To seize the natural harvest and bring in the grain
Against the cold, keen winter and the clinging frosts
And against the dropless drought in the dead months later.
But you take yourselves to the tavern at the end of the town,
Each one eager to blear both eyes with a bowl
And pay out all you have, as your heart may please,
For the wife or widow or wench who happens to live there.   280
And then it's 'Fill up!' and 'Fetch 'er!' and out comes Florie,
And 'Whee-hee!' and 'Whoa-up!' are words enough.
But when all your pleasure is finished, the bill must be paid.
Then you must lay down pledges and sell off your land.
For all such wicked works may God give you worry!
And as the Lord took His own, and left all the others,
So each should be more eager to work on his land.
Teach your people to till, and to fence their fields;
Raise up good tenant houses, make roomy lawns;
Otherwise, have what you have, and hope for still worse—   290
First the failing of food, and fire soon after
To burn you down at one blast for your baleful deeds,
And after that, cold ice, as scholars tell me."

"Pah, Winner," said Waster, "mere empty speech!
With our feasts and with our riding we feed the poor,
And that is pleasing to the Prince who made Paradise.
Christ would far rather his people have part of the wealth
Than see it all huddled and hidden and hoarded in chests
Where no sun falls on it for seven winters,
Or that friars should come and fetch it when you fall dead   *300*
To paint their pillars with it, or plaster their walls.
Your son and all your executors each sue the other,
And after your day they grieve, for you never dared
To feast, fill heads with ale, or find any pleasure.
And grief after your death does no more good
Than a lighted lantern late on a dark night
Carried behind your back, pretty sir, I swear!
Oh would to God it were all as I would have it,
And you, Winner, you wretch, and Despair your brother,
And also Ember-days and the Eves of Saints   *310*
And Friday and also that fellow who follows soon after,
Were drowned in the deep sea where no drought stirs
And Deadly Sin were indicted in court for their death,
And these barons of the bench with their nightcaps on,
Who are widely known and acclaimed as the noblest of clerks,
As good as was Aristotle or Augustine,
Would they were all of them shamed, and Shareshull among them,
Who claims I came with armed power to trouble his peace!
        "And therefore, noble king, having heard our case,
Allow us swiftly to strike out with swords together;   *320*
For I see that it is true as has often been said,
The richer the man is, the quicker he is to fear,
And the more he has ahold of, the feebler his heart."
        Now wretched Winner wrathfully looked round
And said, "It's empty noise to speak such words.
Waster, damn your soul, it's widely known
No kaiser, king, or knight is in your train,
And you've no love for barons, squires, or burgesses;
No one owes faith to you but four or five roughnecks,
And yet these few you feed with so many fine dishes   *330*
That every man in the world might weep for sorrow!
        "You bring the boar's head in with bays aloft,
Then in broad bucktails come, with broths beside them,

Venison next with fruments and glorious pheasants,
And baked meats stand near by, set on the sideboard,
Great dishes heaping with chopped up meats, grilled chickens,
And each single guest has six men's share.
As if that weren't enough, another course follows:
Roast with the richest of sauces and royal spice,
Kids cleft down the back, and quartered swans,   340
And tarts ten inches broad! It tortures my heart
To see a table spread over with blazing dishes,
Arrayed like Christ's own cross with rings and stones.
And then your third course comes, a marvel to me,
For mainly all I know of is Martinmass dinners—
Nothing but garden foods, flesh, and no wild fowl
Except perhaps a hen to the owner of the house—
You bring in basted birds that are broiled on a spit,
Barnacle geese and bitterns, and many billed snipes,
Larks and linnets lapped all over in sugar,   350
Woodcocks and woodpeckers, warm or hot,
Teals and titmice—take all the helpings you please!—
Then caudels of conies, and sweet rich custards,
Dariols and dishmeats that cost a man dear,
Malmsey pottage, as they call it, to cram men's maws;
Twelve dishes at a time between two men,
To eat though the bowels within you burn for sorrow.
Your trumpeters torture my head with their terrible noise,
And every man on the roadway can hear their rattling,
And they say to themselves as they ride there side by side,   360
'Those horns have no need of help from the heavenly King!'
Thus are you rightly scorned, and you'll suffer more later
Who pay out for one repast a ransom of silver!
I heard in the hall one time from the tongue of a shepherd,
'Far better many meals than one merry night!' "

Let any who wish to hear anything more of this work
Fill up his cup and quickly, for here ends Fitt Two.

OH YES, Winner," said Waster, "I know, myself,
What will become of the people within a few years.
Lo, the great plenty of grain that the people sow   370

God will allow to grow on earth, by His grace,
Till it gluts the market and prices cannot go too high,
And you shall be driven mad and made to despair,
And hoping for a hard year you'll hang yourself.
Would you have great lords go live like footloose lads,
And prelates live like the priests of the parishes,
Or proud and wealthy merchants like peddlers of the town?
Then let lords live as they please, and lads as fits them,
These on bacon and beef, these, bitterns and swans,
These on the rough of the rye, and these on rich wheat,   *380*
These upon thin gray gruel, and these on good sauces;
Thus may the people have a part, now cruelly impoverished,
And be given some morsel of meat that can mend their cheer.
If birds should fly about free and should never be troubled
And if wild beasts wallowed in the woods the length of their lives,
And if fish floated free in the flood, each feeding on the other,
Then a ha'penny'd buy a hen within half a year,
And not a lad left in the land to serve a lord!
This, surely, you can see, in truth, for yourself:
The man who would win wealth must find some waster,   *390*
For that which grieves the one must gladden the other."

    "In truth," said Winner to Waster, "I wonder in my heart
At these poor penniless men who buy precious furs,
And saddles made of sendal and richly encircled!
For fear of the wrath of your wives, you follow their wishes
And sell wood cord after cord in a little while,
Both the oak and the ash and everything else that grows;
Only the sprouts and the saplings are saved for your children,
And you say God will grant, by His grace, that they grow in the
                                                             end
To give some shade to your sons. The shame is your own!   *400*
And you need not save the soil, for you're sure you will sell it.
Your forefathers were glad, whenever a friend came,
To take them into the thickets and show them the coverts,
And in every holt they knew they could find a hare
And knew they might lure in many fat bucks to the lawn
To catch and release once more, to lighten their hearts.
But now all is auctioned and sold—ah, more's the pity!—
And wasted willfully, to please your wives.
All those who before kept splendid lords and ladies,
Now they're the freaks of the fashion, in fancy attire,   *410*

With great long trailing sleeves that sweep to the ground,
The borders edged upon every side with ermine.
It's as hard, I swear, to put on such clothes in the dark
As it is for a country wench to get into close silk.
    "Let whoever likes look on her, our Lady of heaven,
How once she fled in fear, away from her people,
And rode on an ambling ass, without any more pomp
Than a baby at her breast, and a broken halter
That Joseph held in his hand, to guard that Prince.
Though she ruled all the world, her robe was poor,   *420*
To give her example to us, and to teach all men
To leave all pomp and pride and scorn, for humility."
    Then, full of wrath, this Waster widened his eyes
And said, "You, Winner, wretch! I wonder in my heart
What any expense of our clothes has ever cost you
That you should upbraid our ladies for brilliant gowns,
Since we ourselves are the people who pay out the silver!
It is only right that a lover should care for his lady
And beautify her form and so bring her heart joy.
She will love him alone as well as she loves her own life   *430*
And make him brave and boldhearted in time of battle,
A man who shuns scandal and shame where soldiers encounter.
If my people are proud, why it pleases me all the more
When I see them fair and gracious before my eyes.
But you, you niggards! —however you sleep at night,
You start in the middle of a snore and spring to your haunches;
At once you look out at the weather and rue the day
You painted your houses and gave a few shirts to your servants.
And therefore, Winner, you wickedly waste your time,
For one good, cheerful day you will never get.   *440*
And after you die, the Devil deals out your goods,
And those you wished might wield your possessions must lose
                                      them;
For the cruel executors shall scatter them all
And you, for all your savings, will win hot hell.
You fail to give any heed to the ancient saw—
'A man is mad to be worried concerning his winnings':
Have what you have, and hold it while you can,
And seize the cup as it comes, the case as it falls,
For however long man lives, he's likely to fetch

Wood that he must waste, to warm his heels, 450
From farther by fifteen miles than his father fetched it.
But I care to chatter no more. Sir king, by your troth,
Judge where we are to go, for the dawn is near.
My heart is heavy indeed, and it hurts me sore
That I still have here in my sight the soul I detest."

    The good king looks with a smile at those two liege men
And says, "Sirs, leave your brawl and great bold words,
And I shall judge today where you two shall dwell
And live in a country where each shall be loved for his worth.

    "Winner, you go your way across wild waves 460
And pass by way of Paris to the pope of Rome;
The cardinals know you well and will serve you nobly
And see that you sleep at night in silken sheets;
They'll feed you, foster you, further your wishes,
And they'd much more gladly go mad than make you angry.
But look, sir, on your life, when I send letters,
Come home to me in a hurry on horse or foot,
And when I know you are coming, the other shall leave
And go to some other man until your stay is over;
For though you abide in the city until you are buried, 470
You never shall walk one foot by the side of Waster.

    "And you, Waster, I judge that your dwelling place
Shall be where the greatest wealth is found and wasted:
Take the road to Cheap and there rear your chamber;
See that the window is wide, and watch all around you
For any man with a purse who may enter the city.
Show him the way to the tun till he's tight as can be,
And make the man drink all night, so he's dry in the morning,
And acquaint him then with Crete, to comfort his veins;
Bring him to Broad Street, and beckon with your finger 480
And show him the shoulders of well-fattened sheep,
Hot and ready for the hungry, and a hen or two.
Set him down softly on a seat, and send out for more:
Bring out of the city the best things you can find
And see that your knave gets a cuff if the cloth is not spread.
But let the man pay before leaving, and pick him so clean
There's devil-a-penny in his purse, and pluck out his eyes.
When that's all eaten and drunk, stay there no longer
But show him the road out of town, and trot off for more.

Then hurry off to the Poultry, where the people all know you, *490*
And tell your steward to stock up well on food,
The herons, the haslets, the hens to be handsomely served,
The partridges, the plovers, and other plucked birds,
The alps, also the ouzels, the costly egrets;
For the more you waste your wealth, the more Winner will love
you.

    "And watch for me, Winner, if you would have wealth,
When I ride out for war with all my army;
For soon at the splendid palace of beautiful Paris
I mean to do it indeed, and to dub you a knight,
And to give away great gifts of gold and silver
To all who are loyal in allegiance and love me at heart;
And I'll come to you, with all I retain in my court,
To the dazzling church at Cologne, where kings lie
entombed." . . .

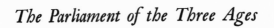

The Parliament of the Three Ages

THE PARLIAMENT
of the Three Ages

❮ Prologue

IN THE month of May, when pleasures are many,
  And the season of summer when the weathers are soft,
I went to the woods to try my fortune
And into the thickets to look for a shot
At a hart or hind, whatever luck might bring;
As God drove daylight out of the heavens,
I lingered along a bank beside a stream
Where the grass was green and flowers grew—
Primroses, periwinkles, rich wild mint,
And dew upon the daisies dripped most fair   10
And all the buds and blossoms and branches were sweet,
And mildly the merry mists began to fall:
The cuckoo and the wood dove sang out keenly
And thrushes called out boldly on the banks—
Each bird in that grove more joyful than the other
That darkness now was done, and day was dawning.
The harts and hinds withdrew to higher ground,
The fox and skunk, they fled away to the earth;
The hare huddles under hedges or hurries home
And bustles into her bed, prepares to sit.   20
I stood in that place, and hunting filled my thought;
Both my bow and my body I leaved like a bush,
And turned toward a tree and tarried there awhile.
And soon, as I looked to the clearing a little way off,
I saw a hart with a great high head of horns:

133

The beam was entirely unburnished, the midsection strong,
Each tine, like a man's foot, glossy in the grooves;
The antlers on either side were amazingly long;
The royals reached out richly from the center
And the surroyals rose out flawless on either side,   30
His head full grown, with a set of six and five,
A stag both broad and stately, and great of body,
A feast fit for a king, catch him who can!
Beside the stag was a buck that loyally served him,
Alerting him and warning when the wind fell off,
So that no one might slip up while he slept and slay him;
And the buck walked ahead on paths where danger threatened.
Lightly I dropped my leash and let it fall
And bid my dog lie down by the bole of a birch;
I checked the wind by the way it stirred the leaves   40
And stalked him stealthily, not snapping a stick,
And crept to a crabapple tree and took its cover.
At last I bent my crossbow, bound to take him,
Drew to the handle, the arrow trained on his heart.
The buck beside him brought up his nose
And stood there sniffing, straining after the scent.
I could only stay where I was, not stir a foot,
For if I twitched or moved or made any sign,
All my wait and all my sport were lost.
The gnats greatly annoyed me and bit at my eyes;   50
The buck stood poised, moved slowly, staring wide;
But at last he bowed again, went back to his eating,
And I hauled the string to the hooks and shot the hart.
I hit him behind the left shoulder, as it happened,
So that the blood burst out on either side:
He balked and brayed, went plunging through the groves
As if he'd have hurled in a heap all that lived in the wood.
The young deer with him fled away then to his comrades,
And they, in terror at the news, turned to the moors.
I hurried back to my hound and got him up   60
Loosed the leash, and let him cast about.
The briar and bracken were bloody where the stag had run,
And the dog leaped after him and lightly pursued
Where he'd crept into a cave and crouched to earth,
And lay as dead as a doornail, brought to the ground.

I caught him by the horns and haled him out,
Twisted his tines and thrust them into the earth,
Turned the fellow over and cut out his tongue
And ripped his bowels out to reward the dog;
I slit his fat to see how well he'd weigh   70
And found the fat a good two fingers thick.
I set about my work then, starting with the jowls,
And slit in a straight line clear to the tail;
After that I opened the stomach at once,
Then raised the right foreleg and carved it off,
And so from leg to leg I leaped about,
And cleanly parted the hide from each
And flayed it down with my fist as far as the backbone;
I took out my trencher then and took off the shoulders,
Removed the corbies' bone and cast it away;   80
I slit him carefully, my finger inside,
Lest the point of the knife should pierce the paunch or guts;
I searched for the suet and scraped it together
And pulled out the paunch and put it in a hole,
Grabbed out the guts and set them to one side,
And then after that I took the numbles next,
And made a cut from the backbone to the middle;
I hacked the haunches cleanly from the sides
And slit by the backbone swiftly and chopped off the neck,
And next I separated the neck and head;   90
I hitched the ends of the haunches through the sides
And heaved them into a hole and hid them with ferns,
And covered the whole thing over with heather and moss
So that no gamekeeper could come upon it later;
The horns and head I hid in a hollow oak,
Where no other hunter would find or even see them;
And then, lest I be caught, I quickly left
And settled not far away, to see what happened
And guard my catch from the swine with their cunning snouts.
And as I sat in my place the sun was so warm,   100
And I so groggy from lack of sleep, I dozed.
In this nervous state I dreamed a strange, long dream,
And all I saw in my soul I'll tell you truly.

I saw keen men in vigorous dispute,
And they spoke of many things, and made themselves lively;
My hearers, if you will listen to me for a moment,
I'll tell you promptly and truly all their array,
And after that I'll name them exactly by their names.
The first was a fierce man, fairer than the others,
A bold knight on a steed and dressed to ride,   *110*
A knight on a noble horse, a hawk on his wrist.
He was big in the chest and broad in the shoulders—
His shoulders and his arms alike were long,
And his waist was as gracefully shaped as a maiden's;
His legs were long and sturdy, handsome to see.
He straightened up in his stirrups and stood aloft,
And he had neither hood nor hat but only his hair,
And a garland on his head, chosen for the time,
Arrayed with bright red roses, richest of flowers,
With trefoils and truelove knots and splendid pearls,   *120*
And there in the center a splendid carbuncle.
He was outfitted in green interwoven with gold,
Adorned with golden bezants and beautiful beryl:
His collar was thickly clustered with chalcedonies,
And many a splendid diamond was set on his sleeves;
The seams were set with many a sapphire,
And emeralds and amethysts on either side,
The hems arrayed with the richest of all rubies;
And well might the price of those gems be many a pound.
The saddle where he sat was of sycamore,   *130*
His bridle all fine gold with silk-braided reins;
The crop was all rich silk and trailed to the ground.
Well grown he was, a man of thirty years,
And young and active yet, and his name was Youth:
And a nobler man I never yet saw on earth.

The second man there sat at ease in his seat,
A man all in russet, corpulent of shape,
In a gray tunic, girt about in the middle,

And every bag on his belt was better than the next.
The man mused much on his gold and all his goods, *140*
And he reckoned again and again his rents and riches—
On spreading fertilizer and fixing his houses,
On the payments of his serfs, on his many benefits,
On presents of poultry, and also parcels of land,
On how to win more plowland, more fair parks,
On profits off his pastures to puff up his purse,
On stewards and on storekeepers to buy heifers,
On clerks and lawyers to serve his manor court;
And all his wit in this world was fixed on his wealth.
By his looks he seemed a man of some sixty years, *150*
And the men of his district called him Middle Age.
The third was an ugly man, who leaned on his side,
All dressed in black, with beads in his hands,
Crooked and curved and contorted with age;
Disfigured was his face, and fallow his hue;
His beard and brows were bleached to white,
And the hair on his head was colored the same.
He was bald and blind, and thick were his lips,
A toothless, woeful wretch; I tell you the truth.
And on and on he mumbled and moaned for mercy, *160*
And cried aloud to Christ and repeated his Creed,
And he said psalms over and over to heaven's saints:
A spiteful, angry man, and his name was Age.
I guess the man was a hundred years old or more,
And all he cared about was his crutch and his bed.
Now I have told you, quickly and truly, their looks
And also named them neatly by their names;
Let me tell now of their talk: listen if you will.

T HE first man, gaily attired all in green,
The man on the noble horse, with a hawk on his wrist, *170*
He was young and active and eager for knightly war,
And he grieved at the lover's lot and piteously sighed;
And sitting up in his saddle, he said these words:
"My lady, my sweetheart, whom I have ever loved,
My wealth and all my worship in the world where you dwell,

My healer of love's bale, with rich, sweet breasts,
All my health and hope, my heart is your own;
I pledge to you this promise: I solemnly vow
That neither hood nor hat shall sit on my head
Till I, steady in my armor, have jousted with honor   *180*
And done great deeds for your love, proved mighty in arms."

Bᴜᴛ the man in gray grew angry at these words,
And said: "My friend, by my faith, you play the fool!
For all your feats are fantasy and folly.
Where is the land and the people that you are the lord of?
For all your regal array, you've no revenue,
And for all your pomp and pride but very few pennies;
All your gold and goods glow there in your clothes,
As long as you've caught your horse, you care for no cartload.
Buy heifers with your steed; make stalls for them;   *190*
Your bright gold bridle would buy you well-bred bullocks;
The price of your jewelry could purchase you lands;
Come, use your reason, man, or you'll ruin yourself!"
The man in the green was greatly angered then,
And he said, "Sir, by my soul, your counsel is feeble.
Except your gold and your goods, you've no other god;
For, by the Lord and the faith that I believe in,
And by the God that gave my ghost to me,
I'd liever linger on in this land awhile,
Enclosed in my armor, on the back of my horse,   *200*
Firmly buckled up in my helmet and hauberk,
With a fierce and sharp lance ready in my hand,
And see some stout knight come and contend with me,
So that I might fulfill what I've solemnly vowed,
And might perform my pledge and prove my strength,
Than get all the goods and gold you ever got
Or all the land and vassals you are the lord of;
And I'd rather quickly ride to the river later
With mettlesome hawks that ring and hurl on high,
And when game fowl are found, and the falconers hurry   *210*
To let their leashes out and release them swiftly:
They snatch off their hoods and cast them up by hand,

138

And then the hottest in haste hurls up and soars
And all their bright bells gaily ring,
And there they hover on high like heavenly angels!
Then fiercely down to the streams the falconers rush,
Down to the river, to beat out the birds with their rods,
And one by one they serve them up to their hawks.
Nimbly then the tercelets strike down ducks,
And lanners and lannerets swoop down to the kill;   220
They meet the mallards, and many a one goes down;
The falcons swiftly, freely, fall to light,
And soon with a *ho!* and a *huff!* they strike down herons,
Buffet them and beat them and bring them to siege,
And keenly they assail them; then they seize them.
Then eagerly the falconers come running
To help the hawks who've hustled faithfully
And with their sharp beaks sharply they strike.
They kneel down on their knees and creep in low,
Catch the wings of the prey and cross them together,   230
Bursting the bones and breaking them asunder;
He picks the marrow out on his glove with a quill
And whoops them down to the quarry they crushed to death:
He quarries them and gluts them, praises them aloud,
Encourages them gaily to leave the checks,
Then holds them on his hand, puts hoods on them,
Draws up the leather thongs to hold the hoods
And loops into their leashes rings of silver;
Then he picks up the lure and looks to his horse,
And he leaps up on the left, according to rule.   240
Then quickly carriers put up the game,
Enduring the tercelets and all their harassment,
For some hold to the check, though some do better.
And speedily the spaniels spring about,
Muddy from splashing when ducks were driven to water;
And then I return again to the court I came from,
With lovely ladies to take in my two arms,
And there I embrace and kiss them and comfort my heart;
And then with beautiful women I dance in the chambers,
And read rich old romances recounting the truth   250
Of warriors and conquerors and noble kings,
How they won in their time great worship and wealth

And rioted themselves with knights in the hall
With part-songs and caroles and many amusements;
And later we go to chess, the chief of games.
Such is the life I'll lead as long as I live,
While you, all worry and woe, keep watch on your goods.
When you're buried and gone, the grief for you will be brief,
And he that you least love will loll in your riches
And spend what you long saved. The devil be with him!"   260
Then the man in russet muttered these words:
"Thrift and you have fought these thirteen winters!
I see there's truth in the proverb said long ago:
'Only a fool deals with fools.' I'll argue no longer"
Then the man dressed in black prepared to speak,
And he said, "Sirs, by my soul, you're both of you fools!
But if you will listen politely to me for a little
I'll stop your argument and end all dispute.
I'll set myself as example, and seek no further:
When I was young in youth and lively in deeds   270
I was quite as eager in arms as anyone else,
And as firm in the stirrups, on my steed's back,
And as gay in my outfit as any man on earth,
And as loyally loved by ladies and maidens.
My form was lovely then, though loathesome now,
And I won as much worship, surely, as either of you.
But later I tired of all this and preferred my ease,
For a man of middle age must have his comforts.
I fertilized then and manured and made up my houses
And purchased good farmland and noble pastures,   280
And I gathered goods and gold most readily to my hand,
And riches and rents came plentifully to me.
But age came over me before I knew it
And disfigured my face and faded all my color,
And both my brows and my beard he blanched to white;
He blurred my sight and brought me sorrow of heart,
Crooked me, bowed me down, and twisted my hands:
I can't lift them to my head or help myself
Or stand on my feet without my cane's support.
Men, make me your mirror, by your troth,   290
And do not shrink from the shadow in your mirror.
The death I dread above all is now at my door,
And I can't tell the day or time of his coming,

140

Or whither I'll go, or where, or what to do after;
But many a prouder man than I in this world
Has passed on the path that I shall soon pass down,
And I shall give you the names of nine of the best
That ever any man on this earth knew of—
Bold conquerors renowned above all others:

THE first and oldest in time was Hector,   300
    In the days the Trojans of Troy were tested in battle
By Menelaus the mighty and men from Greece:
Fiercely they struck and assailed that splendid city
To win his own queen Helen, held in those walls,
Whom Paris, that proud knight, passionately loved.
Sir Hector was eager for renown, as the story tells,
As clerks relate the truth in the chronicles:
By estimate there numbered ninety-nine
True kings in crowns that he killed with his hands,
And he murdered many another as mighty besides.   310
Then Achilles destroyed his enemy by his deeds,
By wiles and without worship he brought him to his death,
As he tended to a man he had captured in war.
So Achilles in turn was slain for that stroke thereafter,
Tricked by a woman's wiles, as Achilles once worked.
Then mighty King Menelaus was merry of heart,
When his enemy Hector had suffered such misfortune;
And with all his Grecian hosts he climbed Troy's walls
And pulled that precious palace down to the earth,
Once royalest in array and richest under heaven.   320
And then the Trojans of Troy were grieved indeed,
And they gathered man by man, and grandly they fought,
But finally misfortune fell on Troy,
For there Priam the prince was put to death,
And Penthesilia passed over before him:
And Troilus, true knight, had trustily fought;
The noble knight Neoptolemus, unfailing in need;
Palamedes, a prized knight proven in arms,
Ulysses and Achilles, eager for glory,
And many more in that company fared the same,   330
As Dictys and Dares both declare.

AFTERWARDS, Alexander won all the world,
Both the sea and the sand and the steady earth,
The Isles of the Orient to Hercules' pillers
Where Elias and Enoch have all this while stayed
And will not come forth till the coming of Antichrist;
And there in knightly fashion was Colchis conquered;
There gentle Jason the Greek won the golden fleece.
Then swiftly he prepared the ways to Gaza,
And there good Gadyfere assembled the Gadres   340
And rode out royally to recover the booty;
Then Emenidas met him and made him tame—
Struck Gadyfere to the ground to writhe and groan;
And when that worthy was dead there was great sorrow.
Then Alexander, Emperor, excellent king,
Arrayed himself to ride on with his ranks:
There was mighty Emenaduse, the Arcadian,
Duke of that army and one of the douzeperes;
And Sir Filot and Floridas, fierce men of arms,
Sir Cliton and Caulus, noble knights,   350
And Sir Garsene the gallant, a good man of arms,
And Sir Lincanor leading his men with a light heart.
And then Sir Cassamus stopped them and asked the king
To go into Ephesia, assist his friends;
For Clarus the king had come in swiftly from India
And he'd frightened Fesonas and besieged Ephesia
For the lady Fesonas, whom he sought for love.
Alexander agreed to go and was soon arrayed,
To do amends for Emenidus, whom he'd mistreated.
He rode then towards Facron and waited by the flood   360
And there he put up his tents and tarried awhile.
And there the brave knights boldly took their leave
To go into Fozayne to see Dame Fesonas
With Idores and Edease, all together;
And there Sir Porrus and his princes swore on the peacock,
And never a boast ever prospered better later,
For all they swore to do they did in full.
There Prince Porrus pricks to the thick of the battle
And bore the battle on his back and bitterly shamed them;

And then bold Bowdrain rode up to the king   *370*
And snatched the gleaming sword from the king's own hand,
And Floridas came quickly in behind him
And cut the helmet from his head and cracked his neck.
Then the good Sir Gadyfere grips his ax
And into the Indians charges again and again,
And he chopped their rigid standard into sticks.
Then Cassamus the bold came up to Sir Carrus,
Who was fighting on foot, and he brought him his steed.
And then Sir Cassamus cut down Sir Carrus,
And for that outrage, Porrus ran him through.   *380*
Then the Indians often times retreated
And fled from the field, and Alexander followed.
And when they were scattered and dispersed and divided asunder,
Our great king Alexander determines to stay
And to go into Fozayne and prepare a feast
And marry the two that desire to be together.
Sir Porrus the prized knight, more praised than all others,
Took Fesonas as his wife, and both were glad;
The bold Baudrain of Banderis, Sir Cassiel himself,
Asked for the fair lady Edias, and wished for no other; *390*
And Sir Betis, best baron of his time,
Took to himself his own love Idores;
Then each man had the love he long had yearned for.
Now Alexander, Emperor, sets out to ride
And turns toward Babylon with the barons remaining,
To seek Queen Candace, his greatest comfort,
And there he besieged and assaulted that fair city,
And the gates were surrendered to him, the keys given up,
And there that peerless prince was murdered by poison.
Dead of a drink—a doleful thing to hear! —   *400*
Brought in a cup by the cursed Cassander.
He had won by conquest twelve great kingdoms,
And dealt them out to his chief knights when he died;
And thus the world's most worthy went to his end.

Then Sir Caesar came, who was called Julius;
All of England he ruled at his own will,

Which after mighty Brutus was called Britain.
He made the Tower of London in his time,
And he craftily devised the aqueduct,
And later he went to Dover, and sojourned there,   *410*
And enclosed a castle with loftly battlements,
And he wisely provisioned it, as all may witness,
For there's honey held in that hold since Caesar's time.
He rode to a province of Rome and ransomed it
And later conquered the great king Cassivellaunus;
And next he rode to Greece, and won it quickly,
And later he seized the city of Alexandria;
Africa and Arabia, noble Egypt,
Syria, Saxony—he seized them all,
And all the isles on the sea on either side.   *420*
And these three men were pagans surpassing all others.
       "Consider now the three most noble Jews
In the Old Testament, as their story is told
In the book of the Bible that tells of monarchs
And which those who read scripture know as KINGS:

T HE first was Joshua, a noble Jew
       Who was carried for his holiness up to rich heaven:
When Pharoah had flayed the people of Israel,
They ran to the Red Sea for fear of him:
Then Joshua the Jew, he prayed to Jesus   *430*
That the people might pass safely at that time;⁻
And soon the sea held back, on either side,
Like a mud wall that was made by human hands;
And the people went over the sea and were safe,
And Pharoah fiercely followed in behind them;
And again Joshua the Jew cried out to Jesus,
And the sea swept back again and sank around them—
A gift for Satan; the devil take their bones!
Then Joshua the Jew bore himself nobly
And conquered twelve great kings and kingdoms,   *440*
The boldest of conquerors, best prized in his time.

THEN worthy David, through God's ordinance,
   Was taken from keeping sheep and crowned a king.
He brought the grim Goliath down to the ground
And he slew him with a sling, and no other art.
The stone shot through his helmet, pierced to his brain,
And at one blow he was dead; the devil take him!
Most dear was David then to God Himself,
And he was a worthy prophet and often praised;
And yet he grieved God greatly after that,   *450*
For into peril he pushed his knight Uriah,
And he died in that sad fight, it's a grief to hear;
And it was a lady, Bathsheba, that brought it about.

AND Judas Maccabeus was another brave Jew,
   A worthy man in war, and wise in arms:
He slew both Antiochus and Appolonius,
And after that another king, Nicanor;
And they called him conqueror, renowned with the best.
These three were gallant Jews and noble jousters,
And they have been laid low for a long time.   *460*
Behold the upshot of all their daring deeds!

AND now I speak of three Christian kings who came after,
   Bold conquerors who captured mighty kingdoms:
The first of these, and oldest in time, was Arthur;
He ruled all shining England at his own will,
And he was king of this people, and held the crown.
He regularly held his court at Carlisle
With all his royal knights at the Round Table
That Merlin made by magic in his time,
And he set the fair Siege Perilous on high   *470*
That none should sit there but should fall to shame
Or should within three days be judged to die
Except Sir Galahad, who won the honor.

There was Lancelot of the Lake, one lusty in arms,
And Gawain the Good, who never wronged a man,
Sir Escanor, Sir Ewain, Sir Eric Fitzlake,
And noble Sir Kay the Keen, renowned for his deeds,
Sir Percival of Wales, who was many times proved,
And Mordred and Bedivere, both men of great might,
And many more of that host, the best of men.   *480*
Then Roystone, that rich king, headstrong in deeds,
Made a garment for his bride from the beards of kings,
And he planned that Arthur's beard should hang with the rest;
But Arthur, our noble king, thinks otherwise,
And he fought with him on the field and left him there dead.
And then Sir Arthur our king prepared to ride,
And on St. Michael's Mountain he wrought marvels,
For there he slew a dragon sorely dreaded.
And soon he sailed over the sea into sundry lands,
While all the people in Britain bowed at his feet.   *490*
Gascony and Guienne he won, in time,
And he conquered many another kingdom and country.
Then he turned to England and to his own people,
And the road towards Glastonbury he rode in haste;
And soon he met Sir Mordred beside a moor
And they fought on the field till all were mortally wounded;
But Arthur our noble king and Sir Gawain his knight,
When all had fled the field or were dead but themselves,
Then Arthur ordered Sir Gawain by his troth
That he swiftly swing his sword far into the lake   *500*
And whatever marvels he saw he should come report;
And Sir Gawain sprang to the sword and swung it to the water,
And a hand rose up and gripped it by the hilt
And brandished the bright steel sword and bore it away;
And Gawain wondered at this, and he quickly returned
To his lord, where he had left him, and looked about
And had no idea in the world where the king was gone.
And then he left in all haste, and headed to the lake
And he saw a boat far out, with people in it;
And Arthur was there, and others of his companions   *510*
And also Morgan le Fay, well versed in witchcraft;
There each last saw the other, for he saw him no more.

Sir Godfrey of Bouillon had such grace of God
That he overran and ransomed the Roman Empire;
And he later cut down the King of Antioch
Called Cormorant, one treacherous of deeds;
And Godfrey was called king, and kept the crown
Of Jerusalem, and ruled the noble Jews,
And honored by all this earth he went to his end.

Then was Charles the Great made chief king of France,   520
With his bold douzeperes, to do whatever he pleased:
The rich Sir Roland and Duke Reiner of Genoa,
Oliver and Aubrey, and Ogier the Dane,
Sir Naimes, who in time of need would never fail,
Turpen and Tierri, two famous lords,
And good Sir Samson himself, of the Royal Mountain,
Sir Berard of Mondisier, a bold man in arms,
And good Sir Guy of Burgoyne, a great man of deeds,
And the four sons of Sir Amion, knights well known,
And others—more than I or any man remembers.   530
Then Sir Charles the Great chose to ride out,
And he passed to Paderborn to prove his power:
He slew with his hands the sultan Salamadin
And again and again he besieged and assaulted that city
Until his desire was granted, the gates thrown open.
The wicked King Widukind would not wait longer
But sped off to Saxony to seek more aid;
And Charles the Great, our chief king, entered the castle
And Lady Niole he quickly took to himself,
And he married her to Sir Mandeville, whom she loved;   540
And swiftly after that he sped into Spain
And got himself settled to camp by the fair river Flagott.
There Oliver the Eager ventured out
And fought with Sir Ferumbrace and made him his captive;
And then they baptized him and called him Florence,
And then he moved on Mandrible to seek Sir Balan,
And the emperor of Egraimort, after that;

And he hoped he might make Sir Balan a man of our faith,
And he caused a font to be brought in in front of his eyes,
And Balan despised it, and spit, and spurned it to earth,   550
And one there swiftly with his sword sliced off his head;
And Lady Florys the fair was christened soon after
And revealed to them the crown Christ had on his head
And swiftly, suitably, showed them the nails thereafter,
Which spiked him once, in passion and pain, to the cross.
And then all these rich relics he promptly took
And placed them at St. Denis, to remain there forever.
And then he boldly sent messages into Marsile
And bade the lord to be Christian, believe in Christ,
Or else he would beat down his battlements and burn him;   560
It was Ganelon drove on that errand, destined to grieve them.
He rode to Roncesvalles then—he would afterwards rue it—
And there the rich duke Roland was robbed of his life,
And Oliver, his own knight, who'd always been true,
And loyal Sir Turpin, trusty in times of need,
And many another as marvelous besides.
He sought out the Saracens seven years and more,
And the Sultan of Sarragossa he found without fail;
And there he beat down the city and captured Sir Marsile,
And that day Marsile died as suited his merit.   570
But by then his men were weary and many were wounded,
And so he returned into France and there took rest;
And then they approached Narbonne, which had greatly annoyed
                                                           them,
And that city he besieged on many sides
Until he had won the gate and was given the keys;
And he made Ameri king there, just at that time,
To have and hold that city, together with his heirs.
And then once more they returned to France for their ease,
And at St. Denis he died when his hour came.

Now I have named you the names of the nine most worthy   580
   That were ever in this world or known upon earth,
And the men who were most doughty in deeds in their day:
But when death comes, no doughtiness endures.

A ND now you shall hear of the ones once known as wise,
All this I'll briefly show you, and then be still.
In Alexander's time there was Aristotle,
A fine philosopher and refiner of metal,
And he got great Alexander what gold he pleased:
And he could multiply metals with mercury waters
And with his ardent spirits and arsenic powder,   *590*
And with saltpeter and sal-gem, and many such matters,
He knew how to mix his metals and make fine silver,
And he could bleach with the best by the blast of his fire.
Then Virgil, in truth, by his supernatural powers,
Made bodies of bright brass to speak out boldly,
To tell what was and what was yet to be,
When Diocletian was named to be emperor
Of Rome and when he ruled the Roman Empire;
And then Sir Solomon was seated apart:
His two books in the Bible are side by side: *600*
The one teaches of wisdom and wit,
And there in the other his proverbs and examples;
And he was the wisest in wit that was ever on earth,
And his teachings will still be believed while the world yet stands
And all the kings and knights and kaisers in it.
Merlin, that marvelous man, made many things
And practiced all the art of necromancy,
And he fashioned a bower to keep his lady Galyan
That no man might possess her or win her away.
These were the wisest that ever the world has seen.   *610*
But mind gives death no pause; he goes where he will.

A ND now of the proudest fighters that ever loved ladies
I'll tell you quickly, and hold you here no longer.
Amadas and Adoine are both in the earth,
Gay in gold and green as they were in their time;
And great Sir Samson himself, once savage in deeds,
And sweet Delilah his darling: Death has them both.
Ipomadon of Apulia, puissant in arms,

The comrade of Calabria—now both are gone.
And gentle Generides, most gallant in his time,   620
And Clariones the clear, now both mere earth.
Sir Eglamore of Artois, most eager in battle,
And Cristabel, clear maid, have crept to their graves.
And Sir Tristan the true, a knight to trust,
Along with Isolt his love, they're laid in the earth.
Where is Dame Dido now, once queen of Carthage?
Dame Candace the comely, Babylon's queen?
Penelope the noble, surpassing all others,
And Guinevere the gay: now both in their graves,
And many more than I or any man remembers.   630

Since when Death comes no doughtiness endures,
Since mind gives Death no pause: he goes where he will,
And since he pulls the pride of lovers low,
And neither riches nor revenue ransom your lives
And nothing at all is assured you in truth but death—
The unexpected guest who suddenly comes—
I think the wealth of all this world worth nothing.
The clerk Ecclesiastes declares in his book,
Vanitas vanitatum et omnia vanitas:
All is vain and vanity, and vanity is all.   640
Quia in inferno nulla est redempcio:
For in hell there is no help, I assure you in truth,
As God in his gospel carefully has taught you:
Ite ostendite vos sacerdotibus,
To shrive you perfectly, and present you to the priests;
Et ecce omnia munda sunt vobis,
And you who have done evil shall soon be clean.
O, man in your middle age, mind what I say!
I am your sire, and you my son, I assure you;
And he is your son, who sits there high on his steed;   650
For age is sire of middle age, middle age of youth;
Now have good day, for I go; I must go to my grave;
Death knocks at my door; I dare wait no longer."

A FTER I'd lingered there and lain a long while,
I heard a bugle blown very loud on a hill,
And quickly I awakened and looked all around,
And I saw the sun was setting, sailing low;
And I hastened on foot, and hurried to the town.
And in the month of May these pleasures were given
As I passed the time on a grassy bank, in fair groves,   *660*
And made myself a bower in the birches with boughs
And sheltered myself in leaves that were light and green.
And may dear God this day give us His bliss,
And Mary, mildest queen, amend us of sin. AMEN. AMEN.

Summer Sunday

Summer Sunday

O N A summer Sunday I saw the sun
    Rising up early on the rim of the east:
Day dawned on the dunes, dark lay the town;
    I caught up my clothes, I would go to the groves in haste;
With the keenest of kennel-dogs, crafty and quick to sing,
    And with huntsmen, worthies, I went to the woods at once.
So rife on the ridge the deer and dogs would run
    That I liked to loll under limbs in the cool of the glades
        And lie down.
        The kennel-dogs quested the kill
        With barking bright as a bell;
        Disheartened the deer in the dell
            And made the ridge resound.

Ridge and rill resounded with the rush of the roes in terror
    And the boisterous barking the brilliant bugle bade.
I stood, stretched up, saw dogs and deer together
    Where they slipped under shrubs or scattered away in the shade.
There lords and ladies with lead-leashes loitered
    With fleet-footed greyhounds that frolicked about and played.
And I came to the ground where grooms began to cry orders,
    And walked by wild water and saw on the other side
        Deep grass.
        I sauntered by the stream, on the strand,
        And there by the flood I found
        A boat lying on the land;
            And so I left the place.

So I left the place, more pleased with my own play,
  And wandered away in the woods to find who I'd find.
I lounged a long while and listened—on a slope I lay—
  Where I heard neither hunter, hound, nor hart, nor hind.
So far I'd walked I'd grown weary of the way;
  Then I left my little game and leaned on a limb
And standing there I saw then, clear as day,
  A woman with a wounderful wheel wound by the wind.
        I waited then.
    Around that wheel were gathered
    Merry men and maids together;
    Most willingly I went there
        To try my fortune.

Fortune, friend and foe, fairest of the fair,
  Was fearful, false, and little of faith, I found.
She spins the wheel to weal and from weal to woe
  In the running ring of the wheelrim running round.
At a look from that lovely lady there,
  I gladly got into the game, cast my goods to the ground!
Ah, could I recount, count up, cunning and clear,
  The virtues of that beauty who in bitterness bound
        Me tight!
    Still, some little I'll stay
    To tell before turning away—
    All my reasons in array
        I'll readily write.

Readily I'll write dark runes to read:
  No lady alive is more lovely in all this land;
I'd go anywhere with that woman and think myself glad,
  So strangely fair her face; at her waist, I found,
The gold of her kirtle like embers gleamed and glowed.
  But in bitter despair that gentle beauty soon bound
Me close, when her laughing heart I had given heed.
  Wildly that wonderful wheel that woman wound,
        With a will.
    A woman of so much might,
    So wicked a wheelwright,
    Had never struck my sight,
        Truth to tell.

Truth to tell, sitting on the turf I saw then
    A gentleman looking on, in a gaming mood, gay,
Bright as the blossoms, his brows bent
    To the wheel the woman whirred on its way.
It was clear that with him all was well as the wheel went,
    For he laughed, leaned back, and seemed at his ease as he lay.
A friendly look toward me that lord sent,
    And I could imagine no man more merry than he
        In his mind.
    I gave the knight greeting.
    He said, "You see, my sweeting,
    The crown of that handsome king?
        I claim it by kind!

    "By kind to me it will come:
    As King I claim the kingdom,
    Kingdom by kind.
    To me the wheel will wind.
    Wind well, worthy dame;
    Come fortune, friendly game,
    Be game now, set
    Myself on that selfsame seat!"

I saw him seated then at a splendid height,
    Right over against the rim of the running ring;
He cast knee over knee as a great king might,
    Handsomely clothed in a cloak, and crowned as a king.
Then high of heart he grew in his gambling heat;
    Laid one leg on the other leg to his liking;
Unlikely it looked that his lordship would fall in the bet;
    All the world, it seemed, was at his wielding
        By right.
    On my knees I met that king.
    He said, "You see, my sweeting,
    How I reign by the ring,
        Most high in might?

    "Most high in might, queen and knight
    Come at my call.
    Foremost in might,

Fair lords at my foot fall.
Lordly the life I lead,
No lord my like is living,
No duke living need I dread,
For I reign by right as King."

Of kings it seems most sad to speak and set down
　　How they sit on that seemly seat awhile, then in wastes are in
　　　　　　　　　　　　　　　　　　　　　　　sorrow sought.
I beheld a man with hair like the leaves of the horehound,
　　All black were his veins, and his brow to bitterness brought;
His diadem with diamonds dripped down
　　But his robes hung wild, though beautifully wrought;
Torn away was his treasure—tent, tower, town—
　　Needful and needing, naked; and nought
　　　　　　　His name.
　　　　　　Kindly I kissed that prince.
　　　　　　He spoke words, wept tears;
　　　　　　Now he, pulled down from his place,
　　　　　　　　A captive had become.

　　　　　　"Become a captive outcast,
　　　　　　Once great kings could call
　　　　　　Me king. From friends I fall,
　　　　　　Long time from love, now little, lo! at the last.
　　　　　　Fickle is fortune, now far from me;
　　　　　　Now weal, now woe,
　　　　　　Now knight, now king, now captive."
A captive had he become, his life a care;
　　Many joys he had lost, and much great mastery.
Then I saw him sorrier still, and hurt still more:
　　A bare body in a bed, on a bier they bore him past me,
A duke driven down into death, hidden in the dark.

The Debate of Body and Soul

THE DEBATE OF
Body and Soul

A s I LAY on a bitter winter's night
     Drowned in the darkness before day,
I saw a strange, unholy sight:
     On a plain bier a body lay
That once had been a splendid knight
     Who'd little cared for heaven's pay;
And now, bereft of life and light,
     The ghost was free to move away.

But when the ghost was risen to go
     It paused a moment more, and stood
And looked at the body stretched below;
     Then, sorrowful and grim of mood,
The ghost cried, "Woe, and greater woe!
     Woe to the flesh and the darkened blood!
Wretched body, now brought low,
     Once so restless, once so proud!

"You whom once it pleased to ride
     High in the saddle, in and out,
Gayest of knights, known far and wide,
     Called lion-hearted, bold in the rout!
Where is all your mighty pride
     And all your boasting, once so loud?
Why do you lie now bare of side,
     For splendid dress a paltry shroud?

"Where are all your worthy weeds,
    Your sumpter with its jeweled head,
Your splendid palfries, riding steeds
    That once you with your right hand led?
Where are your hawks that cried on the leads,
    And the greyhounds that you one time fed?
The Lord has turned on you indeed,
    For all your former friends are fled!

"Where are your castles, lofty towers,
    Gleaming chambers, rooms, and halls
All painted bright with flaming flowers—
    Where are your splendid garments, all?
All your quilts and covertures,
    Your candles and your purple palls?
Poor wretch, there's darkness in your bowers,
    And into darkness you must fall.

"Where are the cooks who served you well,
    Who formerly prepared your meat
Sprinkled with spice so sweet to smell
    That nothing seemed too rich to eat,
And nothing served not fit to swell
    The flesh that one day worms would eat?
Alas! You've won the plagues of hell
    For me, whom once you held so cheap!"

"God made you, ghost, in His own form
    And offered you both wit and skill;
In your safe-keeping I was borne,
    To serve according to your will.
I wrought no witchcraft, thought no harm,
    For I knew neither good nor ill;
I was a creature mute and dumb
    Except as you made cold clay thrill.

"I served you as you might require,
    Both at evening and at morn;
But I was pressed toward desire
    Ever since you first were born.

You who might have judged my fire
    Might have risen up to warn
And check my folly; leave your ire:
    You stand alone at last, forlorn."

The ghost made answer, "Corpse, be still!
    Who has taught you all this wit,
Hurling at me taunts so cruel,
    You, swelled up as if to split!
Can you think, wretch, that though you fill
    With your foul flesh a graveyard pit,
For all the work of a life done ill
    Your hire can be so lightly quit?

"And can you think you'll rest in peace
    Where you lie rotten in the clay?
Though you be rotten whole and piece
    And all your dust be blown away,
Yet still you'll come from hills and trees
    And stand with me on Judgment Day:
We'll enter court and take our place
    And there receive our heavy pay.

"I was your teacher first, and taught,
    But you heard what the devil said;
His bridle in your teeth you caught
    And rushed to do what I forbade.
And sin and shame were all your draught,
    And evil to the scorn of good.
I stood against you long and fought,
    But still you would not turn your head.

"And when I tried to tame and teach
    Of what was evil, what was good,
You'd hear of Christ and the church no speech
    But reared and brayed like one stark mad.
Oh, long, long might I pray and preach,
    But never might I change your mood!
You would not hear of heaven's Judge
    But thundered away wherever you would.

"I warned you, think on the ghost's needs,
    On matins, masses, evensongs;
But you must first do bolder deeds,
    And thought the church bells idle gongs;
To rivers and woods the body speeds,
    Or off into court to do men wrongs;
For the body's pride the poor ghost bleeds,
    Oppressed by evil deeds in throngs.

"What man can do more treachery
    Or more distress his sovereign lord
Than one who holds authority
    And need not ask his master's word?
Since first you reached maturity
    I taught you all I'd seen or heard
To give you peace and make you free,
    And bitter pain was my reward!

"For now you hunt where wild beasts flee,
    And now sprawl out in the forest's eave
Or fly your hawks past stream and tree,
    And split your heart, and let me grieve;
Your eyes are stone and cannot see,
    Your mouth is dumb, your ears are deaf;
And now you're all solemnity
    And fill the room with the stink of death.

"Where is the lady bright of hue,
    Who once would gladly give assent,
That now would lie one night with you
    For any mortal's land or rent?
No longer are you fair to view,
    Or sweet for the kiss you once were lent;
What friend now wouldn't flee from you
    If you strode in where once you went?"

The body answered, "Ghost, I swear
    You're wholly in the wrong in this,
Blaming me for your despair,
    Whom you have robbed of untold bliss.

Where did I ever, by tarn or weir,
    Sit or stand or ride at ease
When you were not beside me there?
    You know well enough where the evil is.

"For whether I rode up or down
    I had you always at my back:
I went, your man, from town to town,
    Obedient to your whipcrack.
Without you there to grant me sound
    I spoke not one word white or black;
Now by my form the truth is shown,
    Here lying silent, dim, and dark.

"For all the while my lord stood near
    I had whatever I might demand,
And I could speak and see and hear,
    Walk, ride, drink, eat at your command;
But now much changed you see me here,
    Since you have left your place unmanned.
Deaf and dumb I lie on the bier
    And cannot stir a foot or hand.

"I might have lived as mute as a sheep
    Or been like a slaughtered ewe or swine
Who ate and drank, then lay in sleep,
    Slain, all pain forever gone;
Brute cattle never yet took keep
    Of what was water, what was wine,
Or tumbled hellwards, plunging deep
    To any grief as fierce as mine!"

The ghost said then, "There is no doubt,
    Wherever you went, I went too;
I had no choice; I was without
    Hand or foot, as I well knew.
But as you carried me about
    I could not make the slightest move;
Thus was I forced to be your lout,
    Like one too weak to challenge you.

"Of one same woman born and bred
     Were both of us, as you well know;
Together we were reared and fed
     Till you found you could rise and go.
For love of you I gently led
     Your steps and seldom caused you woe,
And loss of you was all my dread,
     For lacking you I'd stir no more.

"You'd do some few slight things for me
     At first, while you were young and small,
In the sight of friends or authority
     Who'd beat and bruise you till you'd bawl;
But you grew bold; when you came to see
     How hunger, thirst, and cold appall,
And how pleasant are rest and security,
     You served your own will first of all.

"I found you fair in flesh and blood,
     And on you all my love I cast;
I saw you thrive and thought it good:
     I let you keep your peace and rest.
That made you still more fierce and proud;
     For good works you cared not the least.
I struggled; you did all you would;
     I lay locked fast inside your breast.

"Gluttony and lechery,
     Pride and wicked covetousness,
Envy, malice, cruelty
     To the God of heaven and all that are His—
All such unholy revelry
     Was now your pleasure nights and days;
For all that, dearly must I pay!
     Ah, woe! how harsh the judgement is!

"You were well cautioned here before
     Of what sharp pain we both should have;
You held it all mere gossips' lore,
     You saw so many thrown to the grave.

On the words of the world you set your store,
　　And sought out all the flesh could crave;
I suffered it; I could do no more—
　　You the master, I the slave."

"Ghost, is your peace so easily bought?
　　Can you excuse yourself for all—
You that were so nobly wrought—
　　Can you say I made you my thrall?
Never in life did I do aught—
　　I neither robbed a man nor stole
Without first finding in you the thought;
　　Let him that purchased pay for the whole!

"What could I know of wrong or right,
　　What to choose or what to shun
Unless you brought it to my sight
　　From whom all knowledge needs must come?
When you inclined to the ways of night
　　And taught mute dust to gasp and moan,
Then surely I worked all my might
　　Henceforth to have them as my own,"

"The fiend of hell has raging envy,
　　Hatred of men, and has ever had;
He crept inside us like a spy
　　And undermined my least command.
He took the world in his company—
　　He by whom many a soul is destroyed;
And thus your folly was worse by three
　　And made you, poor wretch, wholly mad.

"When I commanded, 'Take your rest
　　And leave your sins forevermore,
Do penance, lie awake, and fast,'
　　The fiend said, 'Don't be a fool! What for?
Such bitter griefs will fill your chest
　　You'll walk in woe from shore to shore!
Take my advice: make joy your quest!
　　And thrive! Live on for long years more!'

"When I commanded, 'Leave your pride,
     Your many feasts, your shining dress,'
The false world standing at your side
     Urged you to wilder worldliness:
'Put on fine robes of red and white,
     Not some old beggar's tattered rags!
Seize hold of a dashing steed and ride
     With a spangled retinue east and west!'

"When I commanded at dawn, 'Arise
     And take for my sake watch of the ghost,'
You swore with heartfelt groans and sighs
     You couldn't forego your morning's rest.
You sealed your contract, chose your prize,
     You traitors three. And I, distressed—
You led me (Oh, but you were wise!)
     As the butcher leads the helpless beast.

"When you three traitors, one in will,
     Were sworn to be my enemy,
You sat about as gossips will,
     Chattering on in absurdity.
You led me over dale and hill
     As an ox by the horn goes docilely
To where he's doomed to stretch out, still,
     His throat cut through, the blood set free.

"For love I followed you in all
     And so I drew towards my doom,
Following you, my former thrall,
     Forever false and cold to shame;
You won your way—I, bitter gall.
     We both knew well what way we'd come,
And therefore we must see our fall,
     Pain and shame and endless gloom.

"Though all the men below the moon
     Were set upon one bench to say
What painful judgement should be done,
   Not half our grief might such minds weigh;

168

No cry can help us now, no boon,
    No one will now draw our grief away;
The hounds will be upon us soon,
    And we can neither flinch nor pray."

The body watched the grief of the ghost,
    Moaning as if its wits might break,
And said: "Woe that I was not lost
    At birth, who lived for evil's sake,
My heartbeat soundless from the first,
    My cold lips sealed, unable to make
A cry! To earth I might have been cast
    Or lain to rot in a silent lake.

"Born dead, I never might have learned
    Of what was evil, what was good;
I neither would have loved or spurned,
    Nor would I know this final shade.
Can no saint see our fortune turned
    And intercede for saving blood?
In cruel hell where we are burned,
    Can Christ's vast mercy do no good?"

"No, body, no! It's now too late
    For any saint to pray or preach;
The wain is waiting at the gate,
    Your tongue is earth too cold for speech.
The searing pain will never abate,
    In all the world no curing leech;
No longer will our dark road wait;
    God's mercy towers above our reach.

"Had you but thought to cry before
    While we were together, you and I,
And had you, lying sick and sore,
    Confessed, and made the devil fly,
And shed at last one rueful tear
    And begged for mercy, should you die,
We might then have no need to fear
    That God would fail to lift us high.

"Though all the men that now bear life
    Were priests to sing our requiem
And all the maids and every wife
    Widows to weep and pray with them,
Not all that host—alas! not five
    Times all that moves on the world's rim—
Since we would not cry out in life,
    Could lift us now to live with Him.

"Body, no longer mayI dwell,
    Nor stand debating hopelessly;
I hear the hellhounds' doleful yell
    And far more fiends than men can see;
They come to bear me off to hell
    And lo! I've nowhere left to flee;
You too shall come; believe it well,
    On Judgment Day to dwell with me."

It made now not another sound
    But stared and wondered where to go;
Then in there burst at a single bound
    A thousand fiends and more, aglow,
Who set on the ghost and, whirling round,
    Clawed and clutched at it high and low;
And griefs to spare that spirit found
    Battered cruelly to and fro.

For they were ragged, rough, sharp tailed,
    A crooked bulge in every back;
Their claws were razor sharp, long nailed,
    Their limbs all twisted as if to crack;
The ghost was on every side assailed
    By hellish creatures foul and black,
And crying for mercy now little availed
    When Christ allowed their wild attack.

Some with their keen teeth tore the ghost,
    And some poured lead on him, white hot,
And ordered him to drink it fast
    And stood all around his place in a clot;

One devil came there at the last
    That seemed the lord of all the lot;
He raised a colter, gave it a thrust—
    The keen point pierced him through the heart!

Then some set many a glowing sword
    To his back and breast and either side
So that the points met round his heart
    And made great gashes open wide,
And they yelled, "Well may you lose the heart
    That raged in life so full of pride!"
Well for him they obeyed their lord
    Or even worse he might abide!

Since dress was once his greatest care,
    They said, and what he'd long loved best,
They brought him a demon's cape to wear,
    All fire, and over him it was cast;
The hot hasps—each one hurt like a spear—
    Clung like claws to his back and breast;
A helmet, because he'd long loved war,
    Came to him now, and a swift horse next.

Soon after, in they brought a bridle,
    And a demon brought him a riding coat—
A grinning creature, gaping a little,
    Dark flames glowing within his throat—
And for the horse's back a saddle
    Studded with spikes those demons brought,
And then, for the ghost to ride on, a heckle
    And every piece was a coal, red hot.

Then up on that saddle the ghost was slung
    Like one who'd ride to the tournament;
A hundred devils slashed and stung,
    Now here, now there, wherever he went,
And through him fiery spears were run,
    And then with knives he was torn and rent.
At every blow bright sparks flew round
    As when on the anvil a sword is bent.

And when he had ridden that bitter road
    There on the saddle where he'd been placed,
They hurled him down on the ground like a toad
    And all the hounds of hell were released;
They wrenched out bites and howled at the taste,
    Dragging him down to the fiery flood;
All the fiends trod on him, left him half-crazed,
    And all their path was slick with blood.

And then they forced him to bugle and hunt,
    Urge on Bauston and Bevis with skill—
The greyhounds who had served him once—
    And they told him he must sound the kill;
A hundred fiends rose up in front
    And jerked him with ropes with all their will
Till they came at last to that loathesome point
    Below which lay the abyss of hell.

When the ghost had come to that monstrous place
    So fiercely did the fiends all yell
That earth was opened up in haste:
    Then up hot stench and black smoke swell;
Pitch and brimstone rose in a blast
    And five miles off you might catch the smell;
O Christ! a man were cruelly cursed
    On whom the mere tenth part of it fell!

When his fate flamed up for the ghost to see,
    And where it must go, it cast a cry:
"O Christ that reigns for eternity,
    Have mercy on me where I lie!
Poor as I am, You created me:
    No more Your own creature than am I
Is he who sits near You, joyfully,
    Whom you have mercifully lifted high.

"You to whom future and past are known,
    Why was I fashioned to writhe in hell,
To be thus fearfully tortured and torn,
    And that other raised before he fell?

Those that are destined to lie forlorn,
    Wretches Your righteous wrath must kill—
Ah, woe!—why do You allow them born,
    The many who fall to the devil's will?"

Then raucously did the fiends all cry
    "Oh wretch, your wail can help no more!
Whether you call upon Christ or Mary,
    You should have called for grace before!
Now you have lost their company,
    And you yourself have closed the door;
Now therefore join us in misery
    With others wise in all our lore."

The foul fiends, eager for its pain,
    Seized the ghost by head and foot
And cast it with all might and main
    Down, down to the devil's pit
Where the sun shall nevermore be seen,
    And they all sank in along with it;
The firm earth locked itself again:
    The fiery dungeon closed up tight.

When the ghost was gone, that gloomy load
    Borne to hell in the hour before day,
On every hair a sweatdrop stood
    And I shook with terror where I lay;
To Jesus Christ in humble mood
    I called, and earnestly did pray
When the hell-fiends hot as flame and mad
    Drew in close to drag me away.

I thanked Him that once had suffered and died
    For His mercy and His abounding grace,
Who shields me from evil on every side,
    A sinful man as I lay in that place.
And to all the sinful I cry, leave pride!
    Accept remorse, be fully confessed!
No sin, though great, can stand outside
    The endless reach of the mercy of Christ.

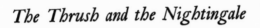

The Thrush and the Nightingale

THE THRUSH
and the Nightingale

SUMMER has come to town with love!
With blossoms and with birds above
    The nut of the hazel springs;
The soft dews darken every dale,
And the longing of the nightingale
    Stirs every bird that sings.

I once heard two birds arguing—
One in joy, one sorrowing—
    Debating shrill and clear;
The one thought women fair and fine,
The other vilified their line—
    All as you shall hear.

It was the nightingale, by name,
Who wished to shield their sex from shame
    And free them from abuse;
The thrush it was that railed away
And boldly bruited night and day
    That all were fiends and shrews—

"For any man who trusts them they
Will turn upon and soon betray,
    As mild as they appear.
They're fickle, false on every hand;
They stir up grief in every land;
    Better if none were here!"

"It's shameful to malign the fair!
They're courteous and debonair;
    Be still, I counsel you.
There'll never be a harm too strong—
Brought about by right or wrong—
    For women to undo.

"They gladden those sunk deep in woe,
Whether highborn men or low;
    They're sly and most discreet.
What good a world without them, then?
For they were made to comfort men;
    There's nothing else so sweet."

"Of women's praises I'll hear nought!
They're treacherous and false of thought,
    And that's one thing I know.
However fair and bright their hue,
Their minds are crafty and untrue;
    For years I've found it so.

"And so King Alexander says;
The world's not seen more wit than his,
    Nor one of richer fief;
Many bear witness, soon and late,
Men whose wealth and power was great
    Till women brought them grief."

The nightingale spoke angrily:
"Bird, you're no fair sight to see,
    With all your lies on show.
Count up a thousand ladies gay
You'll find not one that's false, I say,
    Sitting in all the row.

"Ladies are meek and mild of heart;
They shield themselves from bad report
    In bowers fair and high.
Nothing is sweeter in arms than she
To him who holds her in his glee!
    Bird, why do you lie?"

"Gentle bird, you lecture *me?*
In many a bower I've chanced to be
    And studied these things well.
For just a little bribery
They're glad to act most sinfully
    And plunge their souls to hell.

"Bird, I can't admire you,
For, though you're mild and peaceful too,
    You blurt out brainless song.
Consider what poor Adam found,
The first that ever walked the ground;
    A lady did him wrong."

"Thrush, I swear you must be mad!
You work as if to help the bad,
    Attacking woman's weal.
She gives the sweetest love there is,
And most bound up with courtesies.
    What could be more genteel?

"No mirth on earth is half so great
As when a man makes her his mate
    And they two have embraced.
It's shameful, slandering them so!
Show some remorse! I tell you, go!
    Travel the barren waste!"

"Nightingale, you're in the wrong!
Would you dare send me from this land
    Because I'm in the right?
Consider the case of Sir Gawain
Whom Jesus Christ gave might and main
    And prowess in the fight.

"As widely as he traveled round,
An honest one he never found,
    Neither by day nor night.
Bird, now for your lying mouth
Your infamy spreads north and south!
    Fly off with all your might!"

"I have permission to be here
In orchards and the gardens near,
    To sing my melody.
I never heard from maid or dame
The slightest hint of any shame,
    And they bring joy to me.

"They tell me splendid things; it's true!
And, friend, so I in turn tell you.
    They live in love-longing.
Yet you, bird, perch in the hazel bough
And carp at them! You'll come to woe,
    And wide your fame shall spring."

"My fame spring wide, indeed that's so;
Tell it to him who doesn't know!
    Your news is hardly new!
Bird, come, listen to my advice;
I'll tell you women's treacheries,
    So little known to you.

"Just think of Constantine's fair queen,
In rich furs splendid to be seen;
    Her deeds she came to rue.
She fed a cripple in her bower
And 'healed' him with her coverture!
    Beware when women are 'true.'"

"Thrush, I swear to you you're wrong!
I too have told of them in song;
    It's known in every clime.
Women are fairer and shine more gay
Than sunrise at the break of day
    In sweetest summertime.

"Come to men with your spite for women
And soon they'll lock you up in prison
    And there you'll sadly wait,
And all the lies you ever told yet
Down in the dungeon you'll soon forget
    And shame shall be your fate."

"Nightingale, say all you please;
You say that women will end my ease.
    I curse them all aloud!
In Holy Scripture it is found
They've brought down hundreds to the ground
    Who once were bold and proud.

"Think of Samson, once so strong,
How cruel Delilah did him wrong
    And sold him for her pleasure—
The fairest little piece of price
Christ ever made in Paradise
    For man to hold and treasure."

At once up spoke the nightingale:
"Bird, you're always ready with a tale;
    But listen to my words.
There is a flower lasting long,
And one most praised in every land
    And lovely in her robes.

"In all this world there's none so sweet,
So mild of thought, so fair of speech,
    So quick to heal man's woe.
Bird, you'll rue your ugly thought;
Your words are base and gain you nought;
    Now say such things no more!"

"Nightingale, you're most unwise
To place on women such high price;
    Your profit will be poor.
Among a hundred, scarcely five—
Whether they be maids or wives—
    Care to keep so pure

"That they do not cause grief or blame
Or bring good men to sin and shame;
    That's clearly seen and heard.
Though we come here for just debate
Concerning both the wife and maid,
    You've said not one true word."

"O bird, your mouth has left you shamed!
Through whom was all this world redeemed
    But a maiden meek and mild?
For from her came that holy one
Born long ago in Bethlehem
    Who tames all that is wild.

"She never stooped to sin or shame,
And Mary was that maiden's name;
    Christ be our Lady's shield!
Bird, for all your words so cruel
You're exiled from the forests cool:
    Go fly the dusty field."

"O, nightingale, I have been mad
Or worked as if to help the bad
    Striving against your tunes.
I grant that I am overcome
By her that bore that holy Son
    Who suffered five cruel wounds.

"I now swear by His holy name
That never more will I cast shame
    On either maid or wife;
And from this forest I'll soar high
And care not henceforth where I fly,
    And wander all my life."

The Owl and the Nightingale

THE OWL
and the Nightingale

(*Incipit Altercacio inter Filomenam et Bubonem.*

As I walked out one summer day
I heard, in a nook well hidden away,
Hot words of disagreement sail
Between an Owl and a Nightingale.
The fight was fierce and strong and proud,
Sometimes soft and sometimes loud;
Each bird swelled up against her foe
And out they let their venom go;
Against what points the one might score
The other said all she knew and more;   10
And hour on hour the two birds' song
Kept the battle going strong.

    The Nightingale began the match,
Off in a corner, on a fallow patch,
Sitting high on the branch of a tree
Where blossoms bloomed most handsomely
Above a thick protective hedge
Grown up in rushes and green sedge.
She was pleased with her lofty place, and she
Sang all her notes most artfully.   20
Like notes from heavenly pipes and harps
She fluted our her flats and sharps:

More like a harp's or pipe's sweet note
Than anything from a mortal throat.

On the stock of a tree devoid of flowers
The Owl intoned her holy hours,
In the shade, where ivy grew immense;
That was the Owl's residence.

The Nightingale looked down and spied
The Owl, and winced, and grimly eyed   *30*
That most contemptible of fowls,
For all her life she'd hated owls:
"You wretch!" cried she, "away there! Shoo!
I've wrecked my day by seeing you!
If I look long at you, you thing,
I won't remember how to sing!
My heart flies up and blocks my tongue
At sight of you, you turtle-dung!
And when I hear you yodeling
I'm more inclined to spit than sing!"   *40*

The Owl endured all this till dusk;
By then she was mad enough to bust;
Her heart was grown so huge and sore
She couldn't breathe right any more;
And so she screeched out, loud and long:
"All right! How do you like *my* song?
D'you think I don't know how to sing
Because I do no twittering?
How dare you so defame my name
And cause me all this grief and shame!   *50*
If I had hooks in you, you know
(O, would to heaven it were so!),
And you were down from your high rise,
You might well sing quite otherwise!"

The Nightingale said instantly,
"As long as I'm inside my tree
And don't fly out in the open night,
Your fancy threats have got no bite.

As long as I'm inside my hedge
Your cutting words have got no edge.   60
I know you're hard enough on such as
Foolishly get in your clutches,
And how you dish out more than words,
When possible, to smaller birds.
That's why they hate you so, no doubt,
And all gang up and drive you out,
And why they squawk at you and chide
And hotly chase you till you hide.
Even the little titmouse, she
Would rip your heart out cheerfully!   70
You'll be a monster all your days
For you're grotesque in many ways:
Your body's short; your neck is small;
Your head's the largest part of all;
Your eyes are black and large and wide
Like splats of woad on either side;
You stare about as if to bite
Whatever your talons chance to smite;
Your bill is hard and sharp and hookèd
And like to an awl that's old and crooked.   80
You clack with it both often and long,
And that's supposedly your song!
Ah, how you rail against my life
And hope to bring me to your knife!
Your closest relative's the Frog
Who sits by the millwheel under the cog.
And what are the natural foods of an Owl?
Snails and Mice and Vermin Fowl!
You sit all day and fly at night:
You know yourself you're quite a sight!   90
You're loathsome, and an unclean pest
(I speak of the matter of your nest
And also of your filthy brood):
You feed your young revolting food.
As for the nest, they sit therein
And foul it level with the chin!
They sit there as if blind as stone—
Whence comes the proverb widely known:

'May evil days befall the pest
That feels no shame but fouls his nest!'   *100*

          "The other year a Falcon bred
And left his nest, or turned his head,
And up you stole, as still as a pin,
And let an egg of yours roll in.
Before too long the eggs all hatched
And out of the shells new babies scratched.
The Falcon brought his children meat
And watched the nest, and watched them eat;
And on one side, it came to him,
One of the birds had fouled the rim.   *110*
The Falcon was cross with whoever did it
And loudly yawked, and fiercely chid it:
'Which of you messed? By all that sings,
It's not your nature to do such things!
It's an act too foul for beast or man;
Tell me who did it, whoever can!'
Then up spoke one and then another:
'In truth, it was our own dear brother,
That one there, with the head on it;
Alas that he's not shed of it!   *120*
Throw him out with the you-know-what
And may that huge head crack like a nut!'
The Falcon believed them and felt no doubt,
And he threw that baby Owl out.
He heaved it out with all his heart,
And the Crow and the Magpie tore it apart.
From which same fable we may draw
A very interesting saw:
Just as it came about with the rude
Young Owl, one born of an ugly brood,   *130*
No matter where he may rise or pass,
Sooner or later he'll show his class;
However high his social peg,
We'll know he came from an addled egg.
And the apple that rolls from its parent limb
To lie with apples unlike him,
However far he may have come,
We know pretty well which tree he's from."

    Thus the Nightingale railed away,
And after she had had her say   *140*
She sang a song so loud and sharp
It sounded like a tight-tuned harp.
The Owl, she harkened thitherward
With both her eyes locked netherward,
And swelled and puffed, upon my soul,
As if she'd swallowed a Leapfrog whole,
For she discerned and was aware
That bird was mocking her up there;
Nevertheless, she made reply:
"Why not come out in the open sky   *150*
So all can see which one of us two
Has fairer color and brighter hue?"
"No thanks! I know who'd be the winner.
I do not care to be your dinner!
I know the hooks behind your songs:
They clutch and hold like a pair of tongs.
But with soft words, like all your kind,
You thought you might confuse my mind.
I'd never do as you say, beast;
It's bad advice, to say the least.   *160*
And shame on you for your treachery!
For I've seen through you, as you see.
Oh, hide such treachery from light,
And bury rot with what's all right;
Or if you must be villainous,
Beware of being obvious,
For cunning that is penetrated
Is naturally despised and hated.
And here with me give up your nast-
y plots. I'm wary, also fast.   *170*
Give up your faith in boldness, too;
I'm seven times as sly as you,
And not afraid of all your strength:
I have up here, in breadth and length,
A castle on a lofty rise.
'Good fight's good flight.' So say the wise.

    "But let's stop brawling, me and you,
For talk like this will never do;

Let us use judgment, soberly,
With genteel words and charity;   *180*
Since we are not in full accord
Let's reason, now, and weigh each word;
Without rough strife or fierce debate,
Let us decently litigate;
Let each of us, in civil fashion,
Speak the truth and show no passion."

"Good," said the Owl, "but whom shall we place
Between us two to judge the case?"
"That's easy," said the Nightingale,
"Let Nicholas of Guildford do it;   *190*
No man's wiser or more astute.
He judges by distinctions nice
And loathes devoutly every vice;
And he has insight as to song,
On which note's right and which is wrong;
And he can tell you wrong from right
As easily as dark from light."

The Owl frowned and thought about
All this, and then at last brought out:
"All right. For once you've told the truth,   *200*
For though he seemed, a while, in youth,
A fancier of Nightingales
And other things with pretty tales,
I see of late his passion's cooled,
And now he's one who can't be fooled.
He might have cheated for you once,
But now he'll weigh my arguments.
Nor shall you please him now, and he
Hand down to us a false decree.
He's most mature—a man to trust—   *210*
No longer drawn by foolish lust;
He neither lusts nor does he play,
But goes the straight and narrow way."

The Nightingale had right at hand
All the lore at her command:

"Now, Owl," said she, "is it not true
That you behave as monsters do?
You sing at night, and not by day,
And all your song is 'Wellaway!'
And all who hear that note of doom   220
Shudder, shake, and sink in gloom.
You screech and shriek at your mate, my dear;
It's something horrible to hear!
Indeed they say—both fools and wise—
She never sings, she only cries.
You fly by moonlight, not by day.
It makes one wonder (well one may!)
For all who shun the true and right
Love the dark and hate the light.
And all things sunk in monstrous vice   230
Find the darkness sweet and nice.
And there's a proverb which (though on
The subject of filth) is widely known;
Alfred the king has set it down:
'All those who know our sins we shun.'
And as for you, is the king not right,
You who fly in the dead of night?
Here's something else that's not quite white:
At night your eyes are sharp and bright,
And yet by day you're blind as stone—   240
Can't see the branch you're perching on.
And you're so dim of sight and wit
We make a saying out of it:
'The evil man who sees no good
Is ever joined with the Owl's brood.
He knows his way in the dark by heart
Yet out in the sun can't even start.'
And so it goes with all your kind,
To the ways of Light you pay no mind."

     The Owl listened a longish while;   250
She answered then, without a smile.
"They call you Nightingale," said she;
"Gossipy viper it ought to be!
I've had enough of your chattering stint:

May your tongue find peace in a wooden splint!
You seem to think you've won the day;
Well I too have some things to say.
But now be still, and sit and hear,
And I'll give tit for tat, my dear;
I'll state my case in a civil way,   260
And simple truth will carry the day.

"You say I only fly at night.
Now I won't say that that's not right,
But I'll contend and show with therefores
All the subtle whys and wherefores.
My mighty beak is stiff and strong:
My mighty claws are sharp and long;
For that is natural and right.
They are my joy and my delight;
They're right and fitting for my race,   270
So who can blame my love of chase?
By my example it is seen
That Nature's law is clear and clean.
And yet it's this small birds decry
In every thicket where they fly!
They scream, attack, and wildly tweet
And say things I shall not repeat.
Therefore I like to sit at rest
In peace and quiet in my nest.
For would it much relieve my mind   280
If I should answer them in kind,
Or foully scold these little birds
As herdsmen do, with dirty words?
All wickedness is foul to me,
So I avoid their company.
All wise men fully understand
And make it known on every hand:
'Never debate with a fool or sloven
Or think you can outyawn an oven.'
And I have good authority   290
That Alfred said once, sensibly:
'Keep thyself away from places
Of loud words and purple faces;

Leave such things to fools! Go hence!'
And so I do; an Owl of sense.
And Alfred said another time
What's now a very famous rhyme:
'Mingle with the foul and mean
And never will you come out clean.'
Does the Hawk sink in your esteem   300
If Crows scold from swamp and stream
And dart at him with angry cries
As if to pluck out both his eyes?
The wise Hawk follows Alfred's saw:
He flies away and lets them caw.

    "You've also said another thing.
You say I don't know how to sing.
You say my music's more a moan
And, in your ears, a grisly groan.
Well you're quite wrong! My singing's fine!   310
Full tone, a grand melodic line.
You judge all music, loud or deep,
Against your own high, vapid cheep.
My voice is bold and not forlorn
But rather, like a mighty horn;
And yours is like a flimsy pipe
Of wood that's neither firm nor ripe.
I sing as well as you, at least:
You jabber like an Irish priest.
I sing at dusk, at vespers time,   320
And then when it's come time to climb
In bed, and then in the dead of night,
And finally, with all my might,
When I see rising from afar
The dawn's first light, or the morning star.
My throat's a tool of righteousness:
I make men mark their wickedness.
But you, you sing throughout the night
From evening until morning light,
Over and over, one same song,   330
On and on, the whole night long,
Again and again, you bray and bray

All night long and then all day;
Forever and ever, on you go
Repelling all who live below;
You think your music much adored,
But really men are vastly bored.
Mirth's all right if the dose is small,
But endless mirth is bitter gall;
And harps and pipes and trilling song   340
Are painful when they last too long.
However bright the note may be
It's tedium and misery
If drawn out past all wish or lust;
Therefore men view you with disgust.
Indeed, it's as King Alfred said,
As everyone has heard or read:
'All things lose their tastiness
When they're indulged in to excess.'
Just overstuff on honeyed things   350
And see what rich disgust it brings;
All mirth becomes its opposite
When one has had too much of it
(Save heaven's bliss, which all men name
Forever sweet and ever the same:
However much you take away
The heap's as high as yesterday).

"Another charge you've laid on me,
Which is, that Owls cannot see;
And you say, since I fly by night,   360
I'm blind as a Bat by normal light.
You lie! For I can quickly show
My eyes are fine—and prove it so.
However dark the night may be
My vision never troubles me.
And yet I cannot see, you say,
Because I do not fly by day!
The Hare lies quiet all day, too,
And yet he sees as well as you.
If Hounds come hunting him by day   370
He very nimbly gets away.

He slips up narrow, crooked paths
And pulls a hundred tricks, and laughs;
He hops and twists with sudden starts
And soon, away to the grove he darts!
He'd never escape, quite patently,
If it were true that Hares can't see.
I too can see with perfect ease
Although I spend my day in trees.
As noble soldiers do in war, 380
Moving down the valley floor
Or through the woods in dead of night,
Creeping close before they fight,
Just so the clever Owl goes,
Out of sight like one of those."

    The Nightingale heard all she said
And turned it over in her head;
For it was hard to get around
The arguments the Owl had found;
And what to say was hard to tell: 390
The Owl was right and argued well.
The Nightingale was much distressed
To see how far the Owl had pressed
And feared she might not find a way
To answer all the Owl could say.
But nonetheless she spoke right out,
Considering it best, no doubt,
To boldly meet her foe's attack,
Not panic or reveal her back;
Yield, and your foe will knock you dead 400
Who otherwise might soon have fled.
Fight on! For if your heart is big,
The Boar may show himself a Pig.
And therefore, though the Nightingale
Was cowed, she scoffed and flicked her tail.

    "Owl," said she, "why can it be
You sing all winter 'Woe is me!'
You sing like a setting hen in snow
Whose only sound is 'O, O, O!'

In winter your song could not be glummer,   *410*
But you might as well be mute in summer:
Your envy makes you grump and fuss
And scorn the joys of the rest of us.
Indeed, you're nearly set afire
With anger at our happy choir.
You act like a lunatic to whom
Every joy is a cause for gloom.
He grumbles, lours, and beats his chest
At sight of someone not distressed,
And nothing lifts his spirits high   *420*
But tears in every mortal eye,
And nothing seems to him more fair
Than tangled wool and thread and hair.
An Owl is very much like that,
For when the snow lies deep and flat
And all the world is sunk in sorrow,
You sing from evening until morrow.
But me, it's joy and cheer I bring,
And men are glad to hear me sing,
And all the world rejoices when   *430*
The Nightingale is come again.
The blossoms quickly spring and swell
On every tree and in the dell:
The lilies with their pure white glow
Welcome me—as well you know—
And bid me by their handsome hues
To come to them whenever I choose.
The rose, too, with her shining red,
Growing off in the thorny wood,
Bids, each time I chance to pass there,   *440*
Some short lyric for her pleasure.
Such is my constant, humble task:
The more I sing, the more they ask;
I sing for all the flowery throng
And sing, for all that, not too long;
When I see all the world in bloom
I do not wish it sick with gloom.
When I've done all for which I came,
I leave again, in wisdom's name.

When men start bringing in the sheaves   *450*
And green leaves turn to yellow leaves,
I hurry home and take my way
And turn my back on winter's gray;
When snow and ice bring misery
I hurry home to my own country.
I praise the Lord with love and thanks
Who sends me round to trees and banks.
There on my errand, round I go;
Stay in one place? Good heavens no!
A bird is neither wise nor clever   *460*
To sit around, unloved, forever."

    The Owl considered all she heard
The whole oration, word by word,
And puzzled long on how she might
Best answer, keeping to the right;
For well one might plan carefully
Who fears sly legal sophistry.
"You have asked," the Owl gave answer,
"Why I sing and cry in winter.
It is the noble way of man   *470*
And has been since the world began
That every man calls friends of his
And asks them to festivities
There at his house and at his board
With fair speech and friendly word;
And hour on hour, in the Christmas glow,
When rich and poor and high and low
Sing Christmas carols night and day
I help however well I may.
But still I bear in mind more things   *480*
Than he who only plays and sings.
(Notice my answer, already planned,
Prepared in a wink and ready at hand.)
The summer time is all too proud
And fills man's wit with a dazzling cloud;
He thinks no more of purity;
His thought is all on lechery.
For none hold firm, but each would rather

Lewdly ride upon another.
The stallion stamps and wheels and tears,   *490*
Out of his head with thoughts of mares.
And you're a part of all that rout,
For lust is all you sing about;
And looking forward to your season
You become all bold unreason,
Yet after you have had your fall
We find you hardly sing at all
But only squawk as a mouse might,
With choking sounds and a throat too tight,
A note that's worse than a hedge sparrow's sound,   *500*
Who skims the stubble, close to the ground.
When all your lust is satisfied
We find your song has also died.
Thus men, deluded by distortions,
Cramp themselves in queer contortions,
And not for love at all, in fact,
But only because the fool is cracked;
For when he's gotten what he wants
All his boldness leaves at once,
And once he's stung that maidenhead,   *510*
His love undying drops down dead.
And so it goes with your gay mood:
The day you find you've got a brood
You start to sing quite otherwise.
And so it goes on your high rise:
When you're all finished with your game
Your merriment turns into shame.
But ah, when chilly nights grow long
And bring the frost on, sharp and strong,
Oh then the case is clearly seen: *520*
Beware ye quick! Beware ye keen!
From your hard times I learn the worst:
Sorrow triumphs last and first;
And by your griefs I see anon
Whom to lay hard penance on;
And now it's I who plays and sings
And cheers himself with chirrupings;
And winter brings no grief to me:

I'm not the weakling some may be.
And also, I bring comfort then   530
To solitary-dwelling men,
Or anxious men, or poor, or old
Who sit and hug themselves for cold.
The more disheartening their grief,
The more I sing to bring relief.
What do you think? You grant you've failed?
And grant that Right has here prevailed?"

    "No!" said the Nightingale at once,
"I'll give you further arguments
Before we go to the judge to see   540
Who wins. Be still and listen to me:
I'll nullify with one bare word
Everything I've just now heard."

    "But that's not fair!" the Owl said.
"You've brought your charge, as we agreed,
And I've replied and borne no grudge;
But now, before we see the judge,
I mean to speak out openly
Of you as you have done of me,
And you reply as you think right.   550
So tell me now, you wretched wight,
Have you got any other note
Besides that shrill one in your throat?
You're of no worth at anything
But what you know of chattering;
You're scrawny, anything but strong;
Your coat is neither warm nor long.
What use are you to mortal men?
Nothing more than the wretched wren!
From you there comes no greater good   560
Than crazy cacklings in the wood;
Discount your endless toodle-oo
And nothing more is left in you.
Thus it's said (and nothing's truer)
By Alfred Rex, with wisdom sure:
'No man who's only known for song

Is loved or honored very long;
Only a dolt or lunatic bore
Knows how to sing and nothing more.'
Then you're indeed a worthless thing: 570
Your only talent is to sing.
You're dim and drab, what one might call
A sooty little chimney ball.
You are not fair, you are not strong,
You're neither stout nor trim and long.
You've no more beauty, on my word,
And no more virtue than a turd.
Let me make clearer what I mean:
You're not just ugly, you're unclean.
For when you come to the meadow's edge   580
Where thistles weave a screen with sedge,
By hedgerows or by thick grown weeds
Where men attend to nature's needs,
There you sit, and may be seen there
Shunning places that are cleaner.
At night when I hunt mice that crawl,
You're pecking by the privy wall;
Among the weeds where nettles meet
You chirp behind the privy seat;
And one can find you if one sends   590
Where men stick out their other ends.
Yet you disparage what I eat
And say I choose unwholesome meat!
You eat (and I will tell no lies)
Filthy spiders, foul black flies,
And worms which you (O, horrors!) seize
From crumbling bark on rotting trees.
But I, for my part, do good deeds:
I guard men's homes and serve their needs.
Indeed, my work is very good: 600
I help men earn their livelihood.
Out in the barn at night I perch
And stomp out Mice. Also in church.
For dear to me is Christ's own house
Where I drive out the wicked Mouse;
And never any harm comes there

While I sit guarding it with care.
And when I choose some other place
It's not some thicket of disgrace:
For there are great trees everywhere   610
With thickset boughs, and no branch bare,
All rich with ivy, thick and green,
And leaves and blossoms in between,
Their colors never wholly lost
Even in snow or bitter frost;
There I shelter safe from the storm,
Cool in summer, in winter, warm.
Where my house rises green and bright
Your foul abode is out of sight.

        "Another thing: your lying tongue   620
Cruelly vilifies my young:
You scoff because their nest's unclean.
On every hand such things are seen;
The horse in his stable, the ox in his stall,
Is forced to live with whatever may fall;
And human children in their bed,
Both peasants and the nobly bred,
Do as they must in their youthful time
But leave it off before their prime.
See here! Have youngsters full control?   630
They do as they must. Yes, by my soul!
This saying's passed from man to son:
'Dire need can make old women run.'
But here's the answer that serves you best:
Come with me and see my nest
And note what its arrangement is.
You'll see, if you exert your wits,
That inside we have so much room
My little ones don't crush a plume;
The walls are braided all about   640
With woven sides extending out;
And there they go in times of need;
What you suggest, I quite forbid.
Our house is like the human one,
As humans do, so we have done;

For just as men in every land
Prefer a privy close at hand,
Not wishing to go out too far,
Our management is similar.
Now, chatterbox, be still at last!   650
My arguments have bound you fast.
You know there's nothing you can say;
Hang up your ax and fly away."

The Nightingale, by any gauge,
Was half out of her mind with rage,
And anxiously she searched her wit,
Hoping she might find in it
Some talent besides singing she
Could use to serve humanity,
For answer this, she knew, she must   660
Or all her argument was lost.
Alas, it's very hard to fight
Against plain truth and patent right;
One must exert one's keenest part
When one is troubled with his heart;
One must distort, pervert, devise
Some means to hide in cunning lies
If by one's mouth one hopes to show
What in his heart he knows not so;
How soon a word can slip awry   670
Where heart and mouth in conflict lie!
How soon a word can fall apart
Where lie in conflict mouth and heart!
But nonetheless and even so,
Here's counsel everyone should know:
Seldom is wit more keen or true
Than when hard put for what to do;
And craft can soonest work things out
When matters stand in greatest doubt;
For Alfred said in olden times,   680
A truth still treasured in our minds,
"When misery is most extreme,
The remedy will soon be seen";
As pain increases, so does wit;

The more of that, the more of it.
Thus we see counsel can't depart
Until all craft has left the heart;
But if one lacks all trace of wit,
The purse of craftiness is slit;
And if all trace of wit one lack,   *690*
Then craft must slip from every crack.
For Alfred said, and well he knew,
For all he ever said was true:
"The remedy will soon be seen
When misery is most extreme."

    The Nightingale with all her care
Used every trick she'd learned all year;
On questions intricate and tough
Her cunning served her well enough,
And, troubled as she was, she found   *700*
An answer that would pass as sound.

    "Owl," said she, "you sit and ask
If I do any other task
But sing all through the summertime
And spread my joy in every clime.
How dare you! For it's widely known
My one art's better than all your own.
And better one sweet song from me
Than all your race's history!
Now listen and I'll give the whys.   *710*
Do you know why man's born and dies?
To rise at last past heaven's door,
Where song and mirth last evermore;
There all who make out anything
Of good will go at last to sing.
Therefore at church my music brims
Inspiring clerks to make up hymns
So men may know by means of this
Where they will go and live in bliss;
Thus men may not too soon forget   *720*
But think on bliss and reach it yet,
And guess, when they hear hymns from me

How merry heaven's song must be.
Monks, clerks, priests, with shining faces
In their holy dwelling places
Rise in the middle of the night
And sing about that heavenly light,
And every country parson sings
When first the light of daylight springs.
I humbly aid them as I may,   730
Singing both by dark and day;
And helped by me, however meagerly,
They sing out all their hymns more eagerly.
Thus I warn them, for their good,
To contemplate in a joyful mood,
And bid them to seek earnestly
The hymn that rings eternally.
Oh, Owl, well may you hunch and cling:
This is no empty chattering!
You want a judgment driven home?   740
I'd try my case with the pope in Rome!
But listen longer, if you can,
And soon you'll wish you never began;
Not for all England will you find
An answer in your empty mind.

    "How dare you mock my want of strength,
And littleness, and lack of length?
How dare you say that I'm not strong
Because I'm neither fat nor long?
You don't know what you're saying there;   750
You blow out words like vacant air!
I'm crafty, quick at reasoning,
And so I need not fear a thing.
I know my wit, and songs to spare;
As for the rest, why should I care?
Thus Alfred says, you recollect,
'No strength can outdo intellect.'
A little wit may win the fight
A giant's power never might:
With a little wit and clever tricks   760
Towns and castles fall like sticks;

By cunning, battlements are burst
And every mighty knight unhorsed;
Brute strength may fail to win the day,
But wisdom always gets its way;
You may discern in everything
That wisdom knows no tiring.
A horse is stronger than a man,
But horses do not think or plan,
And so they bear great weights on them   770
And drag together with their team
And suffer both the whip and spur
And stand tied up at the miller's door.
Thus feebleness restrains great force:
For lack of brains, it stays a horse:
And all its strength is no great shield;
It must obey the merest child.
But man, by both his strength and brain,
Makes everything admit his reign.
And if all things had equal strength,   780
Even so, he'd win at length;
For man, with all his crafty skill,
Can bend all creatures to his will.
Just so, I do with my one song
More than you can all year long:
Men love me for my skill at once,
But for your strength they shun your haunts.
What more, I ask you, can you say
Of talent tending all one way?
If two men wrestle in a game—   790
The strength of both about the same—
If one knows tricks in great profusion
But then forgets that he can use them,
The one who knows just one can throw
His man, for all he doesn't know.
The hold well used may well prevail,
And tricks not used must surely fail.
Why should he mourn his ignorance
If one hold ends his man's defense?
You talk of what great works you do.   800
Thank heaven, I am not like you!

Do all your splendid works together,
My one service still is better.
And often when the Foxhounds drive
The Fox, the Cat can stay alive,
For though he knows no trick but one
It beats the Fox's ten-times ten:
The Fox's wiles convince him he
Can dodge the hounds quite easily,
For he knows straight and crooked ways;   *810*
The Cat climbs up a tree and stays,
And so the Hounds soon lose his track
And leave, while he comes walking back.
Meanwhile, through hedges slinks the Fox
And glides along his former tracks
And pretty soon turns back again
So that when all the hounds rush in
The Fox's scent is mingled so
They can't make out which way to go.
If this trick proves of no great worth,   *820*
The Fox will huddle to the earth;
But nonetheless, for all his wit,
He does not reap much benefit:
No matter how his tricks begin,
He ends by giving up his skin.
The Cat may have but one slight skill,
Both in the swamp and on the hill,
But since he climbs with such alac-
rity, his pelt stays on his back.
Just so, though I say so myself,   *830*
My one trick's better than your twelve."

"Stop it, stop it!" cried the Owl;
"Your filthy lies are false and foul!
You paint it all in such a hue
That what you say at first seems true,
But every word you say's fallacious,
Merely a pretty surface which is
Aimed at making all who view
The case believe your nonsense true!
Then stop! No more! Hear what I say: *840*

I'll make it all as clear as day,
And show what ugly tricks you try,
For I'll expose you lie by lie.

"You say you sing to men from love
And teach their hearts to look above
To music which forever endures.
I'm shocked at this vile trick of yours!
How dare you lie so openly?
Will you bring men so easily,
All twittering, to the heavenly land?   *850*
Not likely! They'll soon understand
Before they reach that happy place
They need to quit their sins, beg grace,
And wring their fingers, howl and groan.
I counsel men that they atone
And weep more often than they sing
If they would see their heavenly king;
No man alive is innocent;
Before he goes he must repent,
Cry out and weep and seek relief,   *860*
And know all earthly joys are brief.
But I—God knows—I help them there,
For my song is no deadly snare;
I cry out woe, and all my song
Is lamentation loud and long,
And all who let my song sink in,
Bemoan their state and shrink from sin;
And all whom my sad notes attack
Tremble, groan, and soon leap back.
And lest you carp about the thing,   *870*
I weep much better than you sing;
If truth shall win and drive out wrong,
My weeping's better than your song.
Although some good men one may find
With no unwholesomeness of mind,
They too wish ardently to go;
To good men, all this world is woe;
For even they, for all their worth,
See only sorrow here on earth.

They weep for others of their race   *880*
And wring their hands to win them grace.
I help them all—that is, release
Two kinds of men to heaven's peace:
I sharpen good men's hungering,
For when they hunger, then I sing;
And as for wicked men, I show
What gloom there is down here below.

"And here's another answer now:
When you sit chirping on your bough
You praise carnality and wrong   *890*
To all who listen to your song.
What do you know of heaven's mirth?
Therefore your song lacks any worth.
All you can sing is wickedness,
For what do you know of holiness?
Nobody thinks, when you're on the perch,
Of some priest singing in the church!
And this too let me offer free
If you've the brains to follow me:
How come you never seek a shore   *900*
Where there are men who need you more?
You've never sung in Ireland yet
Or Scotland, where it's cold and wet;
You never fly to Norway or
To Galloway, where the peasants are;
Yet there they hardly know a thing
About the art of how to sing.
Then why are you averse to telling
Them the ins and outs of trilling,
Revealing there, by your fine voice,   *910*
How angels in the sky rejoice?
You're like those useless springs, it seems,
That stand beside swift-running streams
And let the ground be parched with drought
While you splash pointlessly about.
But I, I travel south and north,
And into every land go forth;
Both near and far, both east and west,

I serve the calling I serve best,
Warning men the whole year long   *920*
Not to heed the devil's song;
And by my song I teach all men
They'd better turn their backs on sin,
And warn them against evil ways
Lest they be fooled for all their days;
Far better weep a while before
Than burn in hell forevermore!"

    The Nightingale was much inflamed,
And also more or less ashamed,
Partly because the Owl had taunted   *930*
Her about the spots she haunted,
Near the privy and in the weeds
Where men take care of private needs;
She sat a while and brooded and
Came to clearly understand
How anger can confuse the head,
For it is as King Alfred said:
"Rarely an angry man succeeds,
For wrath twists words as well as deeds";
And wrath can turn and churn the blood   *940*
And change it to a troubled flood,
And soon the heart so swells and strains
That only panting breath remains;
Thus all her wit grew dim as night
And could not make out wrong from right.
All this the Nightingale discerned
And calmed herself although she burned,
For she could argue with more wile
When joyful than when full of bile.

    "Oh, Owl," said she, "grant me one word.   *950*
Take care; you choose a slippery road!
You say we fly behind the house;
Quite so. Men's homes are dear to us.
And where my lord and lady lie
I sing to them and stay nearby.
Can you believe that decent men

Would leave the highway for the fen?
And can you think the sun put out
Because in you dark's all about?
Should I, because of your sad case,   *960*
Go from my right and noble place
And cease to sing beside the bed
Where my lord has his lady led?
It is my right—indeed, my law—
That from all evil I withdraw.
And yet you boast about your song
Because you shriek so fierce and strong,
And say you teach our human friends
That they should weep for all their sins.
Shall each man weep and mourn his lot   *970*
Like some lost wretch which he is not?
If all men howled as you do here
They might drive even priests to fear;
Men ought not moan: they should keep still
And mourn for sins as Christians will.
Is gentle Jesus glorified
By those who've howled and yelled and cried?
Better to cry not loud or long
But measure it to a church's song.
You tell of woe; meanwhile I sing,   *980*
And joy, not woe, is what I bring.
Forevermore you yell and weep
As if afraid to go to sleep;
So fiercely do your yawlings rise
They burst as tears from both your eyes.
But which of the two's the better path
For men to walk in—joy, or wrath?
Yet so we go, each one his way,
You lamenting, I all gay.

  "Do you indeed not understand   *990*
Why I seek out no foreign land?
Come now! What can I hope to do
In lands hope never will come to?
Where everything stirs up distaste
For all is wilderness and waste?

Where crags loom close to heaven on high
And sleet and snow cut through the sky?
A doomed land, grisly and half mad
Whose savage men are forever sad!
They scorn both peace and friendship too   *1000*
And live the way wild creatures do;
And all their meat and fish is raw,
Like wolves, they tear it with their jaw;
And all they drink is milk and whey;
And so they drag on, day by day;
They rise to neither wine nor beer
But get along as do wild deer;
They run around in pelts that smell
Like devils risen out of hell.
If any good man comes to them—   *1010*
As some did long ago from Rome—
To guide them to a gentler course
Or part them from their sins by force,
He might far better not have come,
For like it or not, they'll murder him.
A man could sooner teach a bear
To fight with both a shield and spear
Than teach those savages such things
As listening when someone sings.
What could my song do, then, for them   *1020*
Although I sang till kingdom come?
I'd waste my notes on empty air,
For neither bridle nor halter there
Nor yet a man with steel and iron
Could turn their madness into wisdom.
But here where all the world is gentler
And where men are of milder temper,
Here fittingly I can employ
My voice on services of joy
And bring mankind the gospel news   *1030*
And sing what hymns the priest may choose.
For thus the old law said in the past
(Whose justice shall forever last)
That men shall plow and later sow
Wherever he thinks grain will grow;

For only madmen sow their seed
Where grass can never lift its head."

    At this the Owl reached such a mood
Her outrage made her eyes protrude:
"You say you know about men's bowers   *1040*
Where leaves entwine with pretty flowers
And in one bed two lovers lie
And hug, unseen by any eye.
Well, once you sang (I could tell where)
By such a bower and hoped to lure
A lady out of honesty;
And now with low notes, now with high,
You taught her to do shamefully
And use her body wickedly.
Her lord found out, before much time,   *1050*
And set out traps and spread birdlime
In hopes he'd catch what caused his shame.
Then pretty soon along you came
And *click!* he had you in his trap,
And how your shins did feel the snap!
Then justice judged you for your art:
Wild horses pulled your bones apart.
Now try again some wife or maid
And see if she's so soon betrayed!
You won't long pour your prattle in   *1060*
Before you find you're caught again!"

    The Nightingale was wild indeed,
And if she had been human she'd
Have seized a sword and spear to fight.
However, she did all she might;
She stabbed right back with her bitter tongue;
"Who talks well fights well," says the song.
She pondered that a while in her head.
" 'Who talks well fights well,' Alfred said,
But how can your talk hurt my name?   *1070*
The lord had only himself to blame!
He was so jealous of his wife
He couldn't stand, to save his life,

To see some man go near and speak
To her; it made his proud heart break.
He locked her up inside a bower
As strong and lonely as a tower.
Then I (who pitied her distress
And grieved to see her wretchedness)
Gave her the solace of my song   *1080*
All the night and all day long.
That's why he was cross, and why
He murdered me maliciously.
He worked his own shame onto me,
But all turned out quite differently:
King Henry judged the matter whole
(May Christ have mercy on his soul)
And banished that uncivil knight
Who had so meanly shown his spite
And in that noble monarch's land   *1090*
From utter malice schemed and planned
And trapped a bird and sentenced him
To painful loss of life and limb.
All this brought honor to my kin;
The knight was punished for his sin
And fined, in fact, a hundred pound;
Meanwhile, my young sat safe and sound
Enjoying bliss and calm delight
And happiness, as well they might.
The vengeance was all mine. Therefore,   *1100*
I speak more boldly than before;
Since I'm avenged by Henry's laws
I'm gayer than I ever was.
I'll sing wherever I may please
And no one can so much as sneeze,
Though you object, you grisly ghost—
For there's no hollow stump or post
Where you can safely sleep or hide
And no one come to break your hide.
For farmers, boys, and hired men   *1110.*
Want nothing but to do you in.
And if they chance to spy you once
They fill their pockets up with stones

And hurl them if they can to crack
Your hunched up, miserable back.
For only beaten to the ground
Do you prove useful to mankind,
For on a pole they set you high,
Your corpse exposed to every eye,
And there your wicked claws alarm   1120
Small birds and keep the crops from harm.
Your life's as worthless as your blood,
But as a scarecrow you're quite good.
Therefore when farmers come to sow,
The sparrow, goldfinch, rook, and crow
Will not come near for the life of them:
Your hung-up carcass frightens them.
And when the trees are burgeoning
And tender shoots burst forth and spring,
No bird will dare approach the place   1130
Where he descries your rotted face.
How foul's an Owl whom all things dread,
Who serves no use except when dead!
And here we all may see for sure
How horrible your features are
Throughout your evil life on earth,
For when you hang there, put to death,
The birds you used to scare so sore
Are just as frightened as before!

        "It's right that men should hate you so,   1140
For all you sing is coming woe;
And all you sing of soon or late
Is some approaching gloomy fate!
When you've cried woo-oo-oo all through the night,
No wonder men are filled with fright:
When some man's dying, there you are,
Always bringing it more near;
Foretelling cruel poverty
Or some dear friend's adversity,
Or else foretelling dreadful fire,   1150
Or war, or robbers creeping nigher,
Or cattle struck by plague and dying,

214

Farms in wrack and ruin lying,
Or how some man must lose his wife,
Or barons fall to bitter strife;
And always, always it's distress,
And thus you bring on wretchedness.
No man has ever heard you humming
Except when there is trouble coming.
No wonder all men hate you so   1160
And pelt you, beat you, bring you low
With staffs and turf and stones and clods
Until you've no place left to dodge.
May evil fall on the messenger's head
Who only comes with news to dread,
Who brings no cheer but cheerfully brings
Tales of grief and wretched things.
O, well may God on high be wroth
With you and wearers of the cloth!"

The Owl sat thinking none too long   1170
But gave her answer stiff and strong:
"What! are you ordained" — cried she —
"Or just some false-frock mockery?
You do priests' holy works, I see,
But I can't say how holily.
I don't know how you sing a mass,
But you can curse like sounding brass!
But it's your old malignity
That's made you put your curse on me.
Remember what the carter said,   1180
'Get over on your proper side.'
Why do you scorn my wisdom's light
And all my judgement and my might?
For all men know I'm far from dumb:
I know all things before they come.
I know of hunger and of war
And who'll live ninety years or more;
I know what woman loves her spouse,
I know when danger nears a house,
I know whose neck the noose will fit   1190
Or what death's coming worse than it;

215

I know wherever two sides fight
Which side will turn at last to flight,
I know when plague will strike the herds
And death will strike down beasts and birds;
I know if trees will blossom out,
I know if seeds of grain will sprout,
I know what house will burn at night,
I know if men will flee or fight,
I know what ship will sink at sea,   *1200*
I know when snow will cover me,
I know all that and plenty more:
For I'm well steeped in bookish lore,
And also I know Scripture, too—
More than I will tell to you.
I go to church whenever I can
And gather truth and wisdom in.
I know what all the symbols mean,
And many things you'd never dream.
And when some man is hunted there   *1210*
I know when the pursuit is near.
Oh, often, thanks to my great wit,
In heaviness and grief I sit,
And when I see that awful harm
Is crawling near, I cry, 'Alarm!'
And sharply I cry out, 'Beware!
Prepare yourselves! Prepare! Prepare!'
That's something wise King Alfred said—
A man should keep it in his head—
'Foresee your grief, prepare for it,   *1220*
And you deprive it of its bite.'
Hard blows will hurt a good deal less
If one is armed with wariness,
And arrows cannot find their spot
If one perceives them when they're shot,
For one can walk away from them
If one anticipates their aim.
Then why should man's adversity
In any way be blamed on me?
Although I saw he would be hit,   *1230*
I'm in no way the cause of it.

For though I see some blind man stray
And wander from his proper way
And head toward a stinking pit
And fall and foul himself in it,
Can you believe, though I see all,
That I, by watching, made him fall?
And so it is, it seems to me,
That when I'm sitting in my tree
I know and see as clear as day   *1240*
That some man's going to have to pay;
Should he, because he never knew it,
Blame my knowing he would do it?
I ask you now, can he blame me
Because I'm wiser than is he?

    "When I see sorrows coming on
I fly in close and moan and groan
And warn him to make ready quick,
For trouble's coming fast and thick.
But I, however loud and shrill   *1250*
I cry, can't turn back heaven's will.
Then why do men complain of me
Who tell them what sad things must be?
Although I warn them half a year
I do not bring the thing more near.
I only warn them because I
Would have them guard themselves and try
To face the danger lurking near;
That's why I moan and groan so clear.
And no man living's so secure   *1260*
That he can ever be quite sure
That no misfortune's creeping close,
However little of it he knows.
And thus King Alfred pointed out
The gospel truth without a doubt:
'The better a person's prospects fare,
The more he should exert his care.
Though all signs say he can't go wrong,
No man should trust his luck too long;
All things grow cool, however hot;   *1270*

217

Nothing's so white it cannot spot;
And love can turn to enmity,
And joy can turn to misery;
For everything upon this earth
Shall pass, in time, like last week's mirth.'
Then clearly it can be perceived,
In all you say you are deceived,
For all you say to bring me shame
In fact dishonors your own name.
Strike as you will, at last you'll own   *1280*
The stroke that fells you is your own;
And all your heaped up scorn and slander
Makes my glory all the grander.
If you can't take some better tack
Our judge will send you howling back."

      The Nightingale sat still and sighed. She
Looked all in, and well she might be,
Given all the Owl had said
And all the telling points she'd made.
She grieved and was supremely vexed   *1290*
And pondered what she might say next;
Then, gathering her wits again,
She said, "What! Owl, are you insane?
You brag to me of a special sense,
But have you ever wondered whence
It comes, if not by sorcery?
You must be purged, and thoroughly,
If you're to be allowed to stay
Near men. If not, then fly away!
For all who study witchcraft are   *1300*
Cursed by the priests, and always were;
It's clear as day you're one of them
And cannot turn to Christ again.
I said a little while ago,
And you asked me if it were so,
That I'm a priest. You asked in jest,
But every man from east to west
Knows you stand under heaven's curse;
You need no priest to make it worse.

218

For even children call you foul,   1310
And men call you The Wicked Owl.
And it's the truth, as I've heard tell,
A man must know the heavens well
To understand the fates' decree
And see what you say you can see.
What do you know about a star
Although you see it from afar?
Why, so does many a man and beast
Who can't foresee things in the least.
An ape can hold an open book   1320
And turn the pages over and look,
But in ten years he'll know no more
Of reading than he knew before.
So you may stare and stare at a star
And be no wiser than you are.

    "And yet, foul wretch, you dare chide me
And criticize me cruelly
And say I sing beside the house
And teach the wife to break her vows.
Foul thing, you lie most filthily!   1330
No vow was ever the worse for me!
It's true I sing as daylight fades
Where ladies are, and pretty maids,
And it's true, too, I always sing
Of love, for it's a splendid thing
That wives should love their husbands more,
Not tumble with some paramour.
And as for maidens, it's no shame
To love, remembering her good name,
Giving her heart and plighting her word   1340
To one whom she may call her lord.
Such is the love I always preach,
And there's no other love I teach.
And though a woman's prone to err
(For she's a delicate creature
And may—if some man hotly sighs
And strongly pleads, and tells her lies—
May, I say, behave amiss)

219

Can I be held the cause of this?
If some one woman turns to wrong,   1350
I cannot therefore quit my song.
Woman may sport beneath the sheet
In marriage or in wicked heat;
And listening to me, she may
Be moved to good or evil play.
What's there on earth that heaven sends
Which can't be turned to evil ends?
What's there on earth that is of use
And can't be turned to some abuse
Where men some evil purpose hold.   1360
Silver is good, and so is gold,
But nonetheless, a man can buy
Injustice and adultery.
Weapons are good to maintain peace,
And yet on every side one sees
Good men are slain in many lands
When bad men have them in their hands.
And so it must be with my song:
Good as it is, men may go wrong
And use it for their lustfulness   1370
And other sorts of wickedness.
Or are all kinds of love, to you,
The same? Oh, Owl, it isn't true!
Love's fine between a man and mate
Except outside the married state.
In that case it's a sin and shame,
And may the Cross come down on them
Who twist desire and misbehave!
It's no surprise such people rave
For surely they must be possessed   1380
Who brood before they build a nest!
But woman always has been frail,
And lust can make her virtue fail;
No wonder if she sometimes slips
With hunger burning in her hips;
Yet she's not lost entirely
Who merely falls from frailty;
For many have sunk into desire
And later risen from the mire;

And not all sin is of one kind;   *1390*
There are two ways to fall, I find:
For some can fall to fleshly lust,
And some fail in their spirit first;
Thus flesh draws men to drunkenness
And lust and to laciviousness,
But spirit runs to envy, hate,
And joy at another's sorry fate;
The spirit longs for more and more
And scorns God's mercy, bars the door,
And climbs the heights of pride to show   *1400*
How vile it thinks all those below.
Now tell me, if you think you can,
Is flesh or spirit worse in man?
You must agree with other people,
Flesh is still the lesser evil.
Many a man is clean of flesh
Whose spirit's downright devilish;
Then I say, let no one degrade
In woman—some poor harmless maid—
The frailty of womanhood   *1410*
If he himself sins more through pride.
And so to wives and maids I bring
New joy in love each time I sing,
And I'll defend the maiden's case
If you'll renounce all prejudice:
Just listen, I'll heap wherefores round
Up to the treetops from the ground:
Whatever joy the maid may find,
She falls according to her kind;
Although she dallies some tonight,   *1420*
She hasn't strayed too far from right:
For all's forgiven when she goes
To church and says her marriage vows,
And later she can have as mate
The same man you would now berate,
And boldly go by broad daylight
Where once she had to sneak by night.

"A young girl hardly knows her sin,
When young desire draws her in.

She goes to some dull fellow who   *1430*
Has said he'll show her what to do;
He comes, he goes, he pleads, he prays,
He leaps about in curious ways,
And so pursues her hard and long—
How can the poor child not go wrong?
She hardly knows what it's about,
Although she's eager to find out,
And wants to understand this game
That makes a big, wild fellow tame.
Oh, pity! I cannot contain   *1440*
My grief when I see drawn with pain
Young faces feeling love's first birth—
Ah, gone is all my song of mirth!
And to all such I teach in song
That young love does not last for long.
My song does not last long, at best,
When love flies down and comes to rest
On such as these, then flits away,
And their hot breathing end with day.
My songs are brief for them, and go   *1450*
From higher notes to notes more low.
The maiden sees, when all goes wrong,
Her love was sadly like my song,
Only a trifling little breath
Born quickly, quickly gone to death.
Then, thanks to me, she comprehends
And turns her lust to nobler ends;
She comprehends, thanks to my song,
That foolish love cannot last long.
But wives! I do wish you could see   *1460*
How loathsome *their* absurdity!
Yet they could learn from my ways too:
I'm silent when my pleasure's through.
All wives should quit their foolishness,
However bad their marriage is.

　　"And it's the strangest wonder yet
How any man can so forget
His vows, that he will brave all strife

And do it with another's wife.
One of two things it's got to be   *1470*
(For no third cause occurs to me):
The man is worthy and nobly wrought,
Or else he's frail and good for nought.
But if he's strong, a worthy man,
No one of sense would dare to plan
To shame him in his lady's bed
For fear of paying with his head
Or, worse, with that which dangles down—
Hence, never yearn for her again
And even lacking all such fear,   *1480*
It's evil and can cost you dear
To wrong a good man in his bed
Or dare seduce the one he wed;
Again, if he's some wretch ill bred,
Not hungry either at meals or bed,
Who can feel hot lust when there's
That ugly lout asleep upstairs?
And how can any love arise
When he, too, sometimes feels her thighs?
And thus you understand the case: *1490*
It's shameful, and it's also base
To steal into another's bed;
For if a worthy man she's wed,
No good will come of it, be sure,
If you dare go and lie with her;
And if he's some great hunk of fur,
You'll get no pleasure out of her.
Recall for whom she spreads her legs
And all your joy will turn to dregs.
Lord, how could any free man, then,   *1500*
Desire to visit her again?
The moment he recalls that lout
His mighty love must peter out."

The Owl was pleased with all this tale,
For she believed the Nightingale,
Although she'd argued skillfully
At first, had ended wretchedly.

So she replied, "Ah ha! I find
You've still got maidens on your mind!
You fight for them and hail their ways   1510
And offer them excessive praise.
But often ladies turn to me,
Poor things, and moan most bitterly;
For time and again I've seen a wife
And husband find themselves in strife;
The man goes out, commits his sin
(Oh, well he loves to thrust it in!)
And spends his all on some slut he
Has followed where he shouldn't be,
Leaving alone his own poor spouse   1520
All desolate in an empty house,
In threadbare clothes and not well fed
While he warms up some other bed.
When he comes later to his wife
She's mute for fear of very life.
He bawls at her and brings her grief
And then can't offer her relief.
All that she does displeases him
And all she says seems to him grim;
And though she's never done amiss,   1530
He puts his fist where he should kiss!
There's no man living who can't force
His wife to sin by such a course.
Too often handled in such ways,
It's no surprise if that wife strays!
God knows, she ought not to be chid
If that man should be cuckolded.
It often happens, soon or late,
The wife is soft and delicate,
Well formed, and fair of face and skin;   1540
Therefore it's all the more a sin
That he should waste his loving care
On one not worth her shortest hair;
Alas, there are too many who
Do not know how to keep wives true:
Men who believe if she should speak
To any man she's bound to break

224

Her marriage vows, or if she chance
To praise some man or throw a glance,
The husband locks her in her room;   *1550*
Thus many a marriage meets its doom.
For when a wife has been imprisoned,
She does things she had never imagined.
Woe to him that thus denies her,
Though at last she'll prove the wiser.
Tales like this they bring to me,
Lamenting it all bitterly.
My heart could almost burst in two
When I see all they must go through.
And I too weep and pace the floor   *1560*
And pray to Christ now, all the more,
That He may quickly set her free
And send her better company.

    "And I'll say this too, on my side—
And you cannot, to save your hide,
Find any answer anywhere;
All you have said will be mere air.

    "Many a merchant, many a knight
Still loves and keeps his lady right;
And so does many a humbler man,   *1570*
And she returns his love again:
At meals and bedtime both she speeds
Him on with blessed words and deeds,
And tries in every way she can
To do what's pleasing to her man.
And when he goes away to war,
No one alive is sorrier;
The parting makes her sob and moan
And grieve because she'll be alone;
And longingly she sits oppressed,   *1580*
Her poor heart breaking in her breast.
And all day long and then all night
She thinks of what gave him delight;
Their years seem but a little while
And every step he goes, a mile!

While others sleep nearby at night,
I listen near her windowlight
And know the cause of all her grief
And sing to bring her soul relief.
It's for her sake I leave my song   1590
Of cheer, and mourn the whole night long.
In all her grief I take some part,
And so grow dearer in her heart.
I give whatever aid I may
Because she goes the Righteous Way.

    "False Nightingale, awhile ago
You nearly crushed my heart with woe!
But though I speak of it with pain,
I'll now confute you and explain.
You tell me man's my enemy,   1600
And every man feels scorn for me
And knocks me down with sticks and stones
And beats me black, and breaks my bones,
And later, when at last I die,
He hangs me, spitefully, on high
Where I scare off magpies and crows
And save the seeds the farmer sows.
For evil, I return them good
And for mankind I shed my blood!
I help them even when I die,   1610
So you're not half so good as I:
For when you clench your claws in death
Your dying isn't worth a breath;
Indeed, it's all a mystery
That such a wretch should come to be.
For even when I'm shot and dead
I do good deeds, as you have said:
When I'm set high upon a stick
In holtwoods where the trees grow thick,
The small birds come up curiously   1620
And men can catch them easily;
Thus even my cold corpse is good
And helps mankind obtain his food.
But you've no talents, as I've said,

To help mankind, alive or dead.
I can't see why you rear your brood;
Alive or dead, they do no good."

The Nightingale took note of this
And flitted to a higher place
And there sat taller than before.   *1630*
"Now, Owl," said she, "you must beware!
How can I argue when I see
You're beaten by yourself, not me!
You brag that all men scorn your sight
And that you're loathesome, day or night.
The yells and clamor you arouse
Show how accursed your whole race is.
You say boys chase you, hot and thick,
And hang your carcass on a stick;
They poke and tear and shake you, too,   *1640*
And make a scarecrow out of you.
Well clearly, then, you've lost the day:
You grant the worst things I can say.
It seems you've come into my hands:
You boast your shame, despite your plans."

The Nightingale abruptly ceased,
And sat there lofty and well pleased.
Soon after, she began to trill
A song so cheerful and so shrill
That others heard it, far and near.   *1650*
Then all around her did appear
Thrustlecocks, woodpeckers, thrushes,
All the birds of trees and bushes;
Since it seemed to them she had
Outtalked the Owl, they all felt glad;
They whistled then, so merry-voiced
That all the woods around rejoiced
As, when you've lost a tennis game,
Men jeer at you and hoot your shame.

At once the Owl was heard to bawl,   *1660*
"What's this? Is this your muster-call?

227

What, wretch! Do you intend to fight?
Come, come, you have too little might!
Then what's the meaning of these screams?
You've summoned all your host, it seems!
Well, you'll find out before you're gone
The power of the tribe you scorn.
For all those birds whose bills are hookèd,
All whose claws are sharp and crooked,
They're my kindred, and if I   1670
Call out, they'll gather instantly.
The cock himself (you've seen *him* fight)
Must naturally uphold my right.
For both our cries are clean and bright,
And both of us stay up all night.
If I should care to raise a cry,
I'd lead so great a company
Against you, you'd go screaming back.
I don't give a turd for all your pack!
I wouldn't leave—if I laid in   1680
To you—one feather on your skin!
But when we came here to this spot,
It was agreed on, was it not,
That we'd resolve this legally,
With one who'd judge it honestly.
Do you take back your former vow,
Perceiving you're the loser now?
You think our judge may judge you rightly,
And so perhaps you'd rather fight me?
Well, if you'll take advice from me,   1690
Before I call my company
You'll drop all thought of war today
And, quick as arrows, speed away.
For by these claws with which I hack,
If you stir up my clan's attack,
You'll sing in quite a different key
And curse the day you fought with me.
There's not one here who dares to try
To look straight at me, eye to eye."
The Owl spoke most audaciously,   1700
But she would not have willingly

Chanced calling in her so-called clan;
She merely wished to try the plan
Of bluffing down the Nightingale.
For many a man who's weak and frail
When fighting with a sword and shield
Can walk out on the battlefield
And hurl such dreadful leers and threats
That every man around him sweats.

But then, just as the dawn came winging,   *1710*
Down the Wren flew, sweetly singing,
Bringing the Nightingale her aid.
Quite modest was the song she made,
But she had such a sweet, clear voice
She made the countryside rejoice.
Besides, she had a clever head,
For she was like one city-bred;
She'd spent her life among mankind,
And worked there to improve her mind.
And anywhere you'd hear her talking,   *1720*
Even where the King went walking.

"Listen," she said, "let all this cease!
What! would you dare to break the peace
And bring his majesty to shame?
Hear this! He's neither dead nor lame,
And you'll pay with your blood and brains
If you commit in his domains
A breach of peace! Then don't you budge
But place your cause before a judge
And let his verdict settle it,   *1730*
For you've both pledged your word to it."

The Nightingale said, "That we'll do,
—Not that I give in to you—
But yes, in court I'll seek redress.
I wouldn't want unlawfulness
To end this quarrel wrongfully.
The judgement does not frighten me.
I've said before, and still advise

That Master Nicholas, the wise
Should serve as judge between us two;   *1740*
And this I trust he'll gladly do.
But where shall we go to look for him?"
Up in a linden sat the Wren;
She said, "You'll easily find him;
He lives right over in Portisham—
In Dorsetshire the place would be
Where the downs glide off toward the sea.
I've never seen a man dispense
More justice or write more good sense.
That's why he's known so far and wide,   *1750*
From here to Scotland's other side.
And finding him will take no fuss:
He's only got one little house.
For this the bishops are to blame,
And others who have heard his name
And know what splendid pains he takes.
Why will they not, for their own sakes,
Add him to their establishments
To hear his wit and common sense,
And, just to have his company,   *1760*
Grant him livings plentifully?"

    The Owl said, "Sigh. It's all too true.
These great men don't know what they do
When they leave frail and in neglect
A man of such fine intellect!
They give good jobs to worthless clerks,
But sadly disregard his works.
To relatives, come soon, come late,
They give each one a fine estate,
But can their intellect surpass   *1770*
The claims of Master Nicholas?
Well, let us hasten to him then
And see what judgment he'll bring in."

    "Yes, let us," said the Nightingale.
But who'll go over in detail
The points the two of us have made?"

The Owl said, "Do not be afraid,
For every word we thought to say
I'll lay before the judge to weigh;
And if in some details I err,   *1780*
You quickly stand up and demur."
And with these words away they flew
Without armed guards or retinue,
And so at last the two were come
To Nicholas at Portisham.
But if you ask me which one won,
I cannot say. My tale is done.

Explicit

COMMENTS ON THE POEMS

NOTES

Comments

ON THE POEMS

MEDIEVAL literature has often been discussed as though it were not to be read in the same way we read the literature of other periods. One sometimes hears that, because of the extraordinary leisure and aesthetic tolerance of the class for whom the more sophisticated poetry was composed, the good medieval poet characteristically made use of extremely familiar plots rather than bothering to make up plots of his own, quoted conversation at length where we might summarize, and spent excessive time on descriptions of dress, landscape, and such activities as hunting, jousting, and lovemaking. The argument seems to be that if we are bored the fault lies less with the poetry than with the hurry of life in our time; or perhaps it is that we too would like such poetry if we were creatures of the unenlightened Middle Ages.

But in fact, poets of every age deal with roughly the same human emotions, and for the experienced reader, whatever his time and place, poetry is interesting or not depending upon the moment by moment intensity of the appeal. The question is not really whether one ought to excuse second-rate poetry on the grounds that once it did not seem unoriginal or thin, but whether one has understood and appreciated all that is going on in the poetry. Unfamiliar techniques, together with qualities we are not in the habit of noticing—both of the poems and of the larger reality which the poems reflect—can blind us to poetic merit.

Working with familiar stories, the medieval poet was in a position the modern writer, restricted by copyright laws, might envy. Whereas the modern writer generally must start from scratch and waste much of his energy simply working out character and action, the medieval writer was free (like Shakespeare, or like Homer or Sophocles) to concentrate his attention on manipulating his traditional material to release its full significance or to find in it new possibilities of meaning. He might play one old plot against another, for instance, or might tinker with the arrangement of scenes, with symbolism and Christian allegory, or with literary allusion. Sometimes medieval poets so arranged their verse that the number of lines in a given poem had symbolic significance—the *Pearl*-poet, Dante in the *Divine Comedy*, Wolfram in *Parzifal*. Sometimes, as in Chaucer's *Book of the Duchess*, they worked out veritable jungles of subtle relationship through the frequent repetition of key words, phrases, images, and events. In short, far from being the crude product of an unenlightened age, medieval poetry was, at its best, as complicated as any poetry to be found. It may seem baffling to the modern reader that poets would go to the trouble to work in this way; but they did, or anyway some of them did. Medieval people took the same pains with the illuminations of manuscripts, with pictures on church walls and windows, and, in fact, with nearly everything they touched. And despite the difficulty of their way of working, they were able to produce far more, in some cases, than any modern writer can, whatever his diligence. We need not pause to brood on the reasons for this. They worked out of an established body of belief; they knew less about the world, with the result that they knew more about what they did know (as the philosopher Hobbes once said, "If I had read as many books as other men I would know only as much as other men"); they depended on an established and systematic rhetoric which was understood not only by the poet but also, at least to some extent, by his audience. Perhaps there are other reasons as well. In any case, they produced poetry rather different from ours.

Of course not all medieval English poetry fits this description. In any age, not all poems are written for the same purposes or for the same audiences, and not all poets are equally intelligent or skillful. The little medieval poem "Thirty Days Hath September," still recited today, has no need for the intricacy of Chaucer's *Troilus and Criseyde;* story ballads from the fourteenth and fifteenth centuries—such as the ballad of the fox who went out on the town one night, a ballad still sung—though much altered—have a directness and simplicity which give them the easy kind of timelessness. Light verse of the sort which comes down to us in the older strata of nursery rimes is equally independent of its original time and place—this, for instance:

> There was a man, he had nought;
> Thieves came and took nought;
> He ran in the street and cried nought;
> Why should he cry? He lost nought!

Comments on the Poems

And some very long and serious poems on religious or patriotic subjects are straightforward and simple, presumably because here the facts and the morality are all.

The poems brought together and modernized in the present book are all of the relatively artful or, in the best sense, artificial kind. The first four poems—*Morte Arthure, Winner and Waster, The Parliament of the Three Ages,* and *Summer Sunday*—represent high points in the "alliterative renaissance," that is, the self-conscious revival, in the fourteenth century, of some of the metrical principles of Old English poetry. (The words *revival* and *renaissance* may be misleading. Some scholars insist that there must have been a long continuum of alliterative poetry now lost. See *Sir Gawain and the Green Knight,* ll. 35–36.) It seems very likely that one reason for the return to the older meter, or at any rate the surge of new interest in it, was that the alliterative method, in which stress is signaled partly by the alliteration of initial consonants or vowels, was perfectly suited to the kind of rhetorical artifice fashionable at the time these fourteenth-century poets flourished. At all events, all four of these poems have that ornamentation and stylistic elevation which immediately marks them as poems of the court. The remaining poems here—*The Debate of Body and Soul, The Thrush and the Nightingale,* and *The Owl and the Nightingale*—are all cast (as are two of the alliterative poems) in the debate genre popular with sophisticated thirteenth- and fourteenth-century poets, and they are all, like the alliterative poems, rich in rhetorical ornamentation.

One of the pleasures to be derived from such poetry comes from watching the poet manipulate conventional materials to achieve novelty or, at best, to release some new meaning. It is conventional, for instance, to introduce a description of a May morning, focusing on the beauty of fields and flowers, on the murmuring of a river, and on the musical rivalry of birds. Sometimes (as in Chaucer's *Book of the Duchess*), the May morning may be firmly established as emblematic of resurrection or the coming of some vision; sometimes, because of the traditional pagan associations of May, the vision is of romantic love or (as in some of the poetry of the blunt Scottish Chaucerians) sex. The *Pearl*-poet twists the convention by substituting August for May and treating each of the conventional images ironically, not as emblems of rebirth but as emblems of death, then taking the conventional images straight at a later stage in his poem, using them now as images of heaven and spiritual rebirth. In the *Morte Arthure* the conventional description of a May morning, with its associations of holiness and love, is intro-

237

duced with grimly ironic effect: the knights who ride through this pleasant morning (though the month is actually not May) are on their way to battle. On the other hand, in *The Debate of Body and Soul*, as in Henryson's more famous *Testament of Cresseid*, we find an opposite convention, so to speak—the winter's night—which gains part of its effectiveness from the extreme familiarity of the emotionally antithetical convention.

Hunting scenes are equally conventional in medieval poetry. Such scenes abound in thirteenth- and fourteenth-century French poetry (a strong influence on the English tradition); and they occur in Chaucer, in *Sir Gawain and the Green Knight*, and elsewhere. As for the poems brought together in this book, hunts occur in *The Parliament of the Three Ages* and in *Summer Sunday* and are briefly referred to in other poems translated here. All of the hunts have roughly the same symbolic purpose, representing the larger quest, man's life; but no two are handled in the same way or lead to precisely the same insights or visions.

We need not dwell on particular conventions or their general significance—the dream-vision, the allegorical debate, and so forth. The point at the moment is simply that the manipulation of poetic conventions is central to the medieval poet's technique, in Italy and France, in Germany, in England. To read this poetry well one must learn to recognize the formulas, and one must watch for the poet's subtle alterations. And needless to say, there is more that is of interest in this poetry than the poets' manipulation of conventions. The poems reflect the dazzle of the courts where they were read. Whether the imagery of a given poem is symbolic or merely ornamental, it is bound to be as richly sensuous and as various as almost anything to be found in the English poetic tradition. Equally important, perhaps, the poems reflect an interest in nature and an interest in the everyday activities of men close to nature, both of which we have to some extent lost. They show a delight in irony and a skill in juggling ironic effects that may for some readers amount to a new way of thinking and feeling. And finally, even the slightest of these poems deal with themes of enduring interest. At best the poems offer new ways of seeing; at very least they give one the pleasure of glimpsing for a moment forgotten attitudes.

The Alliterative Morte Arthure

The *Morte Arthure* has sometimes been ranked with the *Pearl* and *Sir Gawain and the Green Knight* as one of the masterpieces of the fourteenth-century "alliterative renaissance." [1] The ranking is defensible, since whatever apologies one may feel one must make for the *Morte Arthure*, it remains a major poetic achievement. But the ranking is nevertheless odd. Only one complete translation of the poem exists — Andrew Boyle's prose translation published by the Everyman Library in 1912 — whereas *Pearl* and *Sir Gawain* have been translated again and again. As for scholarship, on the *Morte Arthure* we have a handful of articles, mostly on textual problems, a few passing references in books on other Arthurian matter, and, at this writing, only one book-length critical study, Professor Matthews's *The Tragedy of Arthur.*[2] On the work of the *Gawain*-poet we have dozens of articles and a number of critical books.[3] Obviously the *Morte Arthure* is not yet a favorite poem of medievalists. In fact, though the poem has been edited from the unique Thornton MS five times, no up-to-date edition of the poem was available in English until 1967, when Professor Finlayson's selective edition appeared, the most recent complete edition in any language being the relatively inaccessible work of E. Björkman (Heidelberg 1915).[4]

The greatness of the *Morte Arthure* is of a different kind from that of *Pearl* and *Sir Gawain and the Green Knight*. The *Gawain*-poet constructs elegant lines, brilliantly manipulating alliterative patterns, rhythms, and consonant and vowel relationships for maximum interpenetration of sound and sense,[5] and he elaborates imagistic and symbolic patterns as well as any poet in the English tradition.[6] He creates vital and unique characters, develops irony, pathos, and, above all, humor with a master's finesse and never slips for an instant into lapses of taste. By comparison, the man who wrote the *Morte Arthure* may seem crude. Rhythm in the *Morte Arthure* is often merely serviceable. Like the *Gawain*-poet, the *Morte Arthure*-poet uses what may be described as a sprung five-stress line with four-beat variants,[7] and he is fond (though less fond than the *Gawain*-poet) of crossed alliteration, superabundant alliteration, and the like; but in *Morte Arthure* the line sometimes lapses from superb music to what must be called slogging through the job.[8] The poet has certain phrases, such as "as hym lykez," which he uses repeatedly (as might an oral poet) to fill out a line, and

Comments on the Poems

even if one grants that these phrases are appropriate to the theme of the poem—for they are—they are obtrusive. The poet's imagery is often powerful and vivid—the dragon and bear in Arthur's first nightmare, for instance—but at times it is mechanical. As for symbolism, it is of a different kind entirely from that of the *Gawain*-poet. Instead of subtle juxtapositions of imagery, which serve to introduce ironic comment or develop allegorical implications, the *Morte Arthure*-poet generally uses bold, stark symbols not easily missed or misunderstood, and bold shifts of genre which throw basic attitudes into ironic juxtaposition—"heroic" against "romantic," "worldly" against "religious." The characterization is carefully worked out but, despite the poet's labor, not impressive compared to characterization in *Sir Gawain*. The humor in the *Morte Arthure* is gallows humor, a far cry from the dazzling, civilized humor of the *Gawain*-poet; and his moments of pathos (for instance when Arthur leaves Guinevere or when Arthur learns of the death of a duchess) are seldom completely successful.[9]

These differences are to a large extent the results of a more basic difference in the way the two poets apprehend reality; in other words, they emerge because of the kinds of subject matter each poet chooses. The virtues of the *Morte Arthure* are those of the medieval warhorse: it is slow and somewhat clumsy, sometimes inelegant, but large and powerful; and like the warhorse it holds with absolute firmness to its course. What the poet directly or indirectly borrows from Geoffrey of Monmouth and Wace, his principal forerunners in the chronicle tradition, he tightens, alters, or expands to suit his own purpose,[10] and his artistic purpose is impressive. If the *Morte Arthure* suffers by comparison to *Sir Gawain and the Green Knight*, the reverse is also true: *Sir Gawain* is a more perfect poem, but one of a lesser kind.

Sir Gawain is a sophisticated Christian comedy—a "romance"—which has little place for the heroic. It is no doubt true that if Gawain had not passed his test at the castle of temptation he would have lost his head; but Gawain does pass his test, in effect (as we were sure he would), and does not lose his head. Indeed, the very idea of the heroic is turned into comedy in *Sir Gawain*. Everywhere in heroic literature we read of centuries-old monsters brought low at last by some outstanding warrior—a Beowulf or Siegfried. How absurd, one might argue, that a monster which has tormented the world for a thousand years should be slain in the end by a paltry mortal! For the *Gawain*-poet, heroic deeds are often "too tedious to tell," or if they must be told are often recounted tongue in cheek. (Gawain does of course be-

The Alliterative Morte Arthure

have heroically at times, and the poet does not always mock him.) The goods affirmed in *Sir Gawain and the Green Knight* are for the most part civilized and Christian values: splendid counterpanes, jewels, dinners; courtly manners and entertainments; charity, loyalty, humility. These are affirmations appropriate to what Edmund Burke would call "the beautiful." They are not affirmations appropriate to "the sublime" —that is, art which seriously concerns itself with the awesome, the terrible, or, in a word, the antihuman. If we accept the general point of view advanced by Professors Höltgen and Matthews, the *Morte Arthure* is a tragedy and affirms the universal human defiance of those outer and inner forces which would destroy all that is best in the human. The poem has what Sir Gawain was never meant to have: power. The *Morte Arthure*-poet makes occasional mistakes, but his large, grim vision and the passion of his affirmation limit the importance of the mistakes.

Moreover, the mistakes are generally defensible because of the difficulty of the thing attempted and the limitation of the poet's models. With a little effort almost any man can achieve sublime vision—the powerfully charged intellectual and emotional sense of the godlike value of the human and the dreadful power of the antihuman, whether we conceive the antihuman as the realm of the old Germanic monsters, or abstract evil, or the indifference of the universe. For a sophisticated man, the difficulty lies in finding a sufficient dramatic vehicle for sublime emotion. Artists have proved repeatedly that it is virtually impossible to make monsters real if one does not believe in them. Compare the fabulous elements in the "Owain," in the *Mabinogion*, to the artifices in Chrétien's *Yvain*. Or compare the monsters in *Beowulf* to the giants of the *Morte Arthure*. We do not see Grendel but only the reactions of the men who see him, for the *Beowulf*-poet (or perhaps the tradition from which he draws) knows for certain that monsters exist but has no clear idea what they look like. The monsters in the *Morte Arthure* are made up—or, to speak precisely, are carefully culled from earlier romances for a new, allegorical use. Not really believing in them, the poet makes them stand primarily as symbols of all that is hostile to man—bestiality, cannibalism, rape, tyranny, ugliness, brute force, stupidity, allegiance to the devil. The most terrible monsters, he suggests, are those inside men, here specifically the monstrousness of spirit in such men as the wicked Lucius of Rome. Such deformity will in time infect even the archetype of royal virtue, King Arthur, whose later degenerate nature the St. Michael's giant foreshadows.

Comments on the Poems

Presenting the St. Michael's giant, the poet works in language which associates the giant with tyranny, identified later with the tyranny of Lucius and that of Arthur at the peak of his power. Consider the language here for instance:

> Then King Arthur answered the ancient woman:
> "I have come from the conqueror, the courteous and noble,
> As one of the noblest men among Arthur's knights,
> A messenger sent to amend these wrongs for the people,
> To speak with this mighty master who guards the mountain,
> And treat of terms with this tyrant, by the treasure of lands,
> To buy a truce for a time, until better may come."
>
> (ll. 985–91)

Speaking of the giant as a "mighty master" (in the original, *maister mane* [11]) and ironically describing himself as a messenger from Arthur's court who comes seeking truce, Arthur sets up an analogy between his dealings with the giant and normal diplomatic dealings. The old woman with whom he speaks answers that the giant "cares for neither rents nor for burnished gold" (l. 994; in the original: *ffor bothe landez and lythes ffulle lyttile by he settes;/Of rentez ne of rede golde rekkez he neuer . . .*). Arthur himself, in his dealings with the Romans and again with Mordred, will care for neither rents nor "rede golde"—but for nobler reasons. Ingenious juxtapositions and grim humor are hallmarks of this poet's technique, and all the subtlety of his thought derives from his fascination with the underlying similarities in things superficially disparate or the essential moral differences within things which outwardly resemble one another. The trouble with the St. Michael's Mountain scene, in short, is that the scene works intellectually as a comment upon other scenes in the poem, but lacks the powerful illusion of reality found elsewhere in the poem. There is, however, good reason for the *Morte Arthure*'s partial failure at this point—its setting in the chronicle tradition and its consequent false realism in the treatment of occasional borrowings from works of fantasy. No other scene in the poem, I think, is flawed in this way, including the romantic Priamus-Gawain scene, and there are many truly magnificent scenes—Arthur's two dreams and the whole of the opening and closing sections of the poem.

The theme of the *Morte Arthure* is pride, a theme intimately related, here as everywhere in medieval literature, to the idea of Fortune—and the poet's chief technique, as I have said, is careful juxtaposition of character against character, scene against scene. The most elaborate critical discussion of the poem is that of Professor William Matthews. It would be a misuse of space here to summarize the whole of Matthews's argument. I will simply outline it and mention certain problems raised by his reading. By internal analysis, Matthews shows that Arthur is a tragic hero whose flaw from the outset is hubris; he argues that the St. Michael's Mount giant is in a sense a figure of what Arthur will become at the height of his pride; and he claims that in the end Arthur tends to think of himself as almost another Christ. He shows in detail that certain elements of Arthur's characterization identify him with Edward III, so that the poem may be read as a criticism of that king (the identification was first pointed out by G. Neilson in 1902).[12] Then, on the theory that no English poet would dare to criticize his king in this way, Matthews suggests unconvincingly that the poem was originally a French work.[13] Two important reviews labored to demolish Matthews's reading—the reviews by J. L. N. O'Loughlin and John Finlayson (see note 2). Both pointed out that if one looks at the *Morte Arthure*-poet's sources in chronicle tradition one finds that this poet consistently heightened Arthur's wisdom and virtue, giving him every possible flattering epithet—"free," "noble," "worthy," and so forth—and by subtler means as well. At least through roughly the first half of the poem it is impossible to take these epithets as ironic. One of the reviewers pointed out that the whole argument that Arthur comes to think of himself as another Christ (an overstatement of Matthews's position) rests on Arthur's single phrase, natural in its setting, expressing a wish that he could "die for you all [his knights]." On this last point Matthews may nevertheless be right, of course; some literary evidence is visceral. Having thrown out Matthews's reading, both reviewers return to the traditional view that Arthur falls because of his sin of incest in engendering Mordred, and for no other cause whatever. (There is no suggestion of Arthur's incestuous begetting of Mordred in Geoffrey's *Historia*, Wace's *Brut*, or Lazamon's *Brut*, nor is it clearly hinted in the *Morte Arthure*.)

But Matthews was essentially correct, and Professor Höltgen, in his article, "König Arthur und Fortuna," supports Matthews's reading. Both Matthews and Höltgen seek to understand the poem by reading carefully what it says, not by imposing on it a meaning assumed from Arthurian tradition. For Höltgen, Arthur falls through trust in Fortune;[14] and what this means, in terms of the medieval tradition of Fortune, is that Arthur falls through mistaken faith in the stability of the things of this world (a form of pride). Riding higher and higher on

Fortune's wheel, Arthur forgets that he must go down again. His trag-
edy is not so much that he proudly climbs to the heights of Fortune (it
is partly that, but the climb is largely an effect on Arthur's very nature
as worthiest of the Nine Worthies). Mainly his tragedy is that he for-
gets that a king acts as God's servant, not as master in his own right. As
a result, he lapses in lawful chivalry (as Finlayson has shown), and so,
when the downswing of Fortune's wheel comes, he goes down raging,
ruining even his own homeland and vassals.

The idea of Fortune is at the heart of the poem, and not only in the
sense that Arthur's dream of Fortune's wheel marks the tragic turning
point. The idea of inevitable change is the central dramatic principle
of the work. The poem begins when Lucius of Rome is at the height of
his power and when Arthur has just finished winning back the vast sys-
tem of holdings and tributes which rightfully belong to his house.
Their clash, the fall of Lucius, and the eventual fall of Arthur in his
turn come inexorably. Again and again, the end of the poem (the fall of
Arthur) ironically echoes the beginning (Arthur's bringing down of
first a giant, then Lucius), showing the change in Arthur's situation.
Some of these echoes take the form of identical actions by Arthur
which have opposite meanings. For instance, in the opening scene King
Arthur's ferocious look terrifies the envoys of Emperor Lucius, who
have insulted Arthur into wholly righteous indignation; near the end
of the poem, when Arthur's fortune has changed and his legitimate
pride has become corrupt, leading him into wars of aggression (Fin-
layson's point), the same look silences Arthur's own Round Table.
Other echoes identify the now-corrupted Arthur with Lucius and his
like. Early in the poem Arthur is advised to put down his arms and
wear only his kirtle as he approaches an unmerciful giant (the dream-
symbol of the giant in Arthur's first nightmare is at the same time a
symbol of Lucius, according to Arthur's interpreters); later Arthur
himself is approached in exactly this way by his victims. Similarly,
the giant savagely demands Arthur's beard, and Arthur later shaves the
beards of his Roman prisoners to shame them. The wanton destruction
wrought by the overweening Lucius has its direct parallel in Arthur's
destructions near the end of his career:

> Now Arthur turns, when the time is right, to Tuscany,
> And he swiftly storms those towns with their lofty towers;
> He casts down mighty walls, wounds gentle knights,
> Topples towers, and torments the people,
> Makes many a splendid widow sing out woe

And often sink down weary, weep, wring her hands.
He wastes all with war, whatever his force rides past,
And all their wealth and their dwellings he turns to destruction.
Thus they spring on and spread, and spare but little,
Spend without sparing what took long years to save.

(ll. 3148–58)

Pivotal details midway through the poem prepare for the king's drastic change. Lucius is unexpectedly ennobled when he behaves toward Arthur's messengers with the same lordly restraint Arthur showed in his dealings earlier with the messengers of Lucius. Lucius, we discover here, is perhaps not as vicious as he seemed. And at about the same time that we are forced to modify our attitude toward Lucius, we must begin to modify our attitude toward Arthur. The Romans crying out against Arthur speak with apparent sincerity; indeed they sometimes echo the very words of Arthur's men in their complaints against Lucius:

> I scorn King Arthur and all his noble barons
> Who thus unjustly occupy these realms,
> Betraying the emperor, his earthly lord,
> All the array of the royalty of the Round Table
> Is cried against with rage in many a realm;
> He holds his revels now with Roman rents,
> But soon he'll explain himself, if all goes right with us.
>
> (ll. 1661–67)

All these sentiments have been expressed against Lucius by Arthur's men, and in almost the same language, in the council in the Giants' Tower at the start of the poem.

The same technique of comparison informs the poet's development of the relationship between Arthur's single combat with the St. Michael's giant and his war with Lucius. Various details, some straight, some ironic, identify Arthur's battle with the giant as a holy cause. The king tells Bedevere and Kay that he is seeking a saint's shrine; later the knights mock the dead "saint" and jokingly compare returning home with his remains to returning with holy relics (ll. 1163–68). The poet dilates on the idea of crossing oneself for safety (ll. 961–68, 1041); and the giant is identified with demonic or infidel forces: he is repeatedly called a "fiend," he "martyrs" children, etc. The fight is associated not only with righteous religious battle, a crusade, but also with war for political order. The giant is a "tyrant," a "powerful master," a bad vassal (cf. l. 1172, *"Be sekere of this sergeaunt, he has me sore greuede!"*—*sergeaunt* here having the meaning "vassal" or "petty lord") with whom Arthur says he will "treat for a truce." Lucius too is a tyrant, a rebel to Arthur's legitimate claim as overlord—if the claim is in fact legitimate—and he has the support of infidels and giants "engendered by friends." (After Caesar's conquest, the legitimacy of Arthur's claim is open to question. The poet's audience probably knew this and could probably consider the claim in the light of its intimate knowledge of more recent claims and counterclaims to continental territories such as Normandy and Guyenne, and even to England.) Lucius and the giant are guilty of the same crimes: Arthur fights both "by-cause of his people," i.e., to protect his people, and also because both seek tribute, Lucius a tribute of rents, the giant a more barbaric and shameful tribute, Arthur's beard. And in both cases it is Arthur's sense of his own proper dignity—as well as his responsibility—which motivates him to fight. There are still other parallels between the two battles. For instance, after destroying the giant, Arthur distributes his treasure just as, after conquering cities, he will distribute treasures and rents. But there is also a significant, though subtle, contrast: Arthur takes no credit for his victory over the giant. It was not a man's deed, he says, but God's or the Virgin's (ll. 1208–10), and in the place of the battle he erects a holy shrine. No parallel details appear when he has won his continental war; on the contrary, he resolves to go "avenge" the man who died on the cross (l. 3215), almost as though he were an equal. The lack of a parallel is no oversight. In a scene emphatically contrasting Arthur's behavior and Sir Gawain's, Gawain does give the honor of victory to God, though Priamus, his victim, would give it to Gawain (cf. ll. 2630–43, esp. l. 2643). And on the other hand, when the two beaten Romans kneeling in their kirtles ask Arthur's mercy "for the love of him who has lent you lordship on earth," Arthur says he will give mercy by his *"own* grace" (ll. 2312–18)—and grim mercy at that. As he moves through the last stages of his invasion Arthur of course himself "torments the people." (l. 3151). Exactly like the giant and like Lucius, he makes women despair and weep and wring their hands, ravages the land, takes treasures, "spoils without mercy." Both Arthur's philosophers and Arthur himself will repeatedly speak later of Arthur's "cruel deeds." Professor O'Loughlin's argument, then, that Arthur did nothing wrong except in engendering Mordred is as untenable as Matthews's argument that Arthur was wrong from the start. Yet it is true, as we shall see, that Arthur's incest is significant.

The Alliterative Morte Arthure

Large structural contrasts of the sort I have been mentioning, all emphasizing change, are supported throughout by details which illustrate in imagistic form the conflicts and oppositions which account for the doubleness of Fortune. On his way to fight the giant of St. Michael's, who has murdered a beloved lady, Arthur and his men pass a beautiful meadow. The poet's description of the place ironically recalls descriptions in the poetry of courtly love:

> They rode along the river that ran so swift,
> Where trees arched out above with regal boughs;
> The roe and the reindeer ran there recklessly,
> Revelling there in the thickets and wild rose trees;
> The groves were all in bloom with brilliant flowers,
> With falcons and cock pheasants of flaming hues;
> And all the birds there flashed as they flew on their wings,
> And there the cuckoos sang out clear in the groves,
> And with every kind of joy they cheered themselves;
> The notes of the nightingales rang out sweetly there
> As they struggled against the thrushes, three hundred at once,
> And what with the murmur of the water and singing of birds
> One might have been cured who had never been well in his life.
>
> (ll. 919–31)

In courtly-love poetry, the image of an earthly paradise where birds sing, flowers bloom, and a beautiful river flows, customarily emphasizes the unchanging nature of the place or at least the apparently unchanging nature. (For a typical example, see Chaucer's *Parliament of Birds,* ll. 183–210.) Similar descriptions abound in medieval literature —elsewhere in Chaucer, in the works of the *Gawain*-poet, in Dante and in the works of lesser continental poets, as well as in several of the poems here in this book. A standard ironic treatment of the image is that in which the garden seems immutable but in fact is not. So in Chaucer's *Legend of Good Women* (prologue), the earth has *forgotten* its "pore estat," has put winter out of mind and now sings with false confidence. It is this strain in the tradition which the *Morte Arthure*-poet employs for his own purpose. His lines on the idyllic scene (just quoted) are built of oppositions: the contrasting images of the swift river and the motionless, regal boughs; the images of hunting bird and game bird; the combative cuckoos, nightingales, and thrushes—traditional debaters. Through this scene where contrasting natures harmlessly war, a scene conventionally associated with love and revelation, Arthur and his men ride to battle far more deadly than that in which the songbirds are engaged.[15]

The same conventional image of the seeming earthly Paradise appears later (ll. 2670–75), immediately—and ironically—followed by a discovery that Sir Gawain is mortally wounded, and afterward followed by a contrasting image of the true Paradise the waters of which can raise the dead. The warning seems clear: beware the beauties and glories of mere earth.

An even more impressive yet simpler imagistic contrast comes when the splendidly garbed King Arthur meets humbly dressed Sir Craddock on the highway to Rome. As Matthews points out, Arthur's dress is an imagistic indication of his overweening pride at this point; or, to put the matter another way, the contrast of Arthur's dress and that of Sir Craddock, newly arrived from England, shows dramatically that Arthur's fortune is not what he thinks it: back home his power is crumbling. In wishing to push on beyond the original holdings of his house, and in taking all the credit himself, Arthur has begun to think with overweening pride. He imagines his power can increase indefinitely.

From the standard medieval point of view, pride is a deadly sin, the chief of the seven. But it would be a mistake to impose the standard opinion, in its usual very simple form, on the *Morte Arthure*. The poem is orthodox, but its vision is not a simple one. Here pride takes three forms. First there is that legitimate sense of dignity and importance a great conqueror experiences after bringing a vast empire to the rule of Christian law. He takes just and reasonable pride not only in his own accomplishments but also in the achievement of his men, and his insistence upon his dignity is not a matter of selfishness but the mark of his power and an effect of his deep love for his people.[16] The opening catalog of Arthur's conquests—a longer catalog than one finds in any of the earlier Arthurian works—is introduced specifically to establish Arthur's legitimate greatness; and the whole scene in which Arthur consults his knights indicates his love for them and theirs for him, as well as the legitimacy of his anger at Lucius's unjustified demand for tribute. The splendid feast Arthur gives for the envoys has in it all the waste and show lamented in *The Parliament of the Three Ages* and in *Winner and Waster*, and perhaps it points forward to that selfish pleasure which will mark Arthur's later corruption, but it is entirely legitimate by virtue of its purpose: by means of this display of wealth and power Arthur hopes to dissuade Lucius from attacking him. Arthur's harsh and vindictive treatment of the messengers from Rome may foreshadow a later cruel streak, but it is not cruelty here; it is justified by purpose. Lucius is to understand that Arthur can make a dangerous enemy. But as the poem progresses—as I have said—the inner or moral meaning of events begins to be obscure. For instance, midway through the poem Arthur delivers a speech on the inappropriateness of a king's ransoming prisoners. His position is unselfish insofar as gathering ransom is mere acquisitiveness—the very fault to which Arthur will come when he adopts his plan of world conquest (or so his philosophers tell him)—but the speech also may reflect the king's exaggerated sense of his personal dignity. Since captives are unworthy of audience with kings, he says, they ought to be exiled or thrown into dungeons to await the king's decision. Soon after this we encounter Arthur's opinion, delivered with great scorn to a soldier at his side, that no mere archer could possibly be so blessed by Fortune as to strike a king or his horse. The notion is not especially uncommon in medieval thought, but Arthur's attitude, his rash faith in his own luck, his faith that it will support him even in technically illegal wars, nevertheless parallels the pride of young Priamus and stands in striking contrast to Gawain's attitude.[17] Having overthrown the "proud" (as the poet insists) young Priamus, Gawain seeks to preserve Priamus's dignity by declaring that he, Gawain, is no one important, merely a tailor to the king, so that Priamus has lost no honor to another knight. Priamus is incredulous at the thought that he might be beaten by a commoner and at last forces Gawain to admit his true identity. But even when Gawain has done so, Gawain insists that the honor is God's, and that the victory is only luck (l. 2642), implying that Priamus might as easily have been lucky.

As Matthews rightly argues, by this time there is a touch of selfish pride even in King Arthur's magnanimity. At the siege of Metz the king graciously grants his peace not only to the ladies who come to beg mercy but to every man, woman, and child in the city; but the poet emphasizes details which throw ironic light on the kindness of the king. Arthur delivers his mercy from high on a splendidly covered horse, and he is dressed in his most glorious apparel. The siege itself, moreover, is presented in curious terms:

> Then boldly they attack and they bend back their engines
> Loaded heavy with stones, and they prove their casts;
> Convents and hospitals they smash to the earth,
> And the fairest of churches and lovely chalk-white chapels;
> Huge stone steeples come smashing down into the streets
> And chambers with wide chimneys, and many chief halls;
> And they smashed and pelted down those plaster walls,
> And the grief of the people was a pitiful thing to hear!
>
> (ll. 3034–41)

Comments on the Poems

These are the only details selected. The siege is just and necessary, but the poet's whole focus is on the accidental destruction of the innocent —converts, hospitals, churches, homes.

The legitimate pride with which Arthur began resulted in defensive, hence justifiable, war against Lucius, a usurper and a tormenter of Arthur's people. But Arthur's decaying pride leads him, as I have said, to plan a war of conquest: he intends to capture all the world, revel on its tributes, and at last avenge the Knight who was murdered on the cross. Mordred's treason cancels that plan—Arthur's wheel has begun to descend—and King Arthur is driven to the final pitch of sinful pride, and emotion at once noble and terrible, which is to say, tragic. Though still described with flattering epithets, he becomes now, as did Achilles once, raw outrage, neither selfish nor selfless in the usual sense of selflessness. He does not fight his final battle for the sake of his people—indeed, the Round Table is against the rash action which is certain to destroy the kingdom. Arthur fights out of personal wrath, to avenge the death of a man he loved and destroy a world intolerable to those who affirm—sinfully, from a Christian point of view—the supreme value of the human. His vengeance vow is profoundly personal, particularly if one compares the formal vows of Cador and the rest at the start of the poem, or the vows of Gawain. Here pride has gone mad, but the madness is unquestionably noble. Vanished utterly is the objective and reasonable concern with justice for his people, the concern displayed in his first formal council in the Giants' Tower; and gone, too, is the concern with wise strategy which once made Arthur lash out at the rash young Sir Cador. What is left is rage: at the pagan and demonic forces which circle his kingdom on every side, at Mordred and all who have betrayed from within, and at himself, finally for his own "cruel deeds," which he takes to be the cause of his downfall. And so he kills Mordred, dies himself, and leaves the kingdom in ruin.

The earlier scenes in the *Morte Arthure,* full of boasts and vows of revenge, battles, deaths, and moments of tenderness, may operate at first mainly as adventure. But these scenes gain new interest when one rereads them after finishing the poem, for nothing here is mere filler. The boasts and vows in the earlier scenes establish the basis for boasts and vows with very different moral implications. The battle scenes set up the favorable view of war which the poem is to reverse and establish the importance of thematically significant characters, especially the model knight, Sir Gawain; and the early battle scenes at the same time elaborate the complex revenge motif. Guinevere's farewell to Arthur intensifies the effect of her later betrayal; but, more important,

The Alliterative Morte Arthure

it lays the groundwork for contrasting farewells—Kay's leave-taking at the time of his death, Gawain's splendid last speech to his men, Mordred's farewell over the dead Gawain, Arthur's angry farewell to Mordred, and the nation's farewell to Arthur at the end of the poem.

Moreover, when one looks more closely at the earlier scenes, one discovers that they are the work of a poet with a keen sense of dramatic method. Consider the glorification of Arthur in the opening movement. The poet's brief "argument" of the poem (ll. 12–25) insists on the virtue and dignity of his characters. They were "loyal in their religion" (*lele in theire lawe*, a phrase which can have wider meaning than my translation preserves); they were circumspect in their works, kind, courteous, aware of the customs of court, and earned many honors. Here as everywhere in the poem, the poet's emphasis is on the greatness of Arthur which makes his fall so terrible. He of course says nothing yet of the reasons for Arthur's fall—they are allowed to emerge dramatically as the poem progresses. But the fact that he does not include them in his argument should not be construed as evidence that he is indifferent to them. The poet's argument ignores the whole final third of the poem—the fall from greatness. In lines 26–51 the legendary sway of Arthur at the height of his power is considerably increased from earlier tradition, and it is moved back in time: the poet gives it to Uther Pendragon, Arthur's father. Arthur is thus transformed from an empire builder, a man who might be suspected of overweening pride, to a defender and protector of his own. Here and elsewhere, the borrowings from Charlemagne and Alexander romances are one of many indications of the English poet's concern with elevating Arthur above all other worthies. Now the poet shifts from a list of conquests already made to conquests being made. And finally, with the pause provided by Arthur's Christmastime revels at Carlisle, the poet shifts from summary to fully elaborated dramatic presentation. His last strictly general remark in this section has the right weight as a terminus and is interesting in other ways as well: "Never in any man's time was more festivity/Made in the western marches in midwinter." The lines (76–77) invite comparison with the lines in the later *Sir Gawain and the Green Knight* (*GGK*, 1380–81) in which Gawain remarks that he has never seen such a kill of deer "this seven years in the winter season." In *Sir Gawain* the emphasis is on the unnatural, perhaps magical winter abundance. In the *Morte Arthure* the emphasis is rather on the extraordinary, even heroic, but not unnatural, glory of Arthur's feast.

Arthur's revels are interrupted by a senator from Rome, and

here the poet finds new ways of glorifying Arthur. The senator addresses Arthur boldly, as he would address a petty vassal in Lucius's name, and Arthur responds with a look of wrath which makes the mighty Romans cower before him. The Romans beg to be forgiven, claiming they merely do their duty to Lucius, whom they fear. Arthur not unnaturally calls them cowards and says: "There is a certain man in this hall [who] if he were sorely vexed, you would not look [at] once for all Lombardy." Thus with a grimly ironic circumlocution and then a direct slap, Arthur answers the senator's excuse. By "a certain man" he of course means himself: the allusion to Lombardy is a bald reference to what Arthur takes for the real reason for the senator's coming—his hope of winning some feudal estate from his emperor. The sneering charge is one Arthur makes repeatedly—for example again at l. 460. The cowardly messenger's next words instantly admit that Arthur is indeed a greater king than Lucius—"You're the lordliest man I have ever looked upon!"—an exclamation easily construed as another lapse in faith to Lucius, motivated by fear of the even greater King Arthur. But the messenger's fear is not introduced merely for comic effect. His fear contrasts with Arthur's respect for the great Lucius, whom he does not fear but whose messengers he honors for the sake of Lucius's noble blood. There is no suggestion, in this early scene, of overweening pride in Arthur: the poet rules that out by every possible means, including Arthur's consultation with his men (a traditional detail). Arthur's wrath is greater here than in the source, but this does not point to a tragic flaw. The poet's heightening of the King's anger increases the importance of Arthur's setting personal vengeance aside (ll. 150–51).

After seven days of feasting and entertaining the Roman senator, showing him an apparent friendliness which encourages him to bring up his business once again with "austeryne wordez"—somber, grave, or grievous words—Arthur suddenly and terribly changes his manner, showing his true colors. Acting with full consent of his parliament, he speaks to the senator with bald scorn. He mocks Rome's power, then directly mocks the senator and his company, comically rushing him out of the country, feigning revulsion at the "obscene" habits of foreigners. The senator again shows his timidity (ll. 467–74). Then the poet rings a change: the senator boldly stands up to King Lucius (ll. 514–52), asserting Arthur's greatness, even his virtue. The senator is not a complete coward after all; what he has heretofore shown is natural fear of a man of extraordinary power.

252

The Alliterative Morte Arthure

The poet's characterization of the senator is only one of many devices introduced for Arthur's glorification. In lines 212–15 the poet speaks of Arthur's goblets, made of gold and studded with gems, which are proof against any poison. The idea here—a medieval commonplace —is that by their nature precious jewels will either cancel the effect of poison or else explode at its touch. (The same idea appears in the alliterative *Purity*.) Notice the lines which immediately follow:

> And the conqueror stood, himself, in gleaming array,
> All clad in clean gold colors, together with his knights,
> And wearing his diadem there on that splendid dais,
> And was judged the mightiest monarch alive on earth.
>
> (ll. 216–19)

The implied analogy between the goblets and the king is difficult to miss: both are clad in gold; whereas the cups have gems, Arthur has his diadem; the cups even share Arthur's most obvious quality in the opening movement of the poem, righteous wrath: "For the bright gold, in its wrath, would burst into pieces." Arthur in his wrath, on the other hand, "casts colors" (*keste colours*) and burns like a glowing coal, as would a gem (ll. 117–18).

But glorification of Arthur is not the poet's only concern in the opening movement. If Arthur is the greatest of the Nine Worthies, a man in whom there can be no poison (as the juxtaposition of the goblets and the king appears to suggest), he will finally prove no more invulnerable to Fortune's power than other men. His eventual fall is foreshadowed and in part explained in the opening movement, and again the poet's main technique is subtle juxtaposition. Consider carefully lines 553–691. At first glance we see only contrast. The poet focuses on Lucius's assembling of his forces (ll. 553–623), then on Arthur's assembling of his. Lucius's tyrannical power is emphasized; Arthur, in contrast speaks with Parliament's sanction at the feast of St. Hilary, one of the four terms when common-law cases were traditionally heard. But the passage on Lucius's preparations ends with emphasis on monstrous progeny—giants "engendered by fiends," witches and warlocks, often viewed in the Middle Ages (as is Malory's Merlin) as the offspring of devils; the Arthurian section ends with focus on Mordred. The poet does not insist on the dangerous potential of Mordred; he does not need to—the story is familiar to his audience. But much is said of his watching over Guinevere (he will later become her lover), and the phrase "childe of my chambyre," which has a number of meanings, is in one sense grimly fitting. For all his great virtue, Arthur is tainted by an old mistake. Gross and obvious bastardy is associated with Lucius's forces, but Arthur's house is also subtly infected.

Arthur's dream of the dragon and bear prepares in another way for his fall. Medieval tradition on the dragon is of a double nature: the dragon is sometimes identified in scriptural exegesis with creative power or monarchy (much as in Chinese tradition), sometimes with destruction and/or evil. See Ezek. 29:3, 32:2, where the dragon is an emblem of Egypt; Jer. 51:34, where it is the emblem of Nebuchadnezzar. In Isaiah it is repeatedly used as an emblem of destruction, as it is in Rev. 12:3 ff and elsewhere. It is sometimes identified with the Eden serpent (see Exod. 7:9-12) or directly with the devil. So in Chaucer, the *Canon's Yeoman's Tale* (Frag. 8, 1435-38).[18] The bear in exegetical tradition is an emblem of ferocity second only to the lion, but unlike the lion it is not used in scripture as an emblem of proper or righteous ferocity. It attacks sheep (1 Sam. 17:34-36), sheep being in turn an emblem of mankind, God's flock; and the fact that it should at last be subdued was one of the wonders of the Messiah's kingdom (e.g., Isa. 11:7). Because of the bear's upright stance, etc., the bear is viewed in folk tradition as a deformed sort of man.

The imagistic identification of the dragon with Arthur, the bear with the St. Michael's giant and also with Lucius's host (ll. 823-25) is carefully worked out. The dragon is beautiful and stately as well as terrible in its strength (ll. 760-72, 786-98); the bear is gross and misshapen, easily identified with the unnaturalness of Lucius's army (ll. 611 ff.) and with the ugliness of the St. Michael's giant, who is also stocky, bowlegged, and foamy-mouthed (ll. 1073-1102). The traditional ambiguity in the image of the dragon—an ambiguity perhaps inherent in the image—is obviously fitting for a king who is the very model of royal virtue but will one day become tyrannical. The ambiguity comes clear, of course, only when we have the hindsight afforded by the last third of the poem. But there are hints, at least, earlier. When the Viscount of Valence charges the Welsh King (ll. 2049 ff.), he carries a dragon "As a sign that our sovereign lord [Arthur] should be destroyed . . . For there can be nothing but death where the dragon is raised." The explication of the heraldic symbol is at least curious set beside the philosopher's explication of the dream symbol.

As a footnote to the above discussion of the poet's sense of the

The Alliterative Morte Arthure

dramatic it might be added that even when the poet is not at his best his scenes have many attractive features. The poet can handle battle scenes better than can many a writer, certainly better than Malory, and he knows how to handle many kinds of fighting—on the battlefield, in the siege of a city, or on warships. The deploying of forces, the skirmishes, mass battles, and single encounters all come through distinctly and forcefully, controlled by a skillful alternation of panoramic and close-up camera shots. To present-day taste the poet's fervent patriotism and partisanship—shown in his frequent use of phrases like "our knights," "our valiant barons," or "our king"—may be distracting; but the poet is surely right. He is not merely cutting down psychic distance but is also insisting that the battle is between the powers of light and the powers of darkness. Lucius's army is an army of pagans, devils, and monsters. His hosts ride not on horses, normally, but on camels and elephants. (The point is Matthews's.) The phrase "our king" and the flattering epithets continue to ring out emphatically even after the fighter of devils has become, himself, a kind of devil, and the tragic irony is impressive.

The poem of course gains additional interest from the fact that its central character is partly drawn from life. As I have said, following Nielson and Matthews, the character of King Arthur is in part based on the character of King Edward III.[19] The list of Arthur's conquests at the start of the poem does not follow the list found in the chronicles but is influenced by the list of Edward's claims or conquests; many of the names in the poem are not Arthurian but belong to Edward's time—the Montagues, for instance—and many of the enemy armies are not traditional enemies of Arthur but enemies of Edward—the Prussians, Lithuanians, and Genoans. Arthur's battle at Sessoynes closely matches Edward's battle of Crécy, and Arthur's siege of Metz parallels Edward's siege of Calais. One parallel pointed out by Matthews is particularly striking. Just as at Metz Arthur grants mercy to the countess and her ladies, so at Calais King Edward, sitting under a scarlet canopy of state, granted mercy to Queen Philippa and her ladies. There are also interesting lesser details, for instance the description of Arthur's beard in *Morte Arthure*, which recalls the description of Edward's beard in *Winner and Waster*. We need not pause over all the parallels. It is enough to say that if the reader takes upon himself as well as he can the psychological set of the poet's original audience, the *Morte Arthure* becomes an even richer experience. The battle scenes lose the repetitiveness they sometimes have as art-in-isolation;

the exclamations of "our king" gather still greater force; and the dissolution resulting from Arthur's pride—and prophesied as the outcome of Edward's pride—takes on greater immediacy. This is not to say that the power of the poem lies chiefly in what may have been its immediate political purpose. It is to say that the reader who enters into the situation behind the poem—here as in the case of, say, Yeats's "Easter, 1916"—will appreciate more than the reader who does not.

Winner and Waster

The sole surviving manuscript of *Winner and Waster* is incomplete and so corrupt that the reading of a line must sometimes be sheer guesswork. Sir Israel Gollancz, who edited the manuscript, suggested that the version we have must have been copied from a manuscript already corrupt and illegible in many places, possibly—Gollancz says—as a result of lying in a minstrel's wallet. There is every likelihood that the poem was originally a tactful political complaint to King Edward III, written for presentation to the king on some specific occasion, perhaps around 1352–53,[20] but the piece was apparently seized by traveling minstrels and used as an entertainment. The lines signaling intermissions for drinking are perhaps the interpolations of a minstrel.[21] They interrupt the poem at more or less arbitrary points, not pointing up structure but merely breaking in without warning or transition to relieve a restless audience—surely not the courtly audience which received *The Alliterative Morte Arthure, The Parliament of the Three Ages,* or *Sir Gawain and the Green Knight.* It would not be surprising to see this political poem turned to wider use, for all that is specific here works beautifully outside the political context which led to its composition.

The theme of the poem, as the title indicates, is winning and wasting.[22] Here the word winning means, finally, any kind of growth, gain, or preservation; and wasting means not merely wanton destruction but any kind of consumption of wealth or goods, whether by the hungry, by revelers, by everyday use, or by time and natural process. Few ideas held more fascination for medieval thinkers than the interdependence of winning and wasting. As Aristotle taught the Middle Ages, generation implies corruption. The seedling implies the rotted flower, hoarding implies spending. What makes the paradox most striking is that while neither can exist without the other, winning (in whatever manifestation) is the deadly enemy of wasting, and wasting the deadly enemy of winning. The careful merchant feels contempt at sight of the profligate; the courtly reveler abhors the skinflint; the rich hate the poor, and poor men hate the rich. The question, then, is how society is to function without open strife between its two necessary components. Ultimately, for this poet, the question is religious. In heaven, the realm of the immutable, no such tension exists, and the more violent the opposition becomes on earth, the nearer we are drawing toward Doomsday. On the political level the question is one of finding the monarch's proper stance as Christian and as lord; on the level of private morality it is a question of finding the good life.

The poet's treatment of the theme is ingenious. He builds his poem out of old conventions: after the prologue, a typical May morning walk leads as usual to a dream-vision; and within the dream come first a conventional scene of armies drawn up in battle array and then, instead of battle, a formal debate followed by the opinion of the judge. Each of the conventions is adjusted to its new thematic purpose. The prologue presents the actual state of affairs in the world, so absolute and violent an opposition between winning and wasting that one cannot make out whether Doomsday is only near or already upon us. On his walk the poet finds the temperate balance of Nature. The "many fair flowers" which make walking a pleasure are bent down as one walks among them, and the pleasant singing of the birds is balanced by the disquieting rattle of the rough, wild stream. In the dream, the hosts drawn up for battle are at once beautiful and dangerous, and the outrage each feels at sight of the other neatly dramatizes the real opposition of the two great forces in the world. On the side of Winner there are men of France, Lorraine, Lombardy, Low Spain, and Westphalia (i.e., merchants granted English free trade in the poet's time); merchants of England and Ireland; and churchmen, evidently more concerned with the treasures of earth than with those of heaven. On the side of Waster are gay young squires, bowmen, many of the landed gentry—those who disperse the wealth and power of the kingdom. The armies are ready to do battle, and once they begin, the poet says, the end must be total destruction. But the world of the dream is not the world of the prologue; it is the world as it ought to be. Here the king is wise and patient—instead of battle, a formal debate and the judgment of the king.

The chief social problem the poet examines is that inevitable and deep hostility of rich and poor which raises the possibility of society's destruction. The poor live off the rich, whom they hate, just as the rich live off the poor, whom they hate; yet by their nature neither the rich nor the poor could survive without the other. On one hand, as Waster points out,

> If birds should fly about free and should never be troubled
> And if wild beasts wallowed in the woods the length of their lives,
> And if fish floated free in the flood, each feeding the other,
> Then a ha'penny'd buy you a hen within half a year,
> And not a lad left in the land to serve a lord!

In other words, economic gain depends upon the seizure of land and oppression of the poor. Allowed to hunt freely, all game preserves and game laws abandoned, the poor would have no need of the rich. But on the other hand, a lack of concern about winning or preserving must lead to the impoverishment of the earth:

> [You] sell wood cord after cord in a little while,
> Both the oak and the ash and everything else that grows;
> Only the sprouts and the saplings are saved for your children,
> And you say God will grant, by His grace, that they grow in the end
> To give some shade to your sons. The shame is your own!
> And you need not save the soil, for you're sure you will sell it.
> Your forefathers were glad, whenever a friend came,
> To take them into the thickets and show them the coverts,
> And in every holt they knew they could find a hare
> And knew they might lure in many fat bucks to the lawn
> To catch and release once more, to lighten their hearts.
> But now all is auctioned and sold—ah, more's the pity!

Society needs its winners, then, who cultivate the land, store up goods, and advance the kingdom. At the same time those psychological qualities which create a winner tend to make the winner a selfish man, an oppressor of the poor, and, worst of all, a man incapable of enjoying anything beautiful or good. As Waster says in righteous indignation:

> But you, you niggards!—however you sleep at night,
> You start in the middle of a snore and spring to your haunches;
> At once you look out at the weather and rue the day
> You painted your houses and gave a few shirts to your servants.
> And therefore, Winner, you wickedly waste your time,
> For one good, cheerful day you will never get.

Winner and Waster

There can be no civilization without winners, but a society of winners would be uncivilized.

To recognize that the opposition of winners and wasters is psychological, a profound difference in ways of thinking and feeling, is to see that the solution of William Langland—a usual medieval solution —will not do. One cannot command individual men, upon peril of their souls, to follow reason and find the mean between winning and wasting. Society must be pluralistic, and order must come from government, the single will (as Dante says) which resolves the many wills.

This is not to deny the value of individual morality. One feels in the prologue the poet's commitment to the old-fashioned values, as well as the poet's painful sense of how old-fashioned his opinions must seem. He laments the loss of old loyalties and the old-fashioned morality through the influence of the cities, and he rails against the decline of art and the triviality of courtly interests. But the poet does not insist that every man should behave in one way. The focus is rather on every man's working honestly in the way that suits him. Whether one is speaking of Troy or of Britain or of the individual soul, the greater danger is "treason from within," and the great sign that times are bad is that

> . . . all our dealings are willfulness and craft,
> All sly and wily words, each tricking the other;
> And there is no friendship, but only faintheartedness.

The good life thus seems not to lie in choosing the side of Winner or the side of Waster, and neither does it lie in a choice of the mean between the two; it apparently comes with knowing one's nature and station, and honestly pursuing one's natural course.

The idea that the good life is not the same for every man provides a clue to the hatred man feels for his neighbor. John Speirs points out that both Winner and Waster accept the Christian code, each explicitly calling upon the seven deadly sins in his attack on the other. Winner accuses Waster of Pride, Gluttony, and Sloth, among other things; and according to Waster, Winner is guilty of Avarice and, worse, "Wanhope," or Despair. Clearly the accusations are just. The irony is that each side dearly loves its own sins, yet honestly finds the other's sins revolting. The poet is not disparaging the Christian standard. He is pointing to the well-known truth that the Christian standard is ideal, impossible perfectly to achieve in a fallen world. (It is righteousness that makes charity necessary.) And if temperamental differences lead to different standards within the Christian scheme, they lead to still sharper differences between Christian values and the values of courtly love. Winner attacks women's expensive dress by holding up the example of the Virgin's humility:

> Let whoever likes look on her, our Lady of heaven,
> How once she fled in fear, away from her people,
> And rode on an ambling ass, without any more pomp
> Than a baby at her breast, and a broken halter
> That Joseph held in his hand, to guard that Prince.
> Though she ruled all the world, her robe was poor,
> To give her example to us.

This opinion is standard in medieval thought, but Waster's reply is equally standard:

> It is only right that a lover should care for his lady
> And beautify her form and so bring her heart joy.
> She will love him alone as well as she loves her own life
> And make him brave and bold-hearted in time of battle,
> A man who shuns scandal and shame where soldiers encounter.

There is no reason to believe that in giving this argument to Waster the poet has any ironic or satiric purpose. One finds the same view of courtly love as a morally uplifting force almost everywhere one looks in medieval literature—in Chaucer, for instance;

> Men reden nat that folk han gretter wit
> Than they that han be most with love ynome;
> And strengest folk ben therwith overcome,
> The worthiest and grettest of degree:
> This was, and is, and yet men shal it see.
> And trewelich it sit wel to be so.
> For alderwisest han therwith ben plesed;
> And they that han ben aldermost in wo,
> With love han ben comforted moost and esed;
> And ofte it hath the cruel herte apesed,
> And worthi folk maad worthier of name,
> And causeth moost to dreden vice and shame.
> (*Troilus and Criseyde*, 1, 241–52)

Where two noble codes stand in conflict, the resolution must again be charity. But in the end one can no more command men to be

260

charitable than one can command them to be reasonable, although one may hope for charity and reason in a few. The wise king's solution is to separate his two servants, Winner and Waster, giving each of them work which suits his talents and sending each to the place in which he will be most loved. Never again are they to meet. Ideally, society ought to be grounded on love and mutual respect, the poet says; but fortunately—given the nature of the world and the nature of man—love and mutual respect are apparently not essential to social order.

Thus the poet reflects that strain of medieval political thought which looks forward, however dimly, to Hobbes and Spinoza. One need not have "good" men to have a good society; indeed, if there are different and mutually exclusive forms of the good life, no man is justified in moral absolutism. What society does require is wise kingship capable of resolving the conflicting forces in the nation for the common profit. Read in its historical setting, *Winner and Waster* is a poem lamenting King Edward's failure to perform such a function. Professor Gollancz has pointed out in his edition of the poem that we may date the work, by internal evidence, as belonging to the year 1352, an opinion supported by J. M. Steadman (see note 20). The king, Edward III, has fostered and fed the disputants these five and twenty years; there is allusion to the apparently recent Statute of Treasons (1352), lines 130–33; and there are many other contemporary allusions. (For details see Gollancz's introduction.)

The king is criticized not only for his failure to bring order (outside the dream world) but also for his personal involvement in the worst features of both winning and wasting. On one hand, Edward's love of magnificent display involved him in heavy expenditure and made him, in a sense, the very emblem of Waster; on the other hand, his ways of covering the expense—his commercialism, his unpopular taxes, his Free Trade policy, etc.,—aligned him with Winner. His emissary in the poem, the Black Prince (if Gollancz's identification is correct), was a profligate hounded by overwhelming debt from the battle of Crécy to the time of his death; and the "wild man" beside the king's pavilion, probably to be considered a Garter Herald or Master of the Ceremonies, fittingly sums up in his own strange figure the disparity between England's two extremes, the hermit or "wight of the woods," on one hand, and, on the other, the splendid life of Windsor Palace, seen at its most extravagant in the ceremonies of the Garter.

The Parliament of the Three Ages

Structurally, *The Parliament of the Three Ages* is one of the more interesting of the short poems that have come down to us from the alliterative renaissance, though it cannot be called a masterpiece of lyricism or moment by moment intensity. It makes a good companion piece to *Winner and Waster*, though it is not a work by the same writer.[23] But whereas *Winner and Waster* is essentially an exploration of political and social questions, the *Parliament* examines winning and wasting in terms of private morality and religion. One result is a major difference in tone. If society is to endure, winning and wasting must find a wise balance; but no balance, however firm, can defend the individual man from death. All the labor of winning and all the pleasures of wasting must at last prove vanity.

The interest of the poem lies not in its complexity or philosophical novelty—it is neither complex nor philosophically original—but, first, in the force and clarity of a few of its images and scenes, and second, in the leisurely but structurally neat development of the argument.

The poem opens with a hunt, a young man's excursion just at dawn on a fair May morning to poach whatever sort of deer his luck may bring him. There is no reason to suppose, as does one critic, that the hunter is Jack-in-the-green or the May King, that the stag he kills has ritual significance, or that the dream which follows the killing of the stag is in fact an "illusion" brought by the stag as messenger from the faerie world.[24] It is certainly true, however, that the realistic hunt has vague overtones, symbolic implications carefully left undefined for the moment. From the outset the hunt is like a man's pursuit of fortune or luck; the stage is "lyally served" by a buck, not because the stag is in fact mythic, but because the shooting of the kinglike stag is meant to suggest very faintly the struggling of men on Fortune's wheel, to be introduced later.

The illegal hunt is a metaphor for life—or at all events becomes such a metaphor for the dreamer. The hunter is both Waster and Winner, the one as proud stalker and destroyer of what is not his own, the other as crafty and avaricious guardian of the hidden meat and horns. But he is something more, too: a man who, after his hunt—his act of sinful concupiscence—is tired and afraid. In the anxiety dream or *somnium animale* which comes to him, the three intermingled qualities of his character and situation, that is Wasting, Winning, and

Summer Sunday

insecurity, are abstracted into the Three Ages—Youth, Middle Age, and Old Age.

In the dream debate, Youth and Middle Age—Waster and Winner respectively—argue their proper virtues, and each shows forcefully the folly of the other. Youth is all idealism and extravagance, Middle Age all practical sense and security. But in Old Age both Youth and Middle Age see their mirror, as Old Age says. Both Wasting and Winning are at last mere vanity; all the pleasures of life—including the pleasure one hopes for but misses in old age, namely wisdom—give way at last to fear of death, remorse, envy, and wrath. Thus life has gone since time began, throughout the Three Ages of the World: Fortune raised up and then struck down three pagan worthies during the Youth of the world; she raised and then struck down three Hebrew worthies in the world's Middle Age; and during the Old Age of the world, now drawing to its close, Fortune raised and Death struck down three Christian emperors.[25]

Thus in two ways, through the history of a man and the history of the world, the poet makes his gloomy case: All is vanity. He does not deny for a moment the beauty of Youth's romantic idealism or the rich pleasure of Middle Age. It is beauty that makes doom terrible, and doom that gives beauty its intensity.

Summer Sunday

Summer Sunday is the most intricate and ornate of the poems modernized here. Stanzas are linked by verbal repetition (as are stanzas in the *Pearl* and some other poems of the fourteenth and fifteenth centuries); alliteration is carried to an extreme, with the result that meter is exploded into a kind of free verse in the long lines; and in the short-line sequences midway through the poem repetition becomes so complex as to defy translation:

> *Be kynde* to it me com
> to cleyme kyngene *kyngdom,*
> *kyngdom by kynde.*
> to me þe whel *wile wynde.*
> *wynd wel,* worþliche wyȝth;
> fare fortune, frendene *flyȝth*
> *flitte* forþ *flyȝtte*
> on þe selue sete to *sitte.*

263

(*Be kynde* is repeated from the last line of the preceding stanza, and *sitte* is repeated in the first line of the stanza following.) As in all the alliterative poems in this collection, *Summer Sunday* makes brilliant use of old conventions—the hunt, the dream vision, the wheel of Fortune scene, and so forth. It seems hardly necessary to comment on how the poem's three main sections are interrelated, both imagistically (through the figure of the circle) and thematically. Suffice it to say that in its gold and silver way *Summer Sunday* is one of the most beautiful lyrics in Middle English.

The original occasion of the poem is a matter of uncertainty. Associating the poem's concluding section with the exile of Edward II, Carleton Brown has urged that *Summer Sunday* was written at the time of that king's death.[26] But some scholars are dissatisfied with this opinion. Some date the poem around 1400 and identify the king as Richard II. The poem shows every sign of coming at the height of the alliterative renaissance rather than at the beginning. Its manipulation of conventions seems to look back, not forward, to the *Morte Arthure*, where another great version of the Fortune's wheel convention is found; to the *Parliament of the Three Ages*, with its similar symbolic use of the hunt; and to *Winner and Waster*, probably the earliest of these poems, and if so, the first to use the kind of symbolic juxtaposition which all the poems have in common.

The Debate of Body and Soul

Most of the poems brought together in this book reflect medieval Christianity at what we now think of as its best—as an advanced religion capable of profound moral, ethical, and social insight, inspired by belief in the actual existence of an absolute good, but untrammeled by superstitious alarm. The side of medieval Christianity which we now prefer, adopted—as much from Neoplatonic thought as from Judaism or the New Testament—a concern with good and a tendency to see evil less as an opposite to good than as a deficiency of good, a departure toward death and chaos, that is, toward mere substance, or Plotinus's "indeterminate principle."[27] But a second and equally vital strain of thought was available to men of the Middle Ages by way of scripture, Germanic myth, classical poetry, the tradition of witchcraft, and the medieval development of Plato's vision. It was a strain popularized by Pope Gregory and later writers, among them Dante,

The Debate of Body and Soul

who found the air full of angels, the ground peopled by monstrous creatures bent upon destroying man or hounding him eternally for his sins. Chaucer usually ignored this strain. The *Gawain*-poet turns to hellfire only once, in *Purity*, where his focus is less on hell's horror than on ways in which hell can be reasonably understood and justified. Dante, however, did not neglect hell's terror and pain, though he turned hell's torture into self-torture and hell into the embodiment of real psychological states.

Numerous surviving minor poems in Middle English celebrate the darker strain in medieval Christianity. There are the splendid, spine-tingling tales told by Robert Mannyng of Brunne in *Handlyng Synne*, there are saints' lives, and much more. From the standpoint of the critic or aesthetician, the interesting question is the extent to which these poems have, for the reader, changed in character with the decline of what we call superstition—in other words the extent to which they remain emotionally effective.

In one respect, *The Debate of Body and Soul* has probably changed as drastically as, say, Halloween. Originally, this poem was both a serious religious exhortation and a brimstone thriller. The ideas are absolutely orthodox—that men go to hell for their sins, that Christ can redeem only those who cry out while yet alive (a point under debate in the poet's time), and that the punishment will be appropriate to the crime. Many of the poem's details on hell's torment can be found in one of the superb Old English homilies. But if a part of the poem's original power may be gone for most modern readers, other qualities remain. The opening debate is extremely well done and concerns an opposition of values still meaningful. What gives the poem its chief interest, however, is the vividness of the imagery, the dramatic conflict of the body and the soul, the sophisticated intelligence of the argument, the fiendishness of the fiends, and the surprise ending. Certainly the medieval reader, like the modern reader, read the poem to frighten himself. We are probably much less frightened, but the essential quality of the poem has not changed.

The poem shows less concern with style than most of the poems brought together here. The rhyme scheme is demanding (and also effective: the frequently recurring rhymes contribute to the darkness of tone) but it is not a scheme so difficult that it explains a shift, in one stanza, from *abababab* to *aaaabbbb*. The syntax is slightly crabbed throughout. The poet's energy has gone mainly into the overall structure of the narrative, the rhetoric, and the imagery, those qualities which tend as much to delight as to instruct.

The Thrush and the Nightingale

The Thrush and the Nightingale is included here not because it has
any great aesthetic merit but mainly because it illuminates *The Owl
and the Nightingale*. In the first place, it is one of the better examples
of the debate, closely adhering to the conventions of the Latin and
French models. Like the formal Latin debates (and like *The Debate of
Body and Soul*), the poem presents speeches completed within the
stanza; it makes no pretense of characterizing the debaters but allows
them to stand as simple emblems; and except in the first stanza, which
is borrowed, it offers relatively little imagistic or lyrical interest. The
discussion itself—a catalog of bad women, on one hand, and, on the
other hand, praise of women's ability to comfort the unhappy, a qual-
ity seen at its best in the Virgin—is thoroughly conventional. Perhaps
the most interesting feature of the poem is its rhetoric, most noticeable
in the poet's neat repetitions and juxtapositions.

It has sometimes been suggested that the poem was influenced by
the Owl and the Nightingale, but only the most general similarities are
discernible. Nothing can be deduced from the fact that the disputants
in both cases are birds, since the device is common; and not much more
can be deduced from occasional similarities of subject matter. Both
poems speak of maidens and wives, for example, but the treatment is
altogether different. Whereas in *The Owl and the Nightingale* we en-
counter first a commentary on maidens, then a retaliatory commen-
tary on wives, the two are lumped together in *The Thrush and the
Nightingale*—as they often are in medieval literature. More important,
perhaps, the three most remarkable features of *the Owl and the Night-
ingale* are all missing from the later poem: *The Thrush and the
Nightingale* has no connective narrative, few personal touches, and no
humor.

If any relationship exists between the two poems it is probably not
one of direct influence but something more distant. *The Thrush and
the Nightingale* may be a late example of an established convention—
the birds' debate on women—which was used roughly a half century
earlier in *The Owl and the Nightingale*.

The Owl and the Nightingale

The Owl and the Nightingale is a comic burlesque, didactic only inso-far as comedy is intrinsically didactic.[28] It is of course hard to talk about humor: one is likely to end up tediously explaining jokes. Per-haps for this reason, discussion of the poem has generally focused on two problems which at first glance seem more manageable: analysis of the opposing positions dramatized in the poem (What do the Owl and the Nightingale really stand for?) and speculation on the authorship question.[29] Both are fundamentally problems of interpretation and can-not adequately be discussed without reference to the most obvious quality of the poem, the quality which gives the poem its enduring in-terest—the humor. If *The Owl and the Nightingale* is indeed a success-ful work of art, containing inherently the reasons why it is as it is and not otherwise, the answer to both of the standard critical questions comes from inside the poem. One needs to recognize that the two birds are burlesque debaters, that Nicholas's virtues are subtly burlesqued, and that in form the poem burlesques the debate genre.

It was once fashionable to read the poem as allegory, finding it a debate between pleasure and asceticism, gaiety and gravity, art and philosophy, the minstrel and the preacher, or the love poet and the didactic poet. The trouble with such interpretations is that the debate is manifestly all of these things and therefore centrally none of them. The Owl is a character, basically but not invariably gloomy, grumpy, reflective, skeptical of this world's value or beauty, and the Nightingale is another character, basically but not invariably cheerful, optimistic, not self-consciously dedicated to Truth. Both are self-important, charmingly egoistic, and as fierce as they dare to be. Indeed, what chiefly distinguishes this debate from others in the same tradition,[30] is the poet's realistic treatment of the birds as they tackle, in helter-skelter fashion, every great question of the poet's time.[31] Clearly, it is the birds themselves we are meant to watch—and the tactics they em-ploy. The great questions to which the birds address themselves are important, certainly, but the birds are not saying anything very impor-tant about them.

It is not enough merely to observe that the birds function as char-acters rather than as emblems, however. Professor A. C. Spearing, for example, has recognized that the birds are complex characters, but he thinks the debate itself serious:

Comments on the Poems

At the beginning of *The Owl and the Nightingale* it is the Nightingale, with its associations with summer and young love, that seems the most attractive of the two birds, but gradually we come to see that the poet is on the side of the moralizing Owl.[32]

It is true that the poet shows a bias in favor of the Owl for piously shunning falsehood while the Nightingale struggles to hold her own in any way she can. After one of the Owl's early speeches, for instance, the poet says:

> The Nightingale heard all she said
> And turned it over in her head;
> For it was hard to get around
> The arguments the Owl had found;
> And what to say was hard to tell:
> The Owl was right, and argued well.
> The Nightingale was much distressed
> To see how far the Owl had pressed
> And feared she might not find a way
> To answer all the Owl could say.
>
> (ll. 386–95)

But the poet's bias is absurd. What has the Owl said, exactly, to trigger the discomfort the Nightingale feels? First, she has claimed that she flies at night because of her nature, which is like the nature of the noble hawk and not like the nature of paltry, chattering smaller birds or pedestrian crows (ll. 269–99). This is a slanted sort of truth at best. The Owl's pretensions to kinship with the race of hawks are an attempt to counter the effect of the Nightingale's story (ll. 101–26) of how an owlet hatched by a falcon fouls the falcon's nest and dies for her base nature (see l. 113). To the end of the poem the Owl is still smarting over this. When all the smaller birds of the country are shouting at her, the Owl threatens to summon her kinsmen and punish them, but the threat is pure bluff, the poet tells us. The Owl is no less afraid of the hawks than are the smaller birds (ll. 1702 ff.).

Another claim the Owl has made is that her music is better than the Nightingale's because it is loud and deep, like the note of a hunting horn (ll. 306–17). Who but an owl would have thought it! She has claimed that she has the good sense to stop singing sometimes, unlike the Nightingale, and because the Owl knows when to stop, she tells us, she does not disgust her listeners as the Nightingale does (ll. 328–55). But this notion depends upon, among other things, the Owl's assertion that the music of an owl can be pleasing at least for a little

The Owl and the Nightingale

while. She has claimed, finally, that she is not blind by day, despite the ugly rumor, and she proves her point by a specious analogy of her behavior and the hare's (ll. 360–81). And lest the notion enter our heads that owls, like hares, are timid, she hurriedly shifts to another anology: she is like a noble soldier creeping up on the enemy by night (ll. 382 ff.).

The poet's seeming bias in favor of the Owl shows up repeatedly, not just toward the end of the poem. Consider another characteristic example:

> The Nightingale, by any gauge,
> Was half out of her mind with rage,
> And anxiously she searched her wit,
> Hoping she might find in it
> Some talent besides singing she
> Could use to serve humanity,
> For answer this, she knew, she must
> Or all her argument was lost.
> Alas, it's very hard to fight
> Against plain truth and patent right;
> One must exert one's keenest part
> When one is troubled in one's heart;
> One must distort, pervert, devise
> Some means to hide in cunning lies
> If by one's mouth one hopes to show
> What in one's heart one knows not so;
> How soon a word can slip awry
> Where heart and mouth in conflict lie!
> How soon a word can fall apart
> Where lie in conflict mouth and heart!
> (ll. 654–73)

To take seriously the Nightingale's lack of talents other than singing, we must begin by taking seriously the Owl's diversity of talents. The Owl sits out in the barn and helps stamp out mice, clearly a noble and helpful occupation, but its value is undercut not only by the comic self-righteousness with which the Owl tells of her work in the barn but also by her pursuit of the same occupation in church, piously "cleansing" if of the "foul mouse." She mentions no other talents until prodded into doing so by the Nightingale, and none of her helpful work is anything but comic—though the Nightingale, who is merely a bird and not clever like us, is impressed in spite of herself.

In the passage quoted above, the Nightingale's fear that all may be lost is rooted in her inability to respond honestly to the single charge that she has only one talent, a trivial one, that of singing. Actually, the Owl has made several points in addition to this one. The Owl has mocked the Nightingale's scrawniness (ll. 558–59 and 574 ff.)—a sore point with her because of the Nightingale's brilliant speech on the ugliness of the Owl (ll. 71 ff.); has referred to the Nightingale's crazy cacklings in the wood (l. 561) retaliating against the Nightingale's description of the Owl as similar to the lunatic (ll. 416 ff.); has charged that the Nightingale is unclean (ll. 579 ff.), thus nullifying, she hopes, the Nightingale's identical charge against her (ll. 90 ff.).

Looking closely, one discovers that throughout the poem both birds make use of two general strategies, the first being that of specious attack or retaliation (name-calling, scornful caricature, and analogies and saws designed to place the enemy in the worst possible company), and the second being that of self-praise or attack on the enemy's self-praise by self-praise on almost identical grounds. Only if one notices the many exact parallels does he see the full humor in each one-sided position. To mention a few, the Owl scornfully describes the Nightingale is a priest (ll. 319 ff.), and the Nightingale gives the same abuse (ll. 117 ff.); the Owl claims that men are disgusted by the Nightingale (ll. 328 ff.), and the Nightingale claims that men are disgusted by the Owl (ll. 1160 ff.); on the other hand, the Owl claims she helps mankind to be properly religious (ll. 848 ff.), precisely the claim the Nightingale has made for herself (ll. 711 ff.).

Surely one can only conclude that if the poet seems to side with the Owl, he must certainly be siding with her for artistic and comic purposes. It is a matter of fact that the Owl is a cheat (cf. ll. 150 ff.). But the serious-minded and self-important Owl would not dream of consciously distorting truth, as both she and the poet insist throughout. It is partly her absolute belief in all she says that makes the Owl comic, and like Chantecleer, a burlesque of the hero as thinker. The Nightingale, on the other hand, does not even imagine herself concerned with truth as the Owl understands it. She knows for a fact that she is a perfectly splendid bird, the best in the world. Having right on her side— in the sense that clearly nightingales are much better than owls, as all nightingales know—she has a natural right to cheat when she cannot win fairly. So all of us are inclined to cheat when, as often happens, the bad side comes up with all the convincing arguments. The poet quite approves, really. When she decides to cheat he says with a flourish of *similitudo*:

The Owl and the Nightingale

But nonetheless she spoke right out,
Considering it best, no doubt,
To boldly meet her foe's attack,
Not panic or reveal her back;
Yield, and your foe will knock you dead
Who otherwise might soon have fled.
Fight on! For if your heart is big,
The Boar may show himself a Pig.

(ll. 396–403)

But it is not simply for the sake of point of view that the poet sides mainly with the Owl. His tongue-in-cheek bias in favor of the side which considers itself most moral, most mature, establishes the poet himself as decidedly moral, decidedly mature. The whole poem, in other words—a poem the climactic section of which deals frankly and hilariously with the sexual adventures of maidens and wives—is spoken in mock sobriety. The poet seems to be none other than Nicholas of Guildford, the clerk who was in youth, as the Owl tells us (ll. 201 ff.), not as serious-minded as he might have been. The pose is a part of his clever plea for preferment. What it might be tasteless (and ineffective) to protest in dead earnest—that he has sobered and is now extremely judicious—Nicholas manages to insist by comic means.[33]

Professor E. G. Stanley has neatly summarized the chief argument against assigning the poem to Nicholas:

> The reason for doubting that Nicholas is the author is in the poet's charge that Nicholas's superiors abuse their power and corruptly and nepotistically make over the emoluments from ecclesiastical offices to those unfit to discharge them. Tact stands high among the poet's characteristics as revealed in his writing: he must have known that, if his superiors were to see O&N, his vague accusations would lead to resentful repression, not advancement.[34]

The position Professor Stanley takes is tenable, certainly, but it misses the tone of the poem. Professor Stanley's language is fierce: "charge," "abuse their power," "corruptly," "nepotistically," "those unfit to discharge them," "vague accusations," "resentful repression." Merely reading the words in isolation from their context, one feels scolded. Nothing in the poem itself has any such bite, however. Asked where Nicholas may be found, the Wren says he lives at Portesham and adds, wide-eyed with comic admiration,

> I've never seen a man dispense
> More justice or write more good sense.

> That's why he's known so far and wide
> From here to Scotland's other side.
>   (ll. 1749–52)

The last line is interesting: a part of the Wren's grandiose claim for Nicholas is that he improves things even in terrible Scotland where, according to the Nightingale (ll. 990–1025), the situation is past repair. Next the Wren says, comically compassionate, that Nicholas is easy to find, for the poor fellow has only one house (ll. 1753–54). However serious the poet may be in wishing for more houses for Nicholas, the idea that he is easy to find because he has only one house is inescapably comic. It is hard to believe that even the most irascible bishop or rich man could take offense at the Wren's charge, coming as it does in this humorous context, that bishops and lords are responsible for Nicholas's shameful situation (ll. 1755–57). The Wren's tone is righteous indignation rising to the comically rhetorical wail,

> Why will they not, for their own sakes,
> Add him to their establishments
> To hear his wit and common sense,
> And, just to have his company,
> Grant him livings plentifully?
>   (ll. 1758–62)

The gloomy Owl agrees whole-heartedly with the Wren, and her remarks are strictly in character:

> . . . It's all too true.
> These great men don't know what they do
> When they leave frail and in neglect
> A man of such fine intellect!
> They give good jobs to worthless clerks,
> But sadly disregard his works.
> To relatives, come soon, come late,
> They give each one a fine estate,
> But can their intellect surpass
> The claims of Master Nicholas?
>   (ll. 1763–72)

The note of grumpy righteousness is one heard before from the Owl, as is, also, the Owl's inclination toward comically extreme positions like the charge here that the bishops (translating l. 1770 literally) "give rents to *little children*." It may be true that Master Nicholas was hurt

The Owl and the Nightingale

by nepotism (the charge would not be here if he were not), but his nudge at the bishops is genial, undercut as it is by his comic exaggeration of the disparity between his merit and the merit of all other contenders for preferment.

In short, even Master Nicholas is a part of the comic burlesque. Though his plea for preferment is serious, and though the whole poem proves his singular merit (as Professor Lumiansky has shown),[35] the comic exaggeration of his worth—explicitly in the speeches of the birds and implicitly in the narrator's comically sober and responsible bias—links him with the poem's larger purpose.

The burlesque begins as a joke on the debate genre later represented in English by such poems as *Winner and Waster, The Parliament of the Three Ages, The Debate of Body and Soul, The Thrush and the Nightingale,* Lydgate's *Horse, Goose, and Sheep,* and, at the height of the tradition, the *Pearl.* The debates are very often inconclusive (this is particularly true of those in Latin), focusing not on the resolution of some problem but on exploration of contrasting positions; they are often allegorical, the disputants representing abstract ideas (in *Winner and Waster,* for example, the battle is between, loosely, hoarding and spending), and a striking feature of most of the debates is the elaborate play of rhetorical devices.

All of these conventional features of the literary debate are handled comically in *The Owl and the Nightingale.* Here as in most debates the argument is inconclusive, but for comically realistic reasons. For one thing, the Owl and Nightingale are not interested in getting at the truth but merely in winning. And for another, the birds fly off to Portisham, so the narrator cannot tell how the argument came out.

The Owl and the Nightingale does begin as though it were to be an allegory. The Nightingale is at first associated with paradise;[36] she sits on a conventional earthy paradise image, "on a fair bough where there were blossoms enough" (translated literally) and her music is like the music of heaven, a point made emphatic by rhetoric:

> Like notes from heavenly pipes and harps
> She fluted out her flats and sharps:
> More like a harp's or pipe's sweet note
> Than anything from a moral throat.
> (ll. 21–24)

All this is undercut, however, by the fact that the bird and the bough are located in the corner of a *breche* (fallow patch)—a word no more elevated than the modern *haylot*. The Owl, too, seems to have allegorical possibilities at first. In her ivy-covered residence she "song hire tide"; but the residence is an old *stoc*—a stump. The splendid grass temple of allegory is shattered the instant the two birds begin to speak: they are mortal creatures, emphatically, and not polite ones.

As for rhetoric, the poem is as rhetorical as anything in the debate genre, but its rhetoric does not aim at elegance. True, in good poetry expert technique is always a quality that delights the reader, but one doubts that anyone in the poet's day ever really thought (as one critic thinks some listeners did): "What a neat traductio!" or "That was a cunning interpretatio!" [37] Partly the rhetorical devices are interesting because, in their very clumsiness, they are funny:

> As long as I'm inside my tree
> And don't fly out in the open night,
> Your fancy threats have got no bite.
> As long as I'm inside my hedge,
> Your cutting words have got no edge.
> (ll. 56–60)

And partly the heavy use of rhetorical devices in this poem is interesting because rhetoric really is one of the chief means by which human beings try to demolish their opponents.

Like all great burlesques, however, *The Owl and the Nightingale* is more than a joke on poetic conventions. It presents, centrally, a comic view of man, whose concern is too often—and all to understandably—not with truth but with winning. In one good medieval word, the Owl and the Nightingale are both, like us, proud. The Owl goes so far as to hint that she is a kind of Christ figure: not only does she return good for evil (l. 1608) she "sheds her blood" for mankind (l. 1609). In a sober moment, the poet might perhaps have made a sermon of all this, but he has chosen a happier course: he cheerfully joins his grandiloquent birds and, moreover, extends the comic melodrama to the larger world, in which the astute, noble, and righteous Nicholas of Guildford contends for preferment against clerks unspeakably less astute, noble, and righteous than himself. It is this larger comedy of human self-importance that gives the poet's burlesque of convention its lasting interest.

Notes

TO COMMENTS ON THE POEMS

[1]   The alliterative renaissance (or "revival") took place in western England in the later fourteenth century. It involved a return to—perhaps an increased interest in—the prosody of Old English verse, wherein beat is signaled in part by alliteration: "Forst sceal freosan, fyr wudu meltan. . . . " In Middle English alliterative verse the rules are much less formal than the rules of Old English verse: indeed, almost no two writers in Middle English use exactly the same rules. Professor Larry D. Benson has recently suggested (in *Art and Tradition in Sir Gawain and the Green Knight* [New Brunswick, N.J.: Rutgers University Press, 1965], pp. 117–26) that the reason for the revival of the old native meter in fourteenth-century England was that it was an ideal vehicle for the then popular "high style" of the rhetoricians. His analysis of rhetorical devices in *Sir Gawain* is excellent and can enrich one's reading of the *Morte Arthure, Winner and Waster, Parliament of the Three Ages,* and *Summer Sunday*—even a reading of these poems in translation.

The principles of the medieval rhetoricians are important in all of the poems brought together here, especially for *Morte Arthure* and *The Owl and the Nightingale.* For a good brief discussion of the rhetorical tradition, see Robert O. Payne, *The Key of Remembrance: A Study of Chaucer's Poetics* (New Haven: published for the University of Cincinnati by the Yale University Press, 1963), pp. 9–59, and for further reading on medieval rhetoric, see Payne's bibliography, pp. 233–40.

[2]   See the reviews by John Finlayson in *Medium Ævum,* 32 (1963), pp. 74–77, and J. L. N. O'Loughlin, in *Review of English studies* n.s. 14 (1963), pp. 179–82.

[3]   Among the important books are G. L. Kittredge's *A Study of Gawain and the Green Knight* (Cambridge: Harvard University Press, 1916); Benson's *Art and Tradition in Sir Gawain and the Green Knight,* cited above; and Marie Borroff's *Sir Gawain and the Green Knight: A Stylistic and Metrical Study* (New Haven: Yale University Press, 1962).

[4]   The selective edition is John Finlayson's *Morte Arthure,* in York Medieval Texts (Evanston, Ill.: Northwestern University Press, 1967). The

most accessible English editions of *Morte Arthure* are those of G. G. Perry (London: EETS, 1865), reedited by Edmund Brock (1871), and the edition of Mary Macleod Banks (London: Longmans, Green, 1900).

⁵ See "Versification and Form" in my *Complete Works of the Gawain-Poet* (Chicago: University of Chicago Press, 1965), pp. 85–90.

⁶ See for instance, the introduction to my *Complete Works of the Gawain-Poet* or Borroff, *Sir Gawain and the Green Knight*, pp. 3–129.

⁷ See "Versification," in my *Works of the Gawain-Poet;* but for a different point of view, cf. Borroff, *Sir Gawain and the Green Knight*, pp. 164–210.

⁸ On this, more anon. One of the poet's favorite ornaments, which can become mere mechanics at times, is alliteration continued through several lines. See, for example, the passage beginning at l. 1884 (Brock edition); see also lines 570–76, 2895–97, 3298–3307, and 2753–63.

⁹ But see John Finlayson, "Arthur and the Giant of St. Michael's Mount," *Medium Ævum* 33 (1964), pp. 112–20.

¹⁰ Professor William Matthews has discussed the poet's practice in *The Tragedy of Arthur: A study of the Alliterative Morte Arthure* (Berkeley and Los Angeles: University of California Press, 1960), pp. 6–31. His discussion, basically sound, sometimes brilliant, needs modification to be found in the Finlayson and O'Loughlin reviews, cited above.

¹¹ The lines quoted read, in the original:

> Thane answers sir Arthure to that alde wyf;
> "I am comyne fra the conquerour, curtaise and gentille,
> As one of the hathelest of Arthur Knyghtez,
> Messenger to this myx, for mendemente of the pople,
> To mele with this maister mane, that here this mounte ȝemez;
> To trete with this tyraunt for tresour of landez,
> And take trew for a tyme, to bettyr may worthe."

¹² See G. Neilson, *Sir Hew of Eglintoun and Huchown of the Awle Ryale, A Biographical Calendar and Literary Estimate* (Glasgow: Philosophical Society, 1900–1901), p. 62, et passim.

¹³ On this point see Finlayson's review, cited above. An obvious proof that Edward could be criticized is *Winner and Waster*, in part an attack on him.

¹⁴ See K. Höltgen, "König Arthur und Fortuna," *Anglia* 75 (1957), pp. 35–54.

Comments on the Poems

[15] Bird debates are conventional. Cf. *The Owl and the Nightingale, The Thrush and the Nightingale,* or, not included here, *The Cuckoo and the Nightingale.* See also the first part of *Winner and Waster.*

[16] It is probably a mistake to think, as some critics seem to do, that the word *pride* invariably connotes sinful pride in Middle English. One encounters "proud steeds," "proud warriors," and the like in many contexts which seem to rule out any such meaning. August Brink has shown [in *Stab und Wort im Gawain,* Studien zur englischen Philologie 59 ed. Lorenz Morsbach (Halle: Max Niemeyer 1920), p. lix] that *proud* is a word of high alliterative rank (*Rang im Stabe*), and for the alliterative poets a word which tended to idealize the characters and subject matter of their narratives.

[17] See lines 2618–39. Testing the hero's virtues against the measure of Gawain is a conventional device in the romances. Consider, for example, Chrétien's *Yvain* or Wolfraim's *Parzival.* The degenerate Gawain represented by, for instance, Malory, is a late development and one which did not have much effect on West Midlands poets. On the illegality of Arthur's late wars, see Finlayson's *Morte Arthure,* p. 12.

[18] See John Gardner, "*The Canon's Yeoman's Tale,* An Interpretation," *PQ* 46 (1967), pp. 14–17.

[19] See Matthews, *The Tragedy of Arthur,* pp. 183–92.

[20] On the authorship and dating of the poem, see J. R. Hulbert, "The Problems of Authorship and Date of *Wynnere and Wastoure,*" *MP* 18 (1920), pp. 31–40; J. M. Steadman, "The Authorship of *Wynnere and Wastoure* and the *Parlement of the Thre Ages:* A Study in Methods of Determining the Common Authorship of Middle English Poems," *MP* 21 (1923), pp. 7–13; and J. M. Steadman, Jr., "The Date of *Winnere and Wastoure,*" *MP* 19 (1921–22), pp. 211–19.

[21] Sir Israel Gollancz, in the introduction to his edition of the poem *Wynnere and Wastoure,* Oxford University Press, 1931 [or Select Early English Poems, III (London: Humphrey Milford, Oxford University Press, 1920)] argues that the intrusive lines are the work of the original poet, a minstrel. According to John Speirs [*Medieval English Poetry: The Non-Chaucerian Tradition,* (London: Faber and Faber, 1962), p. 267] the drinking signaled in the poem "is clearly in the tradition of the ritual drinking that had originally been an essential feature of the old religion of the Scandinavian and Teutonic societies and that explains the obstinate practice of heavy drinking in northern Europe against which preachers inveighed throughout the Middle Ages." Hm.

[22] Except for the work of Gollancz and Speirs, cited above, no detailed interpretation of the poem exists. The interpretation I offer, which em-

Notes

phasizes the poem's apparent concern with order as a system of natural checks and balances, would be interesting to examine in the light of Chaucer's similar attitude toward order, worked out in Fragments 2–5 of the *Canterbury Tales*. For this reading of the Fragments, together with references to parallel thought in the Middle Ages, see John Gardner, "The Case Against the 'Bradshaw Shift'; or, The Mystery of the Manuscript in the Trunk," in John Gardner and Nicholas Joost, eds., *The Art and Age of Geoffrey Chaucer* (PLL, Supplement 3, 1967), pp. 80–106.

[23] J. M. Steadman, "The authorship of *Wynnere and Wastoure* and *The Parlement of the Three Ages*," cited above.

[24] Speirs, *Medieval English Poetry*, p. 292.

[25] The history of the "Nine Worthies" is a stock poetic topic in the Middle Ages and after. See R. S. Loomis, "Verses on the Nine Worthies," *MP* 15 (1917–18), pp. 211–19; and J. H. Roberts, "The Nine Worthies," *MP* 19 (1921–22), pp. 297–305.

[26] For brief discussion of Brown's interpretation see Rossell Hope Robbins, ed., *Historical Poems of the XIVth and XVth Centuries* (New York: Columbia University Press, 1959), pp. 301–2.

[27] I have discussed this strain of medieval Christianity in the introduction to my *Complete Works of the Gawain-Poet*.

[28] A recognition of the humor is implicit in the introductory discussions found in the editions of J. E. Wells (1907, rev. 1908), and J. W. H. Atkins in *Aberystwyth Studies* (Aberystwith, 1922). In their edition, J. H. G. Grattan and G. F. H. Sykes, EETS, e.s., no. 119 (1935), suggest that a joke at the end of the poem would be out of keeping with the otherwise serious tone. As Richard Hazelton has pointed out in his excellent study, "*The Manciple's Tale:* Parody and Critique," *Journal of English and Germanic Philology* 62 (Jan. 1964), 1: "Of all medieval literary traditions none is more vigourous or more durable than that of parody." For the tradition of parody in the Latin texts, see Paul Lehmann's *Die Parodie im Mittelalter* (Munich: Drei Masken-Verlag, 1922) and his supplement, *Parodische Texte, Beispiele zur lateinischen Parodie im Mittelalter* (Munich: Drei Masken-Verlag, 1923). Robert Bossuat comments on parody in the Renard poems in *Le Roman de Renard* (Paris: Hatier-Boivin, 1957), pp. 109–38. For ample evidence of parody in the fabliaux see Per Nykrog, *Les Fabliaux: Étude d'histoire littéraire et de stylistique médiévale* (Copenhagen: E. Munksgaard, 1957), pp. 72–104, et passim. Italo Siciliano treats Villon's use of parody in *François Villon et les thèmes poétiques du moyen age* (Paris: Nizet, 1934), pp. 115–99, et passim. All of these works, together with others less familiar, are cited in Hazelton's notes, q.v. The list might be greatly expanded. A major contribution since the appearance of Hazelton's article is

Comments on the Poems

Marie Borroff's discussion of stylistic parody in *Sir Gawain and the Green Knight*, in the stylistic section of her book, *Sir Gawain and the Green Knight: A Stylistic and Metrical Study* (New Haven, Yale University Press, 1962). In recent years reawakened interest in the literary implications of patristic exegesis has led to a reassessment of the extent to which parody and burlesque inform medieval literature. For instance, in his analysis of Chaucer's "Book of the Duchess," B. F. Huppé suggests the presence of serious religious parody in the Black Knight's remarks on his lady; see *Fruyt and Chaf: Studies in Chaucer's Allegories* by B. F. Huppé and D. W. Robertson, Jr. (Princeton: Princeton University Press, 1964). I have on various occasions pointed out similar punning in the Wakefield plays, and I have mentioned the *Gawain*-poet's use of this technique; see my introduction to *The Complete Works of the Gawain-Poet*, especially the analyses of *Pearl*, *Purity*, and *Patience*.

[29]   For a good, brief summary of the arguments on what the Owl and the Nightingale represent, see R. M. Lumiansky, "Concerning *The Owl and the Nightingale*," PQ 32 (1953), pp. 411–17. On authorship, see, in addition, Eric Gerald Stanley, *The Owl and the Nightingale* (London: Nelson, 1960), pp. 19–22. Good bibliographies on authorship, date, and theme appear in Wells, cited above, pp. 184–85; Atkins, cited above, pp. 182–86; Grattan and Sykes, cited above, pp. xxiii–xxiv. These are supplemented by Lumiansky, p. 411*n*. The most important study of authorship, prior to Lumiansky's, is Kathryn Huganir, *The Owl and the Nightingale: Sources, Date, Author* (Philadelphia: University of Pennsylvania, 1931). Lumiansky's discussion is much less detailed than Huganir's but summarizes Huganir's best points.

[30]   On the debate tradition, see Eric Gerald Stanley's brief discussion in his edition, *The Owl and the Nightingale*, pp. 25–27. The standard treatment of medieval Latin debates is H. Walther, *Das Streitgedicht in der lateinischen Literatur des Mittelalters*, Quellen und Untersuchungen zur lateinischen Philologie des Mittelalters, vol. 5, pt. 2 (Munich: Beck, 1920).

[31]   See Stanley's *The Owl and the Nightingale* for a summary of the scholarship, pp. 22–26, and Lumiansky's "Concerning *The Owl and the Nightingale*" for an analysis of the significance of the wide range of subjects covered, pp. 414–16.

[32]   A. C. Spearing, *Criticism and Medieval Poetry* (London: E. Arnold, 1964), p. 66.

[33]   It has sometimes been suggested that an argument against assigning the poem to Nicholas is that if he were the author he would be praising himself too much; see Stanley, cited above, p. 21. The answer to this argument is not, as Stanley thinks, that "If he were writing to gain preferment he would have to state his merits, and bring them to the notice of his superiors in an

Notes

acceptable manner." Stanley's observation is valid enough, but irrelevant to the poem. The poet does two things at once: by his ingenious introduction of every important subject of the day, his demonstration that he knows legal process, poetic theory, and so forth, and his brilliant organization of the whole burlesque, he demonstrates his real merit; at the same time, by comically exaggerating his virtue, both through what the birds say about him and through his own mock-solemn pose, he wryly apologizes for calling attention to himself. In other words, he is not praising himself too much, because he admits that his self-praise is (exactly like the self-praise of the Owl and the Nightingale) comically excessive.

[34] Stanley, *The Owl and the Nightingale*, p. 21.

[35] Summarizing and analyzing earlier commentary on the poem, Lumiansky, in "Concerning *The Owl and the Nightingale*," first demonstrates that the poem proves the writer's "skill as a poet, his penetrating analysis of two superficially conflicting views of life, his wide knowledge of legal process, and his sane judgment, evinced by his ability to examine both sides of such questions as love, poetry, astrology, preaching, and violence" (p. 416). Speaking to the authorship question, Lumiansky argues that "the poem exists as a plea for preferment for Nicholas, and the debate proper is present primarily to illustrate to some powerful person or persons the outstanding qualities which recommend Nicholas for such preferment. If anyone other than Nicholas wrote the poem—say, a friend—then the poetic skill, the knowledge of legal process, and the ability to examine both sides of contemporary questions would all be attributes of the friend rather than of Nicholas" (pp. 416–17).

[36] H. Hassler, in *"The Owl and the Nightingale" und die literarischen Bestrebungen des 12. und 13. Jahrhunderts* (Leipzig, 1942), pp. 94–97, suggests that the stump and bough symbolize, respectively, somberness and joyousness. Reasonable as this interpretation is, I question it; but at all events, the important point is that the stump and bough do set up allegorical possibilities of some kind, which the poet explodes into comic realism. The next occurrence of the potentially allegorical harp image is a comically realistic comparison of the nightingale's shrill note and the sound of a tightly tuned harp. (ll. 139–42).

[37] Spearing, *Criticism and Medieval Poetry*, p. 66.

Notes

TO THE POEMS

The Alliterative Morte Arthure

The modernization is from the edition of M. M. Banks (London, 1900), with some corrections from E. Brock's edition (London, 1871) and some from the edition of E. Björkman (Heidelberg, 1915) and from the few available studies of the text which have appeared in scholarly journals, especially the important note by J. L. N. O'Loughlin, "The Middle English *Morte Arthure*," *Medium Ævum*, 4 (1935), pp. 153 ff., which provides the theoretical grounds for my conservative reading of the text. I have also consulted the Everyman translation by A. Boyle (New York, 1912).

These notes are meant to serve two main purposes. First, they give literal translation of some words and phrases I have translated freely, so that students interested in using the translation as a crib may not be thoroughly discouraged. But I by no means note every minor change made. For instance, though constant tense shifting is common in alliterative Middle English verse ("He went to his tents, he awakens his barons"), and though I follow the poet's practice in a general way but not line for line, I make no note of my departures from the tense in the text. Again, I do not note every departure for alliteration, tone, or convenience, especially if the departure should be obvious to anyone checking the modernization against the original. Such departures include free renderings of nonessential words, distortions for alliteration, and intrusive phrases which (a) fill out rhythm and/or (b) clarify pronoun reference or sentence structure when these, though clear in Middle English, are necessarily obscure in a modernization. (E.g., line 92, *That on Lammesse daye thare be no lette founden* is translated "And command that on Lammass Day you give no excuses." "And command" is intrusive, and the idea in *lette* (hindrance) is rendered freely for the sake of slant alliteration on *c* and *g*.) I do not note renderings made only for alliterative convenience. Examples are *kene* ("bold"); *beryns* ("men," often rendered here as "barons"); *steryne* ("brave," "strong," "inflexible," sometimes rendered as "stern"); *burelyche* ("grand," "stately," "dignified," or, with reference to weapons, "stout," often rendered metaphorically, by "boarlike"—which I admit may seem mildly insane—but the choice preserves *b* alliteration, maintains the long syllables of the original, and has clear advantages over, for instance, "burly").

Notes

The second purpose of these notes is to explain an occasional obscure detail or to call attention to interesting subtleties.

1–11. The preliminary prayer is common in the more serious kinds of oral medieval verse. Notice the openings by some of Chaucer's pilgrims—the Prioress, the Second Nun. Lines 9 and 10 perhaps suggest not simple recitation but oral-formulaic composition. The poet's frequent use of such filler phrases as "as hym lykes" perhaps suggest the same thing, that the poem was composed orally.

9.   *werpe owte some worde,* literally, "cast out some words." *MA* is clearly intended for oral delivery, presumably at some courtly festivity. Cf. lines 12, 15. Many ME poems which have survived were certainly oral. Note the lines signaling intermission in *Winner and Waster* and the opening of the debate proper in *Parl. of the Three Ages* (ll. 104–8) And cf. *Sir Gawain and the Green Knight,* ll. 30–36.

13.   *awke dedys,* lit., "out of the way, or strange deeds."

14.   *lele in theire lawe,* lit., "loyal in their religious law or custom."

26–51. The legendary sway of Arthur at the height of his power is considerably increased by the poet. He borrows place names from various sources, not only chronicles and romances but also Edward's list of claims. For the poet, as for nearly every English writer on King Arthur down to Spenser and beyond, Arthur was the embodiment of the British national spirit. Indeed, it was apparently in response to the rising spirit of nationalism that in the twelfth century, with the release of Geoffrey of Monmouth's *Historiae Regum Britannical,* Arthur was turned from a folk hero (probably the subject of lost Cornish, Welsh, and Irish tales) to one of the world's great monarchs.

29.   Uther Pendragon—King Arthur's father.

32.   *Scathyll Scottlande,* lit., "hurtful Scotland."

35.   "were held of him," i.e., were ruled by men who acknowledge Arthur as overlord and reigned by his consent or at his delegation.

55.   *Bretayne þe braddere,* lit., "Britain the broader." "Britain," as distinguished from Little Britain (Armorica).

60–61. Actually the ruins of a city built by the Romans. Such ruins are very commonly assigned to Arthur.

62.   The river Usk.

64.   *Carlisle.* Often identified in the Middle Ages as the chief seat of Arthur.

66. .   *douzepeers*—"twelve peers." Charlemagne and Alexander, too, had their twelve peers, or, as Chaucer called them *ferses twelve,* i.e., twelve counsellors. I retain the archaic *douzeperas* throughout for obvious reasons, one of which is convenient alliteration.

68.   *banerettes nobille* (freely, "noble standard bearers"), glossed by Brock as "Knights of the higher order."

70–80. Notice the parallel with *Sir Gawain and the Green Knight.* There Arthur gathers his knights for Christmas festivities, and when they are all feasting, at New Year's, the Green Knight rides in to challenge them.

78.   *at the none euyne,* lit., "at the ninth hour"—ninth hour after equinox, or 3 P.M.

The Poems

81. *sextene Knyghtes in a soyte*—sixteen Knights in a retinue or "suit." *Sixteen* suggests great power here—an idea ironically twisted later (l. 471).

83. The word *king* is often used loosely in Middle English verse. It may refer to any great feudal lord, from wealthy knight to emperor.

84. *as hym lykyde,* "as pleased him," or, to suggest the reflexive force, "as pleasured him." This phrase, with innumerable variants (*as hym best lykes, whenne* or *where them lykes*) and such near-equivalents as *at hys wille,* is extremely common in *MA;* so common, in fact, that it may seem obsessive padding. But the phrase has covert significance in a special sense which is reflected in, for instance, Henri Bracton's *quod principi placuit,* i.e., "what the king pleases," or "the king's pleasure." The assumption is that what pleases the king is the welfare of the state, not what delights his personal whim. [See Ewart Lewis, "King Above Law? Quod Principi Placuit in Bracton," *Speculum,* 39 (1964), pp. 240–69.] This idea, if reflected in the *MA*-poet's *as hym lykes,* etc., must sometimes be straight, sometimes harshly ironic, at other times something between. Needless to say, lesser feudal lords (common knights) exercise a similar "pleasure" in what is good for their vassals. But clearly the phrase does not *always* have feudal nuances in *MA.* It sometimes means just what it would today (Cf. l. 186). This range of meaning, from private or selfish to public and unselfish pleasure, is essential to the poem's theme.

87. *undyrne his sele ryche,* "under his [noble or rich] seal," i.e., in a letter carrying the Emperor's seal.

89. *his targe es to schewe!* loosely, "his shield (or charter) is to be seen." A pun may possibly be intended, "His shield of battle is uncovered," i.e., he stands prepared to strike.

95. Prime: the first hour.

105–9. Interesting lines. The "hole in the earth" suggests the hiding place of a fox or some other hunted animal. In the *Mactacio Abel,* in the Wakefield cycle of mystery plays, the image has exegetical overtones: the hole suggests hell, where Cain, like a hunted animal, will hide. The same exegetical overtone may be present here, brought in by the contrastive phrase "rest under heaven." Lucius, then, presents himself as God-like, usurping the station Arthur himself will later usurp, according to Matthews's reading. What is probably involved here, however, is not subtle irony by the poet but dramatic hyperhole in which Lucius, for scornful effect, suggests that he is as superior to Arthur as God is to man, or as the hunter is to the fox or rabbit.

120–21. Literally, "The Romans for dread rushed (dropped quickly) to the earth,/ for fearfulness of his face, as if they were fated men."

125. *corounede of kynd,* loosely "crowned by Nature," i.e., by your very nature a king. "Summer Sunday" has the same idea.

127. *in thy manrede,* lit., in thy service or homage.

129. *lengez,* lit., "dwells."

137. *voute of thi vesage,* lit., "mein of your visage."

154. "in Britain" inserted for "in these low lands."

157. *steryne mene,* ME *steryne,* from OE *styrne,* may suggest either strength (with overtones of "galantry" and "noble inflexibility") or cruel

283

Notes

irascibility, thus here works with fine irony. Making his grudging peace
with the messengers from Lucius, he employs a word which would honor
them were they not so obviously flexible and given to harsh rant.

170 ff. As in some other Arthurian poems from Western England and
Scotland, the Round Table here is not round. It allows for higher and
lower stations. (Cf *GGK*, ll. 107–15.)

176 ff., cf. *GGK* 121 ff., and *WW*, ll. 330–64; see also Chaucer, General
Prologue to the *Canterbury Tales*, Frag. 1, ll. 335–54. Note also the follow-
ing examples of alliteration taken from lines 176–91 of the original version
of the *Morte Arthure*. Here is an example of crossed alliteration.

There *c*ome in at the *f*yrste *c*ourse, be*f*or the *K*ynge *s*eluene
Crossed alliteration and secondary *s*-pattern:
   Bareheuedys that *w*are *b*ryghte, *b*urnyste with *s*yluer,
Secondary *r*-pattern:
   Alle with *t*aghte mene and *t*owne in *t*ogers fulle *r*yche
   Of *s*aunke *r*ealle in *s*uyte, *s*exty atones; \
Superabundant alliteration:
   *ff*lesch *f*luriste of *f*ermysone with *f*rumentee noble
   Ther-to *w*ylde to *w*ale, and *w*ynlyche bryddes,
Extended alliteration:
   *P*acokes and *p*louers in *p*laters of golde,
   *P*ygges of *p*orke des*p*yne, that *p*astured neuer;
Secondary *f*-pattern:
   Sythene *h*erons in *h*edoyne, *h*yled *f*ulle faire;
   Grett *s*wannes fulle *s*wythe in *s*ilueryne chargeours,
   *T*artes of *t*urky, *t*aste whanne theme lykys;
   *G*umbaldes graythely, full *g*racious to taste;
Extended alliteration:
   Seyne *b*owes of wylde *b*ores with the *b*raune lechyde
   *B*ernakes and *b*otures in *b*aterde dysches
   Thareby *b*raunchers in *b*rede, *b*ettyr was neuer,
   With *b*restes of *b*arowes, that *b*ryghte ware to schewe.

183. i.e., "young porcupines that were not yet weaned"—Brock.

191. *that bryghte ware to schewe,* lit., "that were bright to see."

192. Lit., "Afterward came many stews (pottages), for pleasure (ME
solace) later."

194. As in Belshazzar's feast in *Purity*, the meats are arranged like hills
and decorated with miniature castles, probably of silver, possibly of paper.
As the alcohol burns off (the "azure waves," l. 193) the visual effect is spec-
tacular—and, for the senators, perhaps, slyly threatening.

212–15. The idea here, that by their nature precious jewels will either can-
cel the effect of poison or else explode at its touch, is a common one in
the Middle Ages. It occurs in *Purity*, in Alexander romances, and else-
where.

222–26. Arthur's speech is, of course, jokingly ironic.

224. Literally, "In these barren lands, of roasts or other things."

247–406. The council, with its formal vows from Arthur's lords, sets up the

The Poems

first of the two main actions in the poem: Sir Cador's rash speech will be echoed in rash action early in the war; thereafter, the war will progress vow by vow until it is won and the second action, the return to fight Mordred, begins. The vernicle is the handkerchief which soothed Christ as he bore the cross; it came away with the print of his face on it. An emblem here of the suffering of the righteous.

249. Literally "eager[one]," not "ogre."

282. A favorite legend to early Englishmen. The great version is that of Cynewulf in the Old English *Elene.*

301. "of fighting age," free for *wyth-in two eldres,* i.e., between the two ages (too young to be a soldier and too old).

312–15. The poet is a master of precise and ironic comparisons of this sort —the falling of weapons (e.g., clubs) and the fall of dew, the sweep of bright swords and the motion of a flower in a field. But possibly something more may be involved here. For the exegetes, and in advent lyrics sung to this day, *dew* is a figure of mercy associated with Christ's coming to earth. (Cf. the well-known Middle English lyric "I Sing A Maiden that is Makeles.") Christ himself, and also such virtues as mercy, purity, etc., are frequently represented by the image of a flower. Brittany's warlike vows to Christ seem undermined by imagery ironically recalling Christ in another more charitable aspect.

322. The translation conveniently adopts Brock. Banks and other editors read *wrethe* as "wrongs," not "wrath."

330. Lit., "I shall surely assure him that never shall we settle [reconcile]."

344. Lit., "agrees to conquer yonder lands."

345. Lit., "by the kalends of June we shall encounter once."

384. The line sums up the vengeance argument throughout the passage (247 ff.). When the British go beyond this "fate" and seek to avenge Christ Himself, Fortune oversets them.

390. If the text is emended to "rerewards [and other]," the meaning is "rearguard and the rest."

413–72. Arthur's speeches are highly ornamented. In the original, ll. 419–22 are all on *l;* ll. 423–24 are on *r* with an *l* carried over; l. 425 is on *f* with an *r* carried over; 426–28 are on *m;* ll. 429–66 develop a complex system of *l,m,r,f,* and *s* patterns (429–30, 454, 457–60, 473–4 on *l;* 435–38, 452, 461 on *f;* 439–43, 447–49, 471–72 on *s* etc.).

433. I translate "make reschewes" in the sense of "make rescues," Brock's reading. Probably Banks and the others are correct, reading "make preparations." But cf. 2243, 3859.

450. The famous old Roman road through central England, mentioned by Chaucer, the Wakefield Master, and others.

458. *Be now lathe or lette ryghte as [the] thynkes.* An obscure line. *lathe* = "a loathed one" Björkman glosses "lied, übel," i.e., "grief, evil"); *lette,* "prevention, hinderance," may mean "a prevented one." I hazard that the sense is, "Either be hated [but allowed to pass] or be stopped [for disobeying my orders], just as you please." By changing *now* to *not,* as some editors do, one gets a different reading. As Boyle has it (p. 10), "Let there be no reluctance or hesitation if thou thinkest wisely."

560.   *Stryke theme doune in strates,* probably "strike them down in narrow passes, straights," but perhaps ". . . in ranks."

566.   Here as sometimes elsewhere I avoid the literal "bannerets," obscure to the modern reader, and "bachelors," which would be misleading.

678.   Mordred's plea here is a detail invented by the poet. It serves to mitigate Mordred's later treason, making even him nearly as much a victim of adverse fortune as a sinner. (He himself blames fate.) Mordred's arguments are fundamentally right, it seems to me: the returning heroes—if he allows them to return—will make him seem a trifle. If so, his request is reasonable, and Arthur's rejection of the plea, grounded on the hasty assumption that his kinship with Mordred will be sufficient glory for the young man, is a mistake. Yet the mistake, too, is natural. Arthur's obscure final phrase, "You know what it means," seems to say, "You know the importance of this office," and perhaps—since Arthur emphasizes the fact that he is childless—the phrase hints at something else: "You know what it may lead to—more than a petty kingdom!" But Mordred will take fate in his own hands, trading bad luck for bad religion.

707.   Lit., "I may not [cannot allow myself to] know of [take cognizance of] this woe." Boyle reads: "I had rather not know of this grief."

750–51. "lodestar"—the compass, which points to the North Star. "craft" —here, mathematics.

764.   Cf. l. 193, the azure waves of the burning "landscape" of meats.

876–78. The text is uncertain—"treason to lords" or "treason to lands." In either case, Arthur with bitter irony equates the behavior of a monster with that of a trecherous lord. The poet thus emphasizes the relationship (already implied by the double identification of the bear in Arthur's dream) between the giant and Lucius.

919–31. The stock natural-paradise description has an obvious ironic function; it may also be meant to serve as a signal to the reader that Arthur and his two knights are passing from one world to another, from realistic adventure to romance adventure.

961.   "unblessed"—i.e., not marked with the sign of the cross, hence unprotected.

963.   Wade is traditionally a monster slayer, among other things. Gawain is traditionally a protector of ladies in distress. He becomes, in *Sir Gawain and the Green Knight,* another monster-slayer, but no general tradition behind this has survived. Fur further details on Wade and Gawain, see Banks, pp. 139–40.

994.   Cf. 465–66 and 537–40. The parallel of course underscores a contrast of motives.

1174.   *montez of Araby;* not mountains of Arabia but a mountain in Wales. See Banks's note, p. 140; Björkman, p. 146.

1195.   *That in couerte the kynge held close to hym seluene.* The phrase *in couerte* (cf. modern *covert*) is obscure. The reading "in secret" makes no apparent sense. There is no indication that Arthur is sneaking up on

The Poems

his enemy or making a secret of who has his favor. An emendation to *courte* would introduce an awkward repetition, since *courte* occurs in l. 1198. *Couerte* occurs as an adjective, meaning "sheltered," at l. 1780. I think *in couerte* means in the sheltering place of Arthur's lords, his temporary hall.

1450–51. Translation doubtful. *"Alle the ferse mene be-fore frekly ascryes,/ fferkand in the foreste, to freschene thame selfene."* *Frekly ascryes*—boldly cry out, or boldly (manfully) descry? Can one notice something "frekly"?

1455. Lit., "And with severity Sir Boys is held in arrest." Boyle translates, for some reason, "with vigour Sir Boys is resisted."

1463–66. Hard lines, it seems to me, though apparently they are plain to other readers.

> Swyftly with swerdes, they swappene there-aftyre,
> Swappez, doune ffulle sweperlye swelltande knyghtez,
> That alle swellttez one swarthe, that they ouer-swyngene,
> So many sweys in swoghe swounande att ones!

Does *That alle* in 1466 mean "who all" or "so that all"? Does *that they ouer-swyngene* mean "whom the Britons now continue swinging above"—as Boyle would have it—or "whom they swing over," that is, swing down upon as these weakened men faint on their saddles or on the ground? And does *So many,* in 1467 (a line Boyle drops), mean "so many" or "Thus, many"?

1671. "accountant"—because the enemy earl has spoken of tribute (rents) and has his facts wrong, from the English point of view. The scornful metaphor is developed further in 1673, 1674, 1677, 1678, etc.

1680. I.e., three single encounters in joust.

1686. The King of Syria turns Cleges's own taunt against him: whereas Cleges called the first enemy speaker a mere accountant, Sextenor asks proof that Cleges is worth the trouble of his Syrian noblemen. Cleges grants that the demand is knightly but attributes it to churlish cowardice (l. 1693). Loftily, scornfully, Sextenor declines the gambit. "Our side will suffer you," that is, tolerate your boorishness; but Sextenor—for strategic reasons—will not encounter these churls. (Sextenor's mission is not random warplay but recapture of Rome's nobleman Peter.)

1697. *Borght.* Probably a mistake for Brutus, legendary founder of Britain (cf. *Sir Gawain and the Green Knight*, ll. 11–12). In which case the meaning is, "Brutus brought us and all our bold elders." *Ffro* must in this case be an error for *ffor*. But *"from* Borght *to* Britain" makes sense if *Borght* is a forgotten place-name or mistake for some place-name.

1717–22. Cador's decision is, as Arthur says later, rash. Though Lancelot may laugh, Cador's job—getting Peter to Paris—does not require him to hold proudly to the highway, meeting an ambush of which he has advance warning.

1733–34. A tactic very commonly used by those who would rather be taken prisoner than killed.

Notes

1785. (and 1836). "Miller's play," or "grain pay"—an allusion to the unfair share of grain taken by cheating millers.

1795. Fulfillment of Cador's oath at the Giants' Tower.

1811. *ffellede at the fyrst come*—"Felled at the first onslaught"?

2027-31. Note the prebattle drinking and war revels, customs strange and alarming to the British, though well known to the earlier Anglo-Saxons.

2282. "destriers"—huge war horses, the tanks of the Middle Ages.

2286. "Llamas" is translation by despair. The original has *Elfaydes*, some unidentified beast. (See Björkman, p. 157.)

2322-27. The translation is faked. Boyle translates, "that we shall be certain to perform: surely by our troth we pledge ourselves to carry thy message: we shall allow no man that lives on earth, no pope nor potentate nor noble prince, to see thy letters—rather than divulge it to duke or knight we shall die in agony." The text is corrupt.

2531. "roaring so loud" is desperately free. The original *profers so large* is hard to translate. To *profer* is to show (by voice and stance) readiness to joust; when one knight speaks of another of doing this *so large*, he is ironically complimenting his antagonist on the apparent might which backs the proffer. Cf. 2536, *for all thy prowde lates*—"for all your proud looks, or bearing."

2574. *blode-bande*, usually glossed "blood-bandage," occasionally "blood-bond," as translated. A pun? Certainly both make sense, but the latter more sense than the former.

2575. Barbers. In the Middle Ages they were also leeches or healers of wounds.

2576. The sword is magical—a common device in the Eastern romances.

2592. "and lord"—not in ms; inserted, following O'Loughlin, on the basis of the parallel line in Malory.

Between 2600 and 2610, two bracketed lines dropped from manuscript. See O'Loughlin, "The Middle English *Morte Arthure*," *Medium Ævum* 4 (1935), p. 166.

2603. Judas Maccabeus.

2627-29. Editors disagree on where to put quotation marks and how to interpret 2630-31. Björkman, usually the most reliable editor, mistakenly gives 2630-31 to Priamus. Thus the original lines—["]*Gife I happe to my hele that hende for to serue,/I be holpen in haste, I hette the forsothe*.["]— are Priamus's statement, "If I should chance, to my good fortune, to come into the service of that courteous [noble] man, I would be quickly helped [i.e., made rich, etc.], I tell you forsooth!" 2632 then works as a comparative statement, Priamus's meaning being, "If you, a commoner, are so rich, think what Arthur would do for a knight like me." On the other hand, if Gawain speaks the lines they mean, "If I chance, to my good fortune, to be of service to that courteous [noble] man [my lord], I am helped [rewarded] in haste, I tell you forsooth." In this case 2632, Priamus's response, is ironic, expressing a doubt made explicit at 2637. This reading seems distinctly preferable. Gawain consistently attributes his successes to luck (cf. 2644) not to his own prowess, and courteously praises his king.

The Poems

Priamus's notorious pride would not ordinarily lead to talk of coming to good luck. Further, Björkman's reading makes the conversation shift awkwardly and cannot adequately explain Gawain's repetition of this same sentiment at 2820.

2642–43. Consider "*Þofe me this grace happen;/It es þe gifte of Gode, the gree es hys awen.*" *Grace* here means favor or advancement given to an inferior by one of higher station (cf. the grace of God, grace of the king, grace of the lady, etc.). Gawain's station and honor are improved by his victory over Priamus, but he claims not to have won this rise, it simply "happened," or came by chance. Or rather it comes from God: the *gree*—court favor, prize, or glory—is God's own. Priamus, in the lines that follow, sounds unconvinced that the glory is all God's.

2648–72. Translated rather freely, mainly for the sake of spelling out uncertain pronouns, etc.

2657. Perhaps rightly, Björkman reads *Sexty thowsande forsothe,* not *Sexty thowsande and ten.*

2671–72. for lykynge of byrdez, lit., "for pleasure at the birds"; *þat lufflyche songen,* "who sweetly sang."

2685. gyffen on erles, lit., "given on deposit."

2702 ff. An Eastern romance device, modified here by Christian allegory. Cf. the four streams which flow from the throne of God in *Pearl* (cf. also, *Ezekiel* and *The Apocalypse*). By the introduction of this romance device, the poet perhaps suggests a Christian alternative to Arthur's way, slaughter. But it is less than certain that any conscious allegory is involved. The scene may be mere adventure.

2723–49. An interesting passage. Sir Florent is technically the man in charge of this hunting expedition, though Gawain is higher in rank and reputation. Gawain's first words to his men (2725–56) plainly reveal his desire to take on the unequal fight; his words about Sir Florent's fearlessness are aimed at making it hard for Sir Florent to refuse the battle; and his next words ("whither he fights or flees we're bound to follow—but not for yonder force will I forsake him") in effect deny that the brave Sir Florent could conceivably flee. Nevertheless, Sir Florent, unlike Sir Cador earlier, is prudent, and despite Gawain's attempt to railroad his own rash plan through, Florent objects. His argument is that in all Gawain's talk of the glory to be won, Gawain ignores the shame that will more probably result when their attack proves an act of folly. He says nothing of Gawain's war-boast (2733–34) or of the rivalry for glory among the Round Table knights which partly motivates Gawain's plan (2727 ff.); instead, he makes elaborate display of his own simplicity and inexperience (points he much exaggerates, of course) and he mentions the vain boasts of the carters and serving boys he and Gawain will be forced to impress to their ranks for the fight. Finally, when he gives his advice he shifts from direct address to Gawain and gives the advice to the company generally. Sir Gawain does not miss all this. He sidesteps the argument that the attack would be folly because of the numerical odds and instead counters the ploy Sir Florent used in presenting his central argument—Sir Florent's alleged inexperience

Notes

and the emptiness of servingmen's boasts. Many here are not inexperienced, Gawain says, and some of the boasters are not mere serving boys. In short, what is important in Florent's advice Gawain lightly dismisses with the words "*I grawnte*"—i.e., "I grant the point."

Gawain's rash action here, like his rash action at the court of Lucius, leads to no great catastrophe; but it seems to be only luck that saves him. The reader at least partly admires the hero's recklessness; but a similar recklessness in Arthur will at last bring the kingdom to ruin.

2769. The MS reads *þat all his breste stoppede*, i.e., as I understand it, "so that his heart stopped beating." Brock and later editors emend to *brethe*, "breath."

2775. And all þe doughtty for dule, lit., "and all the doughty (ones) for sorrow (dole)."

2838. See note, l. 462.

2854–55. Translation is free for "Be not afraid of yonder oafs nor of their bright clothes; We shall falsify their boast, for all their bold proffer (i.e., their show of willingness to engage in battle).

2868. That is, the Virgin is Arthur's emblem. In *Sir Gawain and the Green Knight* she is Sir Gawain's sign; he carries her image on the inside of his shield.

2954. The idea, explicit here, of war as a gamble with Fortune, is persistent in the *Morte Arthure* fight scenes. Gawain's oath at 2967, obscured in translation, has the same overtone—lit., "I shall wage (bet) for that man all that I wield."

2998. "hunt"—an ironic allusion to Gawain's original foraging mission, altered by Lorrain's ambush.

3011. Björkman reads not "the best of lords" but "at the behest of lords." Though his grounds for emendation are invalid (as O'Loughlin has shown), the emendation improves the rhythm and sense.

3031. "miner-sheds"—lean-to's to protect those who attack the bases of the walls.

3114–21. Few passages in the poem show more clearly than this superb touch the poet's keen sense of dramatic irony or his mastery of story-telling technique. And note in the lines immediately following the Homeric shift of person, from they to we.

3251. For "ermine" see O'Loughlin's note on this line in his "The Middle English *Morte Arthure*," *Medium Ævum* 4 (1935), p. 167. Other editors say "embroidery."

3352. The apple image shows the view of Fortune taken in the poem and, for that matter, in the Middle Ages generally. The apple recalls the fruit Eve took in Eden. (The fruit is variously identified in medieval paintings and writing—as a pomegranate, as a pear, etc.,—but the apple is perhaps the most common choice.) Eve's eating of the apple is often read as an act of "concupiscence," a desire for worldly pleasures without adequate recognition of their meaning or source. To look beyond worldly things is to look beyond the realm of Fortune to that of Providence—beyond substance to spirit, or beyond selfishness to the selflessness of "charity," i.e., proper love of God and man. As long as one looks no higher than Fortune, one has no free will but is "chained" in carnality and fated, like all things merely physical, to die. Looking to Providence one does have free will and a choice of ultimate death or life. Compare Merlin's statement, in Malory's *Morte D'Arthur*, that he created the Round Table as a figure of this world—in other words, as a temptation. (For detailed treatment of Fortune as the Middle Ages understood it, see Boethius's *Consolation of Philosophy*.) Arthur's concupiscence, the apple-world image suggests, is not simply for things of the world but for the world itself. If the frequent references to Arthur's "cruel deeds" imply that his sin lies in a malfunction of his irascible soul (the part reflected in Plato's metaphor of men of silver), the apple-image here suggests he is guilty of avarice, or greed, as well—a malfunction of the concupiscent soul (cf. Plato's men of iron). Though Plato's own writings were largely unknown in medieval Europe, Platonism powerfully influenced Christian thought. A standard view was that man's fall involved first a perversion of reason, or the rational soul, then a seizure of power by the irascible and concupiscent souls. Note that King Arthur in the present poem begins as a man who wisely controls his passions by wisdom but slowly degenerates.

Winner and Waster

The poem is modernized from Sir Israel Gollancz's edition of *The Parlement of the Thre Ages*, Roxburghe Club, no. 132 (London: Nichols and Sons, 1897), in which this poem, *Winner and Waster*, is given in an appendix. The dialect of the poem is North Midland; it was probably composed in 1352 (see line 206).

1 ff. Compare the opening of *Sir Gawain and the Green Knight*. Brutus, legendary founder of Britain, was one of the Trojan nobility who sought other lands after the treason of Antenor and, in some versions, Aeneas.

7–8. In comparison to London and the trade towns, the West in medieval England (Langland's country) was agrarian and conservative.

45–49. Strongly reminiscent of *Pearl*, stanzas 6 ff.

61. According to Gollancz, the besants of beaten gold may be an allusion to Edward III's memorable coinage of gold in 1343.

63. A version of the famous motto of the Order of the Garter, *Honi soit qui mal y pense*. Edward's expense in connection with the Order was not universally pleasing in his day.

70–83. This iconographic identification is a typical medieval device. The combined hearldic arms of England and France, leoþard and lily, allude to Edward's victory over France at Crécy. On one of Edward's famous coins, the "noble," Saint George holds a shield with the arms of both countries.

129. "the king's peace"—i.e., the peace of the realm, guaranteed by the king.

130–33. The reference to Lorraine, Lombardy, Low Spain, and Westphalia

Notes

alludes to those merchants granted English free trade in the poet's time. The Englishmen and Irishmen mentioned next are also, presumably, to be seen as merchants, warriors only allegorically.

206. Apparently the twenty-fifth year of Edward's reign, or 1352.

290–93. A neat shift from the literal to the allegorical, from the wasted manor destroyed by fire to the fire and ice of hell. The lines may, in addition, allude to some great drought and fire—1315–16, 1322, 1325, and c. 1347 were famous drought years.

317. Shareshull—William de Shareshull, Chief of the Exchequer and Justice of the King's Bench under Edward III, apparently more politician than man-of-law. The point of the poet's allusion is obscure.

330–57. Feasts are a stock topic in medieval poetry. Cf. the feasts in *Purity*, *Sir Gawain and the Green Knight*, or the *Prima Pastorum* pageant in the Wakefield Cycle.

474. The tavern or hostelry district.

479. Crete—i.e., the wine of Crete.

The Parliament of the Three Ages

The modernization is from the EETS edition of M. Y. Offord (London, 1959), with occasional use of Sir Israel Gollancz's Select Early English Poems, 3 (London: Humphrey Milford, Oxford University Press, 1920). The original dialect of the poem was probably North Midland, though the text is inconsistent, no doubt partly through scribal corruption but perhaps also because the poet may have lived in the southern part of the North Midland dialect region. The poem may be dated 1370 or shortly before. (See Offord, p. xxxvi.) It exists in two versions, the Thorton MS and the corrupt Ware MS, both printed by Offord. My version follows Thornton, generally.

1 ff. The opening (like the poem as a whole) is loaded with apparent borrowings. See *The Destruction of Troy*, 12969, "Hit was the money of May when mirthes begyn"; *Piers Plowman*, 2, "In a somer seson whan soft was the sonne." Various details here recall *Roman de la Rose*, and there are parallels to the (perhaps later) *Gawain and the Green Knight*, e.g., "a bonke þe brymme by-syde," 2172.

21–99. Cf. the hunting scenes in GGK, esp. 1319 ff.

27. The correct meaning may be that from a distance the outlines of the branching off the beam suggest a foot.

34. "buck," lit., *soar*, a reddish brown four-year-old male of the fallow or red deer species.

50. A unique image in Middle English hunt poetry.

51–3. The narrator apparently shoots *after* the stag lowers his head because, according to medieval huntsmen, a stag cannot hear well with his head lowered. See Nicholas Cox, *The Gentleman's Recreation* (1677), p. 52.

68–9. An imagistic opposition: the tongue is a delicacy, the bowels mere dogfood.

The Poems

70.   *I s[lit]te hym at þe assaye.* The *assaye* is the part of the chest where the deer's flesh is tested. (Not preserved in the modernization.)

71.   Fat the breadth of two fingers. Cf. *GGK*, 1329.

80.   "corbies' bone": a small piece of gristle at the end of the sternum which was thrown up into a tree for the crows as a luck offering or as pay to sighting falcons.

86.   "numbles." The liver, kidneys, and entrails.

101–2. Cf. *Destruction of Troy*, 2378–79.

105.   *and maden thaym full tale.* The correct reading may be "and explained themselves fully," *tale*, in this case, being a noun (story, explanation), not, as translated, an adverb.

109 ff. Cf. *GGK*, 136 ff.

120 ff.   The jewels may be meant to recall (ironically) Paradise as seen in the Apocalypse. Cf. the jewels in *Pearl*, and see R. J. Menner's list of parallels in alliterative poetry, in his edition of *Purity*, note to 1464 ff.

130.   Medieval saddles were usually of wood, often richly painted.

132.   "crop," ME *cropoure* (crupper), a leather or silk strap fastened to the back of the saddle and running under the horse's tail.

133–34. In medieval tradition, thirty usually meant approaching middle age; forty to sixty was old age. But there are, as here, exceptions to this scheme in medieval writing. (Cf. l. 151 and see Offord's note.)

137.   "russet"—reddish brown coarse woolen cloth.

147.   "store-keepers": *store* in the sense of herds, harvests, etc.; hence the meaning is "herdsmen and the like," or "under-stewards."

176.   Translated freely. The idea of the lady as physician is stock, a part of the "allegory of love" in which terms appropriate to religion are transferred to the sphere of love. (Cf. "Christ the Physician.")

209–45. With hoo and howghe: traditional cries of falconers.

224.   *brynges hym to sege:* i.e., drives him to the open, to a defensive position by the waterside. (Cf. an army settling down to besiege a castle.)

228.   "their sharp beaks" refers to the heron, the prey, not the falcon, probably. But the line is ambiguous.

229–30. "they kneel" i.e., the hunters, helping their hawks by crossing the wings of the prey. By beating its wings the dying heron could kill a valuable hawk. It was important to medieval falconers (and to the falcons) that the falcon himself make the kill.

234.   "quarries them." Technical. It means "allow them to eat the quarry as long as they like." When the hawk took the wrong prey he was punished by being refused quarry.

235.   "checks." Technical. Unwanted prey (crows, rooks, magpies, or other worthless birds).

237.   *Cowples vp theire cowers* (lost in translation): "pull the two strings or braces which tighten the hood like the neck of a sack."

239.   "lure." An object of leather, cloth, or wool, with talons or wings and a piece of fish as bait, used to draw the hawk back when it seemed about to stray.

242.   "tercelets"—male peregrine falcons or goshawks. Fierce, troublesome when the hunting is over.

Notes

258. *dole,* translated "grief," may mean "alms or charitable gifts," may mean "wealth."

280. "farmland," originally *ploughe-londes,* perhaps a measurement, roughly 120 acres (as much as can be plowed in a day).

286. *sowed myn hert:* lit., caused my heart to sting.

312–13. In medieval tradition Achilles was a sneak who killed Hector when he was tending to a captive.

314–15. A tradition preserved by Dictys Cretensis, iii, 29.

329. MS reads *arculus* (Hercules), a mistake.

331. Dictys Cretensis and Dares Phrygius were alleged to have written eyewitness accounts of the fall of Troy, brought down by Benoit de Sainte-Maure and Guido delle Colonne. They, not Homer, were the standard authorities on the fall of Troy for the Middle Ages.

335. The tradition is that Elias and Enoch live on the Isles of the Orient (the Earthly Paradise) and will stay there until they come out to fight the Antichrist on Doomsday.

338. Thorton MS reads *Iazon þe Iewe* (Jason the Jew), Ware, *Iosue þe Iewe* (oshua). Gollancz emends to [Gr]efe, i.e., Greek.

344 ff. These hasty retellings of familiar Alexander tales assume an audience who know longer versions like those preserved in English and French, especially Jacques de Longuyon's *Vœux du Paon* (c. 1312) and the Scottish *Buik of Alexander* (Scottish Text Society, NS (1921–29). Briefly, Gadyfere the Elder is slain by Emenidus. Cassamus, Gadyfere's brother, wants vengeance and goes to Alexander, who reasons him out of it. Cassamus tells Alexander that Gadyfere has left two sons, Gadyfere the Younger and Betis, also a daughter, Fesonas; and that Clarus, King of Ind, seeks to dispossess the heirs and marry Fesonas against her will. Alexander helps the sons when Clarus attacks Epheson, one of Gadyfere's properties. During the siege, some of Clarus's men, including his handsome son Porrus, are captured and taken prisoner. Walking in a courtyard, Porrus finds and kills a peacock, roasts it, and carries it in to the feast. Cassamus, according to custom, proposes that vows be made to the peacock, and Porrus vows that he will take Emenidus's horse from under him in battle (avenging the fair Fesonas's father). He later does so, kills Cassamus, is rebuked for pride by Alexander, and then, with Alexander's blessing, marries Fesonas.

426. The story of Joshua and the Jordon has been confused here with the story of Moses crossing the Red Sea.

430. Anachronistic prayers of this kind are common in medieval mystery plays, unusual elsewhere.

459. "jousters." The unwitting medievalization of classical and Biblical figures is common in early English writings. Cf. the sieges, etc., in *Purity*.

513 ff. The poet distorts chronology to place the famous Charlemagne after the less spectatular Godfrey of Bouillon.

520 ff. Cf. *Chanson de Roland.*

522–23. Duke Reiner, father of Oliver, Roland's companion. Aubrey of Burgogne: not mentioned in the OF *Roland,* but found in the fragmentary *Song of Roland* (c. 1400). Ogier the Dane: a popular figure in Charlemagne romances and a baron in the *Chanson.*

524.   Naimes (of Bavaria): Charlemagne's friend and chief advisor.

525–26. Turpin and Tierri: brave fighters in the *Chanson*. Samson: one of the douzeperes in *Chanson*.

527.   Berarde de Moundres: a great lover in later Charlemagne romances.

528.   Guy of Burgoyne (Burgundy): another late romance hero, associated with love and magic.

529.   The four sons' adventures appear in a French prose romance, *Les Quatre Fils Aymon,* translated by Caxton, c. 1489.

532.   *Polborne* (Paderborn, in Saxony): site of one of Charlemagne's victories, where he later built a palace.

533.   *Salamadin:* not found in Charlemagne tradition.

536.   Widukind, a Westphalian chieftain who led Saxon revolts against Charlemagne but was later baptized and tamed.

539.   Niole and Mandeville: unknown outside *The Parliament of the Three Ages.*

546.   Balame (Balan): a character borrowed from the *Ferumbras* cycle. *Mandrible:* site of a bridge across the river Flagot.

547.   The Emperor and Balan are probably the same. A confusion in the poem.

561.   Ganelon the traitor. Cf. *Book of the Duchess,* 1121–23; *Monk's Tale,* 2389.

608.   Galyan. Malory's "Nyneve," Lady of the Lake.

614.   Amadis and Adoine, among the most famous of lovers in the Middle Ages.

Summer Sunday

Modernized from Rossell Hope Robbins's *Historical Poems of the XIVth and XVth Centuries* (New York: Columbia University Press, 1959). The dialect is West Midland, possibly Cheshire or Shropshire. Some scholars date the poem c. 1327, associating it with the death of Edward II and noting certain words used in a distinctly fourteenth-century sense; a few associate the poem with Richard II and urge a later date, c. 1400. See Robbins, pp. 301–2.

10.   *Kenettes questede to quelle:* lit., "Kenetts (a kind of hunting dog) gave their warning bark, sighting the prey."

26 ff. The waterway which the narrator crosses is clearly one of those mysterious borders between two worlds, reality and dream, earth and earthly paradise, etc., common in medieval poetry. King Arthur, in Malory, crosses such a stream in pursuit of a white deer and finds Merlin. The *Pearl*-poet has a similar waterway. In other respects, cf. the dreamer's visionlike experience in *Book of the Duchess.*

The Owl and the Nightingale

The modernization is from the edition of Eric Gerald Stanley (London: Nelson, 1960). The poem is preserved in two MSS, Cotton Caligula

Notes

A. ix, in the British Museum, and Jesus College 29, in the Bodleian Library, Oxford. A lost MS is listed in the medieval catalogue of the Library at Titchfield Abbey. Stanley follows the Cotton Caligula MS. The dialect of the poem is South Western or Southwest Midlands, though the text shows scribal corruption from surrounding dialects. The MS can be dated paleographically as early thirteenth century, and the poem's allusions to King Henry—almost certainly Henry II—support a date after 1216.

1 ff. Very freely translated. l. 22 "flats and sharps" is obviously anachronistic and not in the original. l. 1 is lit., "I was in a summer valley"— a typical seasonal reference at the beginning of dream-visions and other medieval genres. Cf. Helen E. Sandison, *The "Chanson d'aventure" in Middle English,* Bryn Mawr College Monographs No. 12 (1913), pp. 26 ff.

26. Cf. note to lines 320.

66f. Accurate naturalism; also a favorite medieval theme. See e.g., F. Bond, *Wood Carvings in English Churches* (London: Oxford University Press, 1910), p. 47; and C. J. P. Cave, *Roof Bosses in Medieval Churches: An Aspect of Gothic Sculpture* (Cambridge: At the University Press, 1948), no. 206 and cf. p. 73, both illustrating the attack of an owl by smaller birds.

94. Lit., "You feed a very foul offspring."

121. Lit., "with the worst muck of all."

203. I have "modernized" whimsically. Lit., "and other things gentle and small." *gente & smale* are epithets characteristic of the idealized courtly lady. Cf. Chaucer's *Miller's Tale, CT,* 3 (A), 3234.

232. A charming instance of the narrator's insistence upon his own gravity and respectability.

234. Alfred's proverbs are roughly the medieval equivalent of our "Confucius say. . . ." A collection, *The Proverbs of Alfred,* has come down to us. On the poet's use of proverbs in *O&N,* see Stanley's notes and appendix.

320 ff. The Owl takes credit for singing, not all night like the Nightingale, but only to call the religious to their hours—Vespers, Compline, Matins with Lauds, and Prime.

348 ff. Parodic of homiletic language. Cf. 711 ff, where the Nightingale echoes the same pious diction.

422 ff. The sense seems to be that the Owl takes perverse delight in that which causes trouble, such as coarse flocks mingled with fine carded wool and hair, hard to disentangle.

432 ff. In the original, a parody of stock medieval lyric devices, both in phrase and subject matter. Dimly visible in modernization.

478. "carols": really the medieval *conductus,* a four-part song often with some popular, nonecclesiastical melody carried in the tenor, which was sung as the priest approached the altar.

502 f. In medieval tradition (wrongly derived by medieval writers from Pliny), the nightingale stops singing after copulation.

499 ff. A stock attack on the chivalric idea (e.g., in *Parsifal*) that courtly love ennobles, making the soldier brave and good.

625 and *633*. Neat permutations, both "obscene," of traditional saws. "A man must live with whatever may befall," and "Need can make old women trot" (not normally in a fecal sense).

702 ff. Apparently a comic allusion to the twelfth- and thirteenth-century scholastic debate on whether one virtue sincerely exercized could, since all the virtues were interconnected, embrace all other virtues—hence, whether one earnest virtue might be worth more than the feeble exercize of all the virtues.

724 ff. Midnight-service hymns (Matins and Lauds) frequently referred to the coming of light.

771. Greater irony in the original: "in front of great teams." The association of the horse and pride is very common in medieval writings. (Cf. Chaucer's "proud Bayard.")

805 ff. O&N scholarship insists that foxes, like cats, can climb trees; that "foxes were treed in the Middle Ages [as] shown by a fourteenth-century misericord in Gloucester depicting a fox on the branch of a tree (reproduced in F. Bond, *Woodcarvings in English Churches,* p. 99); that "foxes are still treed." [Stanley's note to l. 816.] From this, scholars move on to questions concerning the precise sources of the poet's knowledge that foxes can climb trees. But obviously the poet, like most fox hunters, is ignorant of the fox's remarkable ability and means to contrast the cat's one trick with the fox's many which do not include that one. The poet's pronouns easily admit the sensible reading my translation gives. Though I once saw a fox climb a ladder.

849 ff. The passage on the necessity of tears is a homiletic commonplace. (See Stanley's note to ll. 854–92.)

900 ff. It was standard knowledge that nightingales do not sing in some countries, among them Ireland. (Stanley's note to ll. 905–10.)

992 ff. A stock medieval description of (imaginary or real) wild lands, handsomely overdone here. Cf. Ohthere's description of Norway in King Alfred's Orosius (*EETS,* O.S., 79, pp. 17–21, et passim.

1009. Stanley notes that because of the furs they wore, inhabitants of the far north looked like devils as pictured in medieval illustrations. But the reference here is to their stench, a standard element of medieval hell descriptions.

1017. The image may come from Neckam's *De Naturis Rerum,* ii, ch. 129 and 130. In 129 apes are trained to fight with swords and shields, and in the following chapter a bear is treated as the type of cruelty. (See Stanley's note to l. 1021 f.)

1140 ff. (original text, 1145–1330). A. C. Cawley points out subtle astrological material here. "Astrology in *The Owl and the Nightingale*," *MLN* 46 (1951), pp. 161–74.

1236 ff. The lines seem to parody the Boethian argument, in the *Consolation of Philosophy,* on free will. Though God sees in advance what will happen, his seeing is not the cause of the event.

1293 ff. Cawley points out in his essay cited above that the Nightingale, overwhelmed by the Owl's defense of astrology, here advances the argument that, although astrology is a real science, the Owl, knowing nothing of the stars, can only be working by witchcraft.

1394 ff. A loose and free-wheeling treatment of the seven deadly sins, according to Gregory's more or less standard list: *Superbia* (Pride), *Ira* (Wrath), *Invidia* (Envy), *Avarita* (Covetousness), *Acedia* (Sloth), *Gula* (Gluttony), and *Luxuria* (Lust). Sins of the flesh usually include Gluttony and Lust; the rest are normally treated as sins of the spirit. The opinion expressed at 1404 is standard, also found in, for instance, the *Ancrene Riwle* or Rule of Anchoresses.

1729. In the time of Henry II and after, the "King's peace" meant a right of trial for all, peace and law as the state's responsibility. Earlier it meant special protection by the king.